THE IMPACT OF EXPANSION ON EUROPEAN UNION INSTITUTIONS

The Impact of Expansion on European Union Institutions

The Eastern Touch on Brussels

Eva G. Heidbreder

THE IMPACT OF EXPANSION ON EUROPEAN UNION INSTITUTIONS
Copyright © Eva G. Heidbreder, 2011.

First published in 2011 by
PALGRAVE MACMILLAN®
in the United States—a division of St. Martin's Press LLC,
175 Fifth Avenue, New York, NY 10010.

Where this book is distributed in the UK, Europe and the rest of the World,
this is by Palgrave Macmillan, a division of Macmillan Publishers Limited,
registered in England, company number 785998, of Houndmills,
Basingstoke, Hampshire RG21 6XS.

Palgrave Macmillan is the global academic imprint of the above
companies and has companies and representatives throughout the world.

Palgrave® and Macmillan® are registered trademarks in the United
States, the United Kingdom, Europe and other countries.

ISBN: 978–0–230–11096–0

Library of Congress Cataloging-in-Publication Data

Heidbreder, Eva G.
    The impact of expansion on European Union institutions : the eastern
touch on Brussels / Eva G. Heidbreder.
        p.   cm.
    Includes bibliographical references.
    ISBN 978–0–230–11096–0 (alk. paper)
    1. European Union.   2. Public institutions—European Union countries.
    3. Political planning—European Union countries.   4. Policy sciences.
    I. Title.
JN30.H39 2010
341.242′2—dc22   2010040756

A catalogue record of the book is available from the British Library

Design by Integra Software Services

First edition: April 2011

10 9 8 7 6 5 4 3 2 1

Printed and bound in Great Britain by
CPI Antony Rowe , Chippenham and Eastbourne

For Ursel

CONTENTS

LIST OF TABLES AND FIGURES

TABLES

FIGURES

ACKNOWLEDGMENTS

This book has traveled a lot and benefited from many recommendations and criticisms by those whom I would like to thank here—and many more who remain unnamed but backed the project far beyond the academic support. The prime "Danke" appertains to Adrienne Héritier, who, with great attention and care, supervised my PhD at the European University Institute. The EUI offered an ideal place to draft the thesis, which this book is based on. During the time in Florence, the intellectual exchange with many a scholar left its imprints on my thinking and on this study. I am especially grateful to Giuliano Amato, Stefano Bartolini, Fritz Kratochwil, Bruno de Witte, Phil Schmitter, and Jacques Ziller. Outside the EUI, "grazie" to Giliberto Capano at the University Bologna. Important preparatory work for this research was conducted before moving to Italy; therefore a very special thanks to Gerda Falkner and her team at the Institute for Advanced Studies in Vienna. Not only in Vienna, discussions with Guy Peters have been deeply encouraging to widen my horizon. Moving on, in particular during my postdoctoral period at the KFG Researchers College at the FU Berlin, Tanja Börzel has been a highly appreciated critic and supporter. But it was my very first professor in European Studies who gave the most instructive guidance. In a telephone call from faraway Osnabrück she once complained: "I read your stuff, Eva, what are they doing to you? You seem so confused! Do not let them confuse you, stick to your initial idea, that was much better." Thank you, Ingeborg Tömmel, and all those who took the effort to fruitfully confuse me or offered assistance in overcoming the inspiring puzzlement.

ABBREVIATIONS

ACCESS	Community Programme to strengthen the Civil Society
AEBR	Association of European Border Regions
AEGR	Arbeitsgemeinschaft Europäischer Grenzregionen
AP	Accession Partnership
AQG	Council's Atomic Questions Group
CAF	Common Assessment Framework
CAP	Common Agricultural Policy
CBC	Cross-Border Cooperation
CEEC	Central and eastern European country
COMECOM	Council for Mutual Economic Assistance
DG	Directorate General
EAEC	European Atomic Energy Community
EC	European Community
EACN	European Anti-Corruption Network
ECJ	European Court of Justice
EFTA	European Free Trade Association
EIDHR	European Initiative for Democracy and Human Rights
ENP	European Neighbourhood Policy
ENPI	European Neighbourhood and Partnership Instrument
EP	European Parliament
EUMC	European Monitoring Centre on Racism and Xenophobia
EURATOM	European Atomic Energy Community
ERDF	European Regional Development Fund
ESA	Euratom Supply Agency
ESF	European Social Fund
FCNM	Framework Convention on National Minorities

GNI	Gross national income
GNP	Gross national product
GRECO	Group of States against Corruption
IAEA	International Atomic and Energy Agency
ISPA	Instrument for Structural Policies for Pre-accession
LIBE	EP Committee on Civil Liberties, Justice and Home Affairs
LIEN	Linking Inter European Non-governmental Organizations
LS	EU Commission Legal Service
MEDA	Euro-Mediterranean Partnership Programme (*Messures d'Accompagnement*)
NEA	Nuclear Energy Agency
NGO	Nongovernmental organization
NIS	Newly independent state
NRWG	Nuclear Regulators Working Group
NSRF	National Strategic Reference Frameworks
OLAF	European Anti-Fraud Office
OMC	Open method of coordination
OSCE	Organisation for Security and Cooperation in Europe
PHARE	Pologne, Hongrie Aide à la Réstructuration Éconmomique
PROGRESS	Community programme for employment and solidarity
RAXEN	Information Network on Racism and Xenophobia
RSWG	Reactor Safety Working Group
PROGRESS	Community Programme for Employment and Social Solidarity
PUMA	Public Management Service (OECD)
SAPARD	Special Accession Programme for Agriculture and Rural Development
SGEI	Services of General Economic Interest
SGI	Services of General Interest
SIGMA	Support for Improvement in Governance and Management
TACIS	Technical Assistance to the Commonwealth of Independent States
TAIEX	Technical Assistance and Information Exchange
TEC	Treaty establishing the European Community
TEU	Treaty on European Union

TFAN	Task Force for Accession Negotiations
TFEU	Treaty on the Functioning of the European Union
TREN	Transport and Energy
UCLAF	Unité de coordination de la lutte anti-fraude
UN	United Nations
UNCAC	United Nations Convention against Corruption
UNTOC	United Nations Convention against Transnational Organised Crime
WENRA	Western European Nuclear Regulators' Association
WPNS	Working Party on Nuclear Safety
WTO	World Trade Organisation

PART I

INTRODUCTION

POLICIES AS THE FOCAL POINT OF POLITY FORMATION: THE PUZZLE OF IMPLEMENTING ENLARGEMENT

The assumption made throughout this is that the nature of political organization depends on the conflicts exploited in the political system, which ultimately is what politics is about. The thesis is that we shall never understand politics unless we know what the struggle is about.

E. E. Schattschneider, *The Semisovereign People*[1]

CHAPTER 1

RESEARCH QUESTION AND EMPIRICAL PUZZLE

Enlargements have been a feature of European integration from the early days. In the 2004/2007 rounds of widening, 12 new member states joined the European Union (EU). Much academic attention has revolved around the effects that accession to the EU has had on the incumbent member states, especially regarding the former socialist states of Central and Eastern Europe. A core question for the course and dynamics of EU integration has, however, remained widely unexplored: what effects has implementing enlargement had on the EU itself?

Studies that focus on the effects of enlargement on the EU concentrate foremost on formal institutional implications, such as the changed organizational compositions of the Council of Ministers (Council), the European Commission (Commission), and the European Parliament (EP), the adapted distribution of voting powers in the Council, or the reform of certain policies to accommodate enlargement. The present study departs from this body of literature in two respects. On the one hand, it is concerned with the implications of policy making—that is, the institutional repercussions that the enactment policies generate—rather than the effect of institutional changes on policy making. On the other hand, it scrutinizes the policy-generated effects on the larger polity development—that is, whether and how enlargement serves as a catalyst for EU integration—rather than the implications of widening on the day-to-day functioning of the Union. In short, this book aims to fill the research gap on the impact of enlargement on integration dynamics: under which conditions does the widening of the EU cause deepening within the EU?

The problem-driven research approach is motivated by an empirical puzzle. In order to implement the so-called eastern enlargement, the EU member state governments delegated extraordinary competences to the Commission that were without precedent in earlier enlargements. On the basis of the leverage of accession conditionality, the Commission super-vised compliance with EU standards in the candidate states. Entry was conditional on achieving the EU accession criteria. Yet, some of the crite-ria went beyond the Commission's competences under the formal legal framework, the *acquis communautaire*. The Commission was therefore involved in policies in the candidate states of which it had no say in the member states. By design of these competences, they should all have ceased to exist at the moment of accession. Yet, we can observe that the Commission was still active in some of these fields after accession, notwithstanding the fact that the competences were initially restricted to the pre-accession phase. The research puzzle that drives this analysis is therefore: why were some policies extended beyond the Copenhagen enlargement framework while others remained, as designed, restricted to the pre-accession policy?

The goal of the book is to shed light on the empirical puzzle under which conditions implementing enlargement led to new supranational capacities. More generally, policy-generated institutionalization processes are traced. To this end, all policies for which the Commission had extended capacities in the enlargement framework will be analyzed. Of the five cases under scrutiny, supranational capacities to act beyond the Copenhagen framework were extended in three cases and remained lim-ited to external states in two policy fields. To discover the conditions that explain the variance, cases are compared in a most similar design. The two sets of cases vary in the dependent variable (institutionalization of new supranational capacities), but in order to identify which conditions explain the different outcomes, all share that they were first established as clearly restricted competences in the Copenhagen framework. The find-ings are complemented by a succinct, most different comparison in order to examine alternative explanations.

In line with the problem-driven approach, the theoretical framework serves to develop expectations about necessary and sufficient conditions that explain the varying outcomes. The theoretical framework conse-quently consists of two levels to conceptualize the necessary and sufficient conditions under which policy making generates new institutionalized capacities. Drawing from neofunctional theories, the necessary condi-tion is identified as functional pressure that derives from successful policy making in the distinct institutional sub-system that the enlargement framework offered. Although necessary for the continued involvement of the Commission in the policies at stake, functional pressure fails to explain the variance between cases. In order to provide a theoretically consistent explanation, the conceptualization of the sufficient conditions also builds on functional theories. What emerges from the analysis is that policies are integrated if they do not entail new political relationships between citizens and the EU level. Put differently, if no political spillover is expected, the sufficient condition is met. The two intervening variables are, accordingly, policy types and modes of governance because they determine the actor relationships between policy makers and policy takers. Only if functional pressure emerges can supranational capacities extend beyond the initial mandate that limits them to the enlargement context. The way competences are established in the enlargement framework proves decisive. If the policy type and the mode of governance do not violate the established political relationships, new supranational capacities will be institutionalized. In contrast, if new policies are expected to reorient citizens' political relationships to the EU level, the relevant representatives of the member states will block supranational institutionalization. The central questions raised relate to three core research topics on the EU: (1) the impact of enlargement policy on the EU, (2) the organizational development of the Commission, (3) and the dynamics of supranational institutionalization at large. I will briefly address each in the reversed order.

POLICY-GENERATED INSTITUTIONALIZATION: DYNAMICS OF EUROPEAN UNION INTEGRATION

The most general theme of this book is the question, what drives the process of EU integration? The topic is tackled by scrutinizing the links between the EU's widening and deepening. The theoretical perspective fleshes out how policy making, in the framework of eastern enlargement, altered the institutionalized powers of the European Commission as a political agent. Generalizations that can be drawn beyond the context of enlargement and the Commission enlighten the broader picture of ongoing dynamics that trigger the supranational institutionalization of policy-making capacities.

The main hypothesis that policies themselves are a source for the institutionalization of supranational capacities builds on the claim that policy making generates institutional change. This argument links to streams in policy theory, which, in the late 1960s, had already noted critically that most of public policy analysis is concerned with "constituent policies," say an institutionalist angle (Salisbury 1968: 163). Recovering the approaches that emerged from this assessment in public policy research responds to the critique that EU scholars have deplorably neglected the role of policies (Panke and Börzel 2007: 138). Along these lines, the book speaks to existing EU literature in a threefold manner. First, the "major point here is that policy has, by and large, been treated as *dependent variable* that is affected in one way or another by political processes" (Froman 1968: 43, emphasis in the original; see also Froman 1967), whereas this book will consider them as *independent variables*. Accordingly, applying Theodore Lowi's classical policy typology (1964, 1972, 1985, 1988, 2008), the commonly assumed causal relationship between policies and institutions is inversed: policies determine institutional structure and processes. On the one hand, this levels the ground for a comprehensive functional explanation to the puzzle about how implementing enlargement fostered the Commission's capacities. On the other hand, the findings that result from this analysis lead to conclusions on the relevance of policy-centered theory in explaining polity formation.

Second, the empirical focus on political steering instruments of the Commission cuts right into the heart of the debate on governance in the EU (Benz 2004; Christiansen and Piattoni 2003; Héritier 2003; Hooghe and Marks 2001; Jachtenfuchs 2001; Kohler-Koch and Eising 1999; Mayntz and Scharpf 1995b; Marks, Scharpf et al. 1996; Scharpf 1999; Schuppert and Zürn 2008; Tömmel 2007; also: Commission of the European Communities 2001). Given the special character of the Union—a lack of the essential means to coerce along the lines of a traditional state—governance has become the most frequently used terminology and widely applied theoretical angle in the analysis of how the EU exerts control across the levels of the layered polity. Governance offers an analytical perspective capable of describing all kinds of modes of governance of and beyond traditional steering. It can produce generalizable statements on structures and mechanisms of coordination; however, it lacks a genuine theoretical underpinning and has been linked to different approaches (Benz et al. 2007: 16; Pierre and Peters 2000: 37). Systematically tracing how policy instruments were developed in the Copenhagen framework and how they moved beyond this distinct institutional setting enriches the empirical body of research on modes of governance. More importantly, because the analysis starts from the relevance of policies and political conflicts that determine which policy tools will be applied, it responds to the chief critique that the governance perspective is faced with, namely its "power blindness" (Benz et al. 2007; Mayntz 2004). Starting from the perspective that *policies matter* opens the analysis to the relevance of actual political problems and societal conflicts that determine institutions whose structure and functioning are consequently explained by the characteristics of the policies dealt with—without narrowing the perspective to traditional state-centered coercion.

Third, besides the insights that the theoretical reemphasis brings to the fore, the empirical findings illustrate mechanisms through which the Commission continues to extend its capacities. In so doing the results challenge research that depicts virtually the "end of integration" after the completion of the single market project. Parallel to a massive increase in legal substance to be administered, the formal extension of treaty-based competences has decelerated, which has been interpreted as a deliberate weakening of the Commission by the member states and "a fundamental change in the nature of European integration as a political issue that occurred in the early 1990s" (Kassim and Menon 2004: 24). Mark Pollack has advocated this claim most prominently in his work on the "creeping competences" (1994) and their alleged end after Maastricht Treaty (2000). The author argues that there was a creeping increase of EC competences throughout the first decades of European integration (1957–1992) during which policy making on the EU level extended into basically all political issue areas. However, this incremental task extension came to a halt because of political and economic backlash in the early 1990s. While my findings do not contradict that there has been such backlash that impeded the formal transfer of competences, it shows that if zooming into policy making, other dynamics come to the fore that hint to a continuation of the creeping competences that are even more stealthy. Below the processes of formal competence conferral, the execution of policies itself creates a dynamic for the continued creeping competences of the Commission. Thus, the political agent attains ever more de facto capacities in the form of soft regulation and distributive policies that are linked to conditions that grant the Commission considerable control powers. This does not suppose a teleological functionalist explanation in that all policy making would generally lead to institutionalization. Unmistakably, member state governments exert effective control and can successfully block the conferral of new supranational competences. Tracing the establishment and execution of single policies provides evidence for the fact that the scope of what member states tolerate depends on the policy type and mode of governance invoked. Integration continues. Yet, it does not necessarily do so by formalized delegation. The specific policies the EU deals with determine the functional extension of steering capacities within the margins acceptable to the member states. In conclusion, this mode of supranational institutionalization raises a whole additional set of questions about democratic responsibility and bureaucratic accountability in the ongoing process of European integration (see also Dashwood 1996; Mörth 2004a).

ORGANIZATIONAL AND INSTITUTIONAL DEVELOPMENTS OF A POLITICAL AGENT: THE EUROPEAN COMMISSION'S CONTINUED CREEPING COMPETENCES

The second theme tackled is the organizational development and institutional role of the European Commission. As the supranational initiator of legislation and the implementing body, the Commission is most prone to be affected by policy-generated institutional change. The exceptional competences that the Commission had in executing enlargement indicate a high likelihood for policy-induced changes. Because of strong uncertainty about how to integrate 12 new member states, the Commission had extraordinary discretion in how to interpret and implement the accession criteria and was endowed with far-reaching independence in developing and applying steering instruments vis-à-vis the candidate states. Addressing the question of how "doing enlargement" affected the Commission's capacities will therefore serve to advance our wider understanding of the Commission's internal organization and interorganizational role as part of the EU polity.

From an organizational development perspective, enlargement policy is a decisive case because it put the Commission in an exceptionally powerful position in relation to not only the candidate states but also the member states that depended on information and skills that only the Commission could deliver. At the moment of delegation in 1993, the task of implementing enlargement lacked precise tactics and a schedule. The pre-accession strategy evolved on the basis of the Copenhagen mandate from the ensuing delegations to the Commission by the European Council. The Commission emerged the main actor in defining how to fill the very broad criteria incrementally with more concrete substance. The major steps in relation to Treaty reforms occurred in parallel to the incremental molding of enlargement policy. While the Maastricht and Amsterdam Treaty as well as the subsequent Constitutional (ultimately the Lisbon) Treaty mark the grand integration steps of the period, key decisions for the EU approach to enlargement were taken at the European Council of Essen (1994) that inaugurated the *pre-accession strategy* under this very label, followed by the Luxembourg Council (1997), which launched the *enhanced strategy* and in which the heads of state and government agreed to open negotiations with a first group of applicants, as well as the Council of Helsinki (1999) that extended the number of states to negotiate accession to include further six applicants. The establishment of the Copenhagen criteria indicates above all an important qualitative innovation. The subsequent decisions established a genuine structured approach to enlargement for the first time, and thus the framework in which the underlying new principles were operationalized into actual steering instruments by the Commission.

Although the different formal steps were acts of delegation to the Commission, the latter had the most central role in the shift from a logic of acquis-based negotiations to a logic of control backed by conditionality. Not only did the Commission spell out the conditions, but it also supervised compliance with them. Besides that, as the conductor of the accession negotiations, the Commission was resolute in deciding whether a chapter could be opened or closed. In the words of a former central European deputy chief negotiator: "In the course of the negotiations the field of application of the principle of conditionality was further widened by applying certain conditions for the opening and closing of the negotiations' chapters. In a majority of cases the European Commission shaped those conditions on an ad hoc basis" (Maniokas 2004: 22). However, the leverage on candidate countries diminished the closer a state approached accession since the threat of rejecting membership lost credibility. Whereas the thrust of conditionality weakened in the eyes of the acceding states, it was in the member states' interest that the Commission pushed its competences to its limits within the Copenhagen framework to exert influence on the candidates before accession. The member states therefore granted the Commission considerable freedom on how to operationalize the criteria, even if this diminished member state control over the process. Through the entrepreneurship of key actors in the Commission, the abstract Copenhagen criteria were incrementally filled with tangible meaning and the Commission established new enforcement tools and structures to monitor and evaluate compliance in areas in which it lacked powers inside the EU. Hence, enlargement policy provided a playground on which the Commission could effectively develop and apply new steering instruments. Implementing enlargement is accordingly a crucial case to understand the organizational development of the Commission related to the innovation of steering instruments.

In organizational terms, the more rigorous approach to enlargement was most immediately reflected in the establishment of a single-standing Directorate General for Enlargement that took on the tasks previously executed by the External Relations Directorate. The new directorate general had a strong coordinating function between the sectoral directorates and as an interface between the EU and the candidate countries. In sum, regarding resources and actual authority, enlargement policy under the Copenhagen framework granted the Commission an unprecedented degree of authority. Although economic and political criteria may be traced back to the demands placed on the candidates during the southern enlargement, making them explicit and insisting on adaptation before accession gave a "quasi-constitutional nature to the Copenhagen criteria" (Hillion 2002: 409). In a nutshell, "in response to the different nature of this enlargement the Union has developed a new method for this process. The new method is based on four new principles: complexity, differentiation, conditionality and asymmetry. . . . [A]ll four principles form a single logic of control" (Maniokas 2004: 33). This control was exercised by the Commission, whose extended authority was based on the special role it had in implementing enlargement. Other than formal institutional changes that result from enlargement, taking seriously that policies matter suggests that executing enlargement itself should have left its marks on the Commission's internal organization and inter-institutional role. To this end, the analysis will trace how the Commission conducted the enlargement policy to filter out the effect of policy making. The empirical findings show how the horizontal enlargement policy, cutting across all policy fields the EU is concerned with, had both organizational consequences inside the Commission and inter-institutional effects on the Commission's overall capacities to act in the multilevel system. The Commission's organizational development was affected by enlargement much more than reckoned in existing scholarly writing. The results developed throughout the book thus open a new field of study next to existing research on the formal institutional impact of enlargement (generally see, e.g., Best et al. 2008; Carrubba 2003; Redmond and Rosenthal 1998; Wallace 2007; on single policies, e.g., de Filippis 2003; Eisl 1999; Fagan et al. 2005; Homeyer Von 2004; Ingham et al. 2005; Kramer 2004; Monar 2003; Rollo 2003; Sjursen 1998).

CONCEPTUALIZING WIDENING WITHIN INTEGRATION RESEARCH: THE EFFECTS OF IMPLEMENTING EASTERN ENLARGEMENT

Eastern enlargement, covering the period between 1993 and 2004/2007, represents a quasi-laboratory context to studying the effect of policy making on institutionalization processes. The incrementally developed strategic accession approach established a distinct institutional framework whose effects on the wider acquis can be distilled to further our understanding of how policies shape institutions. Enlargement policy since 1993 departs from earlier approaches to widening. The most relevant difference is that—backed by pre-accession conditionality—new supranational responsibilities were created that applied only to candidates, but not member states. The study will focus on policies that entered the EU agenda anew in the Copenhagen accession framework to trace under which conditions the implementation of these policies resulted or failed to result in the institutionalization of new genuine supranational capacities of the Commission.

Enlargement is an elemental feature of European integration. Just as much as the EU has intensified internal cooperation and harmonization between states, it has expanded territorially initially from 6 to 9 (1973), to 12 (1981, 1986), to 15 (1995), to the current 27 member states, with further states currently negotiating their entry to the EU. The so-called eastern enlargement was completed in two steps. The first big wave of candidate states joined in 2004, followed by two further countries in 2007.[2] Eastern enlargement differed from the earlier ones in some vital respects. Apart from the sheer number of candidate states, the majority of the applicant countries was in a process of economic, political, and social transformation and had a gross national product decisively below the average of the member states'. This posed novel challenges that were tackled by the adoption of a strategic accession approach. Unlike the "classical enlargement method" (Preston 1995), conditions were defined that, for the first time, went unequivocally beyond the full application of the acquis communautaire. What was the general setup of this Copenhagen framework in which the Commission implemented enlargement?

The official starting point of the eastern enlargement process was the Council of Copenhagen in 1993. After a period of dispute over whether the EU should enlarge at all, the decision to do so was linked to conditions for the candidates to be met before admission to the club. The Council affirmed that "[a]ccession will take place as soon as an associated country is able to assume the obligations of membership by satisfying the economic and political conditions required" (European Council 1993). The requirements of the economic and political Copenhagen conditions went beyond the adoption of the acquis communautaire. The criteria covered three issues: the stability of institutions guaranteeing democracy, the rule of law, human rights, and respect for and protection of minorities; the existence of a functioning market economy as well as the capacity to cope with competitive pressure and market forces within the Union; and the ability to take on the obligations of membership, including adherence to the Union's aims. The European Council of Madrid (1995) supplemented these criteria by mandating that attaining the membership criteria also included the adjustment of administrative structures.[3] In essence, the accession conditions meant that the applicant states had to adopt more rules than those applicable to the member states. The approach of linking accession to conditions to be met before entry was the most relevant departure from the previous incorporation of new members. For that reason, the Copenhagen mandate marks the introduction of a new principle that shaped the preceding incremental policy change from the *classical* to the *Copenhagen* enlargement method. The policy instrument at the heart of the new approach was conditionality: no compliance, no accession.

To pinpoint the traits of the *Copenhagen method,* Table 1.1 juxtaposes the five principles underlying the *classical enlargement method* until 1995 with the specific features of the EU's approach developed since 1993. Apart from the first principle, the full application of the acquis that was reinforced by the Copenhagen criteria and handled with a decisively higher level of restraint by limiting opt-outs for entering states, the logic of pre-accession conditionality marked a departure from the classical

Table 1.1   Principles of the Community/Union approach to enlargement

Classical Method (till 1995) (Preston 1995)	Pre-Accession Strategy (as from 1993) (Maniokas 2004)
Acceptance full acquis *Entering states have to comply with the rules applying to all member states without being granted permanent opt-outs.*	**>Reinforcement of principle** *Entering states have to comply with the rules applying to member states, reduced options for opt-outs, pre-accession criteria.*
Negations focus on acquis *Formal accession negotiations focus solely on the practicalities of the applicants taking on the acquis.*	**<Complexity** *Extension to pre-accession criteria and increased emphasis on implementation beyond formal legal adaptation.*
New policy instruments (instead of reform) *Problems created by an increased economic diversity of the enlarged Community are addressed by the creation of new policy instruments overlaid on existing ones rather than by a fundamental reform of the inadequacies of the latter.*	**<Asymmetry** *Explicit goal to reform policies before accession, differentiated application of critical policies for new member states (CAP, Structural Policy) instead of introduction of new policies.*
Incremental institutional adaptation *New members are integrated into the Community's institutional structure on the basis on limited incremental adaptation which is facilitated by the promise of a more fundamental review after enlargement.*	**<Conditionality** *Candidate states have to undergo major adaptations before accession, reforms of the EU structures likewise before accession.*
Negotiation with groups *The Community prefers to negotiate with groups of states that already have close relations with each other.*	**<Differentiation** *Each candidate is evaluated and negotiated with separately, stressing the bilateral character of EU/candidate relations.*

Source: Own table, cf. Preston (1995); Maniokas (2004).

approach: Instead of only focusing on the acquis, the agenda was extended by the Copenhagen criteria. Instead of introducing new policy instruments, reform of the existing instruments was made a condition sine qua non for taking on board new members. Equally, adaptations in candidate states were to be completed before accession and held more relevant than stabilizing the democratizing systems through quick integration, and negotiations were to be conducted by stressing the bilateral character of relations since the central and eastern European states rejected developing closer links before starting negotiations. The new bottom line of the Copenhagen strategy was to use the logic of conditionality to achieve adaptations before accession.

Given that enlargement policy extended supranational competences without fully institutionalizing these into the acquis, the Copenhagen framework is best conceptualized as a distinct institutional sub-system that is linked to but not fully incorporated into the acquis. Supranational actors apply rules that endow them with real competences, while the validity of these competences remains limited in time and scope. Conceptualizing enlargement policy in this manner has two advantages. First, methodologically, it equips us with clear distinctions to separate competences exercised in the enlargement context from capacities that emerged outside this distinct set of rules. The effects of policy making can therefore be traced. Second, enlargement is theorized as an integral feature of EU integration. Generalizations from the findings are therefore possible and should hold for other distinct institutional sub-systems that exist around the institutional core of the acquis. This conceptualization of enlargement policy therefore pitchforks the phenomenon out of the still prevalent lack of theoretical connectivity (Schimmelfennig and Sedelmeier 2002: 501), which is linked to the subordinate empirical attention or even complete theoretical negligence of enlargement in European integration theories (Wiener and Diez 2009: 235).

THEORETICAL FRAMEWORK AND RESEARCH APPROACH

The theoretical research interest in the impact of policies on institutionalization processes is tackled by resolving the empirical puzzle of how the implementation of enlargement affected the Commission's capacities. To this end, comparative analysis of five qualitative case studies will be conducted. Change is measured over time, and outcomes are compared across two groups of cases in which change occurred or failed to materialize. Methodologically, I will trace how policies were first established and implemented in the Copenhagen framework in order to investigate into the processes in between the two points of measurement before and after implementing enlargement. The following pages outline the conceptualization and measurement of the dependent variable as well as the systematic case selection before providing an outlook on the structure of the book. The underlying conceptual and methodological question that will be answered is, how can we observe and measure policy-generated institutionalization processes?

THE DEPENDENT VARIABLE: ACTION CAPACITY OF THE EUROPEAN COMMISSION

So far, I have referred to the dependent variable in rather unspecific terms as supranational capacities. This concept needs to be defined and operationalized more precisely. What we are interested in is, in the most abstract terms of proceeding EU integration, the accumulation of policy-making competences on the supranational level. The notion of policy-making competences is narrowed down by the cases under perspective. The cases are concerned with the competences the Commission had vis-à-vis the (candidate) states; the policy-making competences we are dealing with are accordingly the Commission's steering capacities. For the empirical analysis, these are operationalized as policy instruments through which the Commission can influence actor behavior inside states. To account for the fact that such capacities can be of hierarchical or nonhierarchical nature, I will refer to the term *action capacity*. The *European Commission's action capacity* in a particular policy field is hence established by the sum of formal or informal steering instruments that it has at its disposal in the multilevel polity, that is, the Commission's institutionalized capabilities to influence actor behavior inside the member states. If the implementation of enlargement had an impact, change must be observed between the status quo ante-policy instruments in a field before enlargement and the status quo post-policy instrument in the same field after enlargement.

Accounting for both hierarchical and nonhierarchical instruments is key to the definition of the dependent variable. The governance school has convincingly argued and illustrated in empirical research on the EU that steering "beyond the state" indeed relies on "policy-making without legislating" (Héritier 2002). While narrowly defined governance is restricted to such nonhierarchical modes of coordination, "[i]n the encompassing sense it implies every mode of political steering involving public and private actors, including the traditional modes of government and different types of steering from hierarchical imposition to sheer information measures" (Héritier 2002: 185). It is the sum of all forms of intentional collective coordination and regulation of societal concerns (Mayntz 2008: 45). This latter definition provides a suitable starting point to define the full range of action capacity that the Commission can possibly possess in a policy field. Empirically, formal competences are encompassed by legal acts that lay down a competence or task. Yet, de facto action capacity depends likewise on the behavioral practice of relevant actors given varying degrees of discretion of legal provisions that need to be interpreted in day-to-day policy making. To create a measure, we therefore have to consider legal and behavioral indicators.

In terms of legal formulation, steering instruments take different degrees of coerciveness ranging from exclusive competences anchored in the founding treaties to shared and auxiliary competences of the Commission to "support, coordinate or supplement the actions of the Member States" (European Council 2007).[4] Obviously, whereas exclusive treaty-based competences of the EU provide a clear-cut measure for the scope of action of the Commission, less coercive steering instruments are less sharply defined. Therefore, reference to behavioral patterns is necessary to distinguish the cut-off point of institutionalized capacities. I define institutionalized action capacity as steering instruments that are embedded in the organizational structure of the Commission and equipped with sufficient resources to be persistent over time. In consequence, ad hoc tasks exercised by the Commission that lack funding and organizational anchoring do not qualify as extended action capacity, since they fall short of institutionalization and do therefore not entail a persistent institutionalization and deepening of the EU polity.

Table 1.2 summarizes the empirical indicators to identify hierarchical and nonhierarchical steering instruments. Action capacity is operationalized as the steering instruments that the Commission has at its disposal.

Table 1.2   Action capacity of the European Commission

Mode of Governance Operationalization	Hierarchical	Nonhierarchical
Steering Instrument	Binding legislation	Incentive setting, voluntary accords, target setting and benchmarking, open method of coordination, informal agreements (networks)
Control Tools	Litigation (ECJ) (binding on policy taker)	"Naming and shaming," positive/negative rewards (optional for policy taker)
Empirical Indicators	Primary and secondary EU law (regulations, directives, decisions)	Organizational and financial resources of the Commission, policy programs, recommendations, inter-institutional agreements

Source: own table.

These instruments can be of hierarchical or nonhierarchical nature, which implies different control tools. These indicators will be applied to trace and measure change in the Commission's action capacity. Empirical indicators to trace steering instruments and control tools are either formal legal acts or informal institutional agreements and financial resources. We can envisage three possible scenarios: (a) member states change their strategy and integrate the competences the Commission had on critical policies vis-à-vis the candidate states by creating new formal competences, (b) the steering instruments the Commission developed in the Copenhagen framework are integrated without extending formal treaty powers, i.e., mainly nonhierarchical capacities result, and (c) authority over new policies remains limited to the context of enlargement policy. While the first two possibilities yield an extension of action capacity in varying degrees, the third option leads to a different outcome—which, by design of the Copenhagen mandate, should be the expected outcome.

CASE SELECTION: POLICY COMPETENCES BEYOND THE ACQUIS

The cases selected represent policies in which the Commission had no competences prior to implementing enlargement. Since competences over these policies were established for the first time in the enlargement framework but not the acquis communautaire, they are expected to create "spill-in" in favor of the Commission. In order to uncover the conditions under which such a spill-in occurs, all those cases in which the Commission had extended competences in the Copenhagen framework compared with its overall responsibilities under the acquis are scrutinized. Triangulating evidence from primary documents on policy programs, the actual implementation and the (external) evaluation of these, five areas emerge as relevant cases: the respect for and protection of minorities, institutional capacity building, cross-border cooperation, nuclear safety, and anticorruption policy. In the first three areas, an extension of the Commission's capacities can be observed, but this does not hold for the latter two cases. The design of the analysis is therefore *backward-looking*, meaning that the specific variance on the dependent variable is to be explained as well as possible (Scharpf 1997). Arguing that in policy analysis it is usually impossible to isolate cause-effect relationships, a backward-looking design offers a pragmatic, *y-centered* research strategy that aims to explain variance on the dependent variable (in contrast to a x-centered perspective that asks which effects a specific independent variable causes) (Ganghof 2005). Correspondingly, the qualitative cross-temporal analysis of the single cases serves to trace and explain the particular conditions that are then compared across the two groups of cases.

The limited number of cases available does not lend itself to a systematic most different case comparison. However, covering different policy issues it is possible to compare, in a second step, the varying independent variables to examine possible alternative explanations based on policy classifications. The theoretical framework that will be developed in Part II hypothesizes that the policy type and mode of governance are decisive for an extension of the Commission's action capacity. The cases under perspective do not systematically vary on the independent variable, the policy types at stake, but they vary regarding the policy issues and hence the treaty bases they build upon. In addition to the main body of the research, an indicative comparison will be added that links to Hoffmann's challenge to neofunctional theory. Hoffmann argued that whether a policy is concerned with "high" or "low" politics determines the likelihood for integration, not functional pressure (1982: 29). Although the findings of the comparisons confirm the crucial relevance of politics, the distinction between high and low politics does not match the pattern observed. Instead, whether a functional policy response on the EU level can be decoupled from the essential political stakes of national actors explains variance.

OUTLINE OF THE BOOK

The remainder of the book falls in three parts that develop the theoretical and empirical argument and provide a comparative summary of the empirical findings in order to draw conclusions on and along the main themes of the book. The second part spells out the theoretical framework. The explanation of how policies generate institutionalization of supranational action capacity proceeds in two steps that form an epistemologically consistent functionalist model. Referring to neofunctional integration theory, the necessary conditions for policies to generate supranational institutionalization derive from functional pressure that is generated by the formulation and implementation of policies in the enlargement framework. Lowi's policy typology is then introduced to identify the sufficient conditions that explain why policies that are under functional pressure will be institutionalized or not. Policies are treated as independent variables to explain why and how supranational competences are institutionalized. As the dependent variable, institutions are shaped according to how actors frame a political problem. Institutions therefore depend on expectations actors hold depending on the political problem and conflict at stake.

Part III substantiates the argument along five case studies to scrutinize the main hypothesis, namely, that the expected political relationships between the Commission and citizens are decisive for member states to tolerate or block the institutionalization of supranational capacities. Political relationships depend on the policy type at play and the mode of governance applied. Tracing the single cases, each chapter falls into three parts: (a) Commission competences under the acquis in a respective policy field before 1993, (b) the establishment and exercise of steering instruments in the Copenhagen framework, and (c) supranational steering instruments under the acquis after enlargement. For every case, the degree of functional pressure for institutionalization and the direction of shifts in the distribution of political authority are investigated. Methodologically, tracing the formulation and execution of policies during the pre-accession phase fleshes out the causal links between the changes observed before and after implementing enlargement. Chapters 4 to 6 illustrate the cases in which the creation and implementation of policies in the Copenhagen framework was extended beyond the initial mandate; chapters 7 and 8 present the cases in which the member states actively refuted extended supranational authority in the EU's framework.

The book closes by discussing the single cases from a comparative perspective, offering a compact summary of the empirical analysis and the main results at the same time. In sum, the conclusions raise far-reaching questions on legitimacy of and political representation in the EU that, in fact, continues to create ever more creeping supranational competences in order to offer functional responses to collective challenges while preempting political spill-over, that is, the establishment of more substantive political relationships between citizens and policy makers on the EU level. In short, member state governments are generous in tolerating new Commission action capacity to produce policies as long as political attention remains in the national realm.

PART II

THEORETICAL FRAMEWORK

POLICY MAKING AS CAUSE FOR INTEGRATION: A TWO-LEVEL FUNCTIONAL APPROACH

> I was attempting to turn political science on its head (or back on its feet) by arguing that "policy causes politics."
>
> Theodore J. Lowi, "New Dimensions in Policy and Politics"[1]

CHAPTER 2

NECESSARY AND SUFFICIENT CONDITIONS FOR POLICY-GENERATED INSTITUTIONALIZATION

The analysis starts from an empirical observation. From a set of restricted competences delegated to the supranational level, some competences recede as foreseen while others extend beyond their initially intended reach. The very design of the Copenhagen framework was to establish new policy-making capacities in a distinct institutional setting to realize enlargement without creating new formal powers for the European Union. Accordingly, the empirical null-hypothesis that the theoretical conceptualization departs from reads: after the completion of enlargement, the additional capacities delegated to the Commission to implement enlargement will disappear. This hypothesis does not hold. As a matter of fact, competences are extended beyond the constrained realm they were first placed in. Why and how?

Over the following pages a two-level functional explanation will be developed to answer this question. Overall, a *neofunctional approach* will explicate why enlargement creates functional pressure and thus the necessary condition for the extension of Commission action capacity. The approach does not, however, capture the sufficient conditions for a single policy to be institutionalized. Hence neofunctionalism provides the starting point of the analysis and is complemented with the *arenas of power approach* that focuses on single policies. On the basis of the latter, the sufficient conditions for the integration of a particular policy are identified.

The institutionalization of new action capacities on the EU level viewed from a neofunctional perspective leads to the following expectation: *if new capacities are established in a distinct institutional setting outside the core institutions, the overall likelihood for further integration increases.* The underlying mechanism is *policy-generated functional pressure* to integrate capacities to the institutional core. This does, however, not mean that each and every policy under pressure will be institutionalized. The expectation for a single policy goes beyond the neofunctional explanation: *whether a capacity under functional pressure will be institutionalized depends on the implicit political stakes at play.* The intervening variables to capture the expected political consequences are the mode of governance and the policy type because both define the relationship between policy makers and individual citizens. It is expected that member state governments support responses to functional pressure, that is, the shift of policy making to the EU level, as long as it does not entail political spillover and hence a loyalty transfer of citizens from the national to the supranational realm. Therefore, certain policy types and steering instruments are integrated while the conferral of other political problems is preempted.

Complementing the *neofunctional* approach by the equally functional *arenas of power approach* increases the explanatory scope of the model. Neofunctionalism alone suffers from a "lack of generalizable micro-foundational basis necessary to support predictions about variation in support for integration across issue countries, and time" (Moravcsik 1998: 16). Unlike the realist school in international relations for which power and the distribution of preferences remain the basic explanatory factors (Morgenthau 1960; Walt 1987; Waltz 1979; Wight 1991), in functional terms the ultimate independent variable are means-ends relations. It follows that for realist approaches bargaining theories offer consistent microfoundations to create a consistent, more holistic theory (Keohane 1984, 1989; Keohane and Milner 1996; Keohane and Nye 1974; Nye 1988). But by the same token, it is not the case that "neofunctionalism lacked explicit theories of interest-group policies, interstate bargaining, and international institutions" (Moravcsik 1998: 16). Proposing a consistent functional argument, the choice whether to cooperate for a particular purpose depends on whether the shared perception suggests that a choice offers the best available means to pursue specific ends. If sticking to a functional logic, the ultimate choice for cooperation or noncooperation must therefore be an inherent characteristic of a policy. Put in a nutshell, *whether cooperation occurs or not depends on the kind of policy at stake because it determines actor expectations and their strategic policy choices.*

Staying within the functional logic, the theoretical microfoundations must be linked to the shared perceptions on built-in qualities of each policy. Whether a policy established in the Copenhagen framework will be extended to the wider acquis must depend on its expected impact on the member states. This again derives from the manner in which a policy is first framed at the supranational level. Following this line of thought, it is necessary to turn to heuristics that classify policies as well as a descriptive institutional analysis in order to categorize policy features that lead policy makers to devise their strategies.

Why opt for a holistic functional explanation? The research puzzle and design lend themselves to a neofunctional explanation. The more general research question about the link between deepening and widening is concerned with the grand themes of EU integration. Neofunctionalism's focus on incremental supranationalization of powers is particularly well suited to analyze the effects of policy implementation over a number of years (in contrast to approaches that focus on "grand bargains"). The focus on policy-generated change, in turn, is best captured by the arena of powers' focus on policies as determinants for politics because it offers conceptual tools to distinguish causal mechanisms linked to different types of policies. In addition, the two angles complement each other and offer a powerful, consistent theoretical approach.

Structuring the analysis along necessary and sufficient conditions deserves an important qualification. The purpose here is not to generalize about necessary conditions more broadly but to resolve a "real-life" puzzle. Neofunctional research backs the theoretical expectation that functional pressure is a necessary condition for the institutionalization of new action capacity. The main focus of this study is, however, not to test whether this necessary condition holds generally. Empirically, functional pressure is observed in all cases under scrutiny, while no systematic comparison with cases in which no functional pressure emerged is conducted—not least because of the absence of such cases. In consequence, the present research design does not provide a thorough empirical testing of necessary conditions, but it offers a theoretically consistent explanation for the underlying research puzzle.

Furthermore, the theoretical framework developed below complements rather than competes with other approaches that, at first sight, seem to offer alternative explanations. *Principal-agent* frameworks offer another reading of the puzzle on focusing on "how rational actors can control the behavior of agents to whom they delegate authority" (see Epstein and O'Halloran 1999a: 698).[2] These approaches have been fruitfully applied to the EU in a number of influential studies.[3] Applying a principal-agent model offers a conceptual framework geared to capture unintended effects of delegation. Framing our puzzle in these terms, an extension of Commission action capacity should be caused by agency loss: the Commission (the agent) is delegated limited capacities by the member states (the principals) and extends its discretion beyond the initial mandate. Agency loss arises because agents can exploit their advantageous access to information. Information asymmetries bare the danger that agents behave opportunistic in favor of their own preferences (shrinking, also bureaucratic drift), or systematically different to the principal's preferences (slippage). Scanning through the empirical evidence, an explanation offered by principal-agent theory does not contradict the findings. It shows, however, also that the member state governments can actually successfully prevent the Commission from acquiring capacities. The Commission does not shirk, but in some cases member states allow an extension of its capacities, which they reject in other cases. What principal-agent theory cannot capture is why and how member state preferences are molded and may change during a policy-making process. The analysis offered in the following does not directly compete with this contention but provides a different angle that asks instead: what determines the principals' preferences regarding Commission capacities?

A second stream of literature that needs to be distinguished is the *new institutionalism* (Hall and Taylor 1996). The model applied shares the basic feature of actor-centered institutionalism (Mayntz and Scharpf 1995a; Scharpf 1997) in that both are concerned with (mainly corporate) actors acting and interacting within institutional frameworks. A central difference to the revised neofunctionalist approach is, however, the role of norms. With direct reference to Scharpf's framework Haas states that actor-centered institutionalism "sounds as if it could combine institutionalism with constructivism: but this is not so. Ideas do not matter. Actors do not change preferences during the game, but rather they recalculate advantages. . . . Rival assessments of benefits, shaped by prior ideas or ideologies, are still excluded. Learning, in the sense of reassessing values, does not operate" (2004b: xlvi). Accordingly, the neofunctional starting point links most directly to sociological institutionalism "that overlaps with neo-neofunctionalism in its emphasis on the formation of transnational class, sectoral and professional associations, and the contestation generated by global and regional social movements" (Schmitter 2003: 49). Other new institutionalist approaches—based on more hard rationality, epistemic, or legal logics—remain outside of the neofunctional explanatory model. Again, it is the specific underlying research interest that suggests a neofunctional approach to identify the conditions under which action capacity is extended beyond the Copenhagen enlargement framework. For this to happen, member state actors indeed have to change their strategies on the basis of expected outcomes to tolerate that the Commission attains new actor capacities: what drives the change in strategies that leads member state actors to tolerate the institutionalization of capacities beyond the initially intended limits?

NEOFUNCTIONALISM: NECESSARY CONDITIONS AND MACROPERSPECTIVE

The neofunctionalist point of departure is that policies created in an institutionally distinct framework outside the institutional core raise the likelihood for further integration. It is expected that the exercise of policies generates functional pressure to institutionalize capacities within the main legal framework. Markedly, "neither functionalism, nor neofunctionalism nor neo-neofunctionalism has or had anything to say about enlargement" (Schmitter 2003: 70). The question under which conditions policy making generates institutionalization is, however, directly linked to neofunctional concepts that explain the progression of integration. To this end, the approach will be extended by the notion of *spill-in* of policies from an institutional subset (the Copenhagen framework) to the institutional core (the acquis). The respective approach allows defining ex ante under which conditions the *likelihood* for an extension of the sum of supranational capacities rises.

I will narrow down the theoretical discussion to the revised versions as last presented by Ernst Haas (2004a) and Philippe Schmitter (2003) in which they revive the theory whose "obsolence" Haas himself had announced in the 1970s (1975).[4] Asserting that "[r]egional integration theory has a new lease; it is no longer obsolete" (Haas 2004a: liii), Haas and Schmitter integrate theoretical developments of the decades since the theory was first introduced (in particular: Haas 1968; Schmitter 1970, 1971b) and provide a sketch for a research agenda based on the strengths and weaknesses of the revised (neo-)neofunctional approach. Before we extend the neofunctional model to apply it to our puzzle, it is worthwhile to consider the following brief summary of the main innovations that are of relevance for our analysis.

Neofunctionalism is a theory of regional integration in which non-state actors play key role in advancing integration. In the case of the EU the Commission was expected to play this role as supranational secretariat, together with other non-state organizations (interest associations, social movements, etc.). In initiating integration, member states are the key actors, but in all subsequent stages member states alone determine neither the direction nor the dynamics of integration. Quite to the contrary, non-state actors can successfully unite their potential influence to promote their own interest for more supranational competences. They do so by exploiting the fact that the initial assignment of limited tasks creates functional pressures to extend supranational activities into other areas as far as this appears necessary to fully achieve the intended goals. In other words, *unintended consequences* and *functional spillover* occur. This process is "intrinsically sporadic and conflictual," but "under conditions of democracy and pluralistic representation, national governments will find themselves increasingly entangled in regional pressures and end up resolving their conflicts by conceding a wider scope and developing more authority to the regional organizations they have created" (Schmitter 2003: 46). The functional spillover from the economic-social sphere will hence eventually lead to *political spillover,* in which national actors and citizens shift expectations to the supranational level. By adding the arenas of power approach below, it will be argued that because certain policy arenas are more prone to evoke political spillover, national decision makers will give in to functional pressures as long as it does not imply the creation of direct political relationships between citizens and the supranational level.

Adhering to the basic neofunctional framework, Haas confronts the approach with related work dealing with multilevel governance, new institutionalism, path dependency, and constructivism to suggest amendments. Likewise, Schmitter offers a self-critical review and spells out an extended "neo-neofunctionalist" research agenda. The revised version of the approach will be summarized along five concepts that the authors raise. (1) The distinction of different mechanisms of integration is outlined and extended by the notion of spill-in. (2) The definition of the dependent variable is critically reviewed to arrive at a more open-ended concept of multilevel and polycentric polity in which the notion of Commission action capacity fits well in as dependent variable. (3) The key actors are outlined, and the persistent role of national governments is highlighted. Accordingly, the discretion of the Commission and effective control capacities of the member states can be qualified. (4) Tapping on the structure-agency problem, the double-role of institutions as context and dependent variable is discussed. This implies for the analysis that institutions both feature as context variables that constrain or motivate actor strategies and are the result of political action. (5) Finally, spillover is distinguished from related concepts, such as the logic of path dependence. This underpins the reasons for opting for a neofunctional explanation.

(1) Early neofunctionalism came soon under attack for assuming that, once initiated, integration would proceed quasi-automatically. Arguing that a theory of integration must also be a theory of disintegration, Schmitter refuted this notion already in 1970 when he introduced a model based on concepts for different modes of integration, stalemate, and disintegration (Schmitter 1970, 1971a) that occur at different rates

of intensity in consecutive upward-moving cycles of integration. For integration to progress the most likely mechanism is *spillover*, that is, the simultaneous and balanced increase of the level of authority (decisional authority) and scope of authority (number of issue areas). The most likely outcome is encapsulation, that is, "to respond to crisis by marginal modifications within the zone of indifference" (Schmitter 1970: 846), which marks the status quo reached in integration.

To account for the integration of a policy from an institutionally distinct but linked subset or spin-off, I will introduce the notion of *spill-in* below. Like spillover, spill-in increases level and scope of authority, yet the mechanism is not that functional pressure links related policies but that functional pressure links different institutional frameworks. The emphasis on the nonautomatic nature of integration is key to the explanation, in which functional pressure is a necessary but not sufficient condition for integration.

The different dynamics of (dis-)integration have further been extended to include different forums altogether. Consequently, not only the European Commission may embody supranationalization. This contention will be reflected in the cases studies. Other international organizations than the EU prove important players that offer alternative functional responses and thus viable, less coercive substitutes for cooperation in the EU framework. Theoretically, this implies that instead of a final statelike entity "it becomes possible (even probable) to envisage other end-states," and hence a " 'Multi-level and Poly-centric System of Governance' is one such candidate" (Schmitter 2003: 69). This guides to the next two points of amendment, the dependent variable and the role of actors, in particular member state governments.

(2) Initially, neofunctionalism aimed to "judge if and how 'political community' results from measures of 'political integration' " (Haas 2004b: 4). Regarding the EU, this *dependent variable* was equated with the eventual formation of a federal state-like entity. Sandholtz et al. (2001) depart from this and redefine the dependent variable more open-ended as "institutionalized governance for an emerging 'European space' " (Haas 2004a: xx). As a consequence, no explicit finalité or end state is implied or defined. Instead of integrating the compatible elements, I propose to use neo-institutionalist language as a heuristic. Accordingly, the dependent variable is a measure of scope and level of institutionalization of single policies. In the EU's constitutional framework, official policy competences are the formal source of supranational power and the key indicator for integration. As outlined above, for the research question dealt with, the dependent variable is defined as institutionalized action

capacities. These embrace both formal competences and nonhierarchical supranational steering instruments. This definition falls into the wider definition of "institutionalized governance."

The definition by Sandholtz/Sweet Stone/Fligstein (SSF) faces Haas's critique that the conceptualization suggests falsely: "institutions are empty of content. What seems to matter to SSF is the creation and multiplication of organizations that make, interpret, and enforce rules, not the interests and actors who 'inhabit' them" (2004a: xxii). For Haas this is problematic since the logic of spillover is driven by interests and ideas that determine the rules actors opt for. Sticking to SSF while paying respect to the role of interests and ideas is, however, no contradiction if we accept the dual role of institutions in the model. Accordingly, the degree of institutionalization is a measure to estimate scope and level of integration, that is, the dependent variable. At the same time, interests and ideas are on the side of the independent variables that are at the core of the explanatory mechanism. Here institutions appear as background variables and are by no means "empty of content." The dual role of institutions will be further illustrated with respect to the agency/structure problem.

(3) In their revisions, the authors do not suggest fundamental adaptations regarding the role of pertinent actors. Yet, they rebalance the emphasis on the impact and importance of different actors with reference to related analytical approaches to EU integration. "An appreciation of multilevel governance implies continued respect for one crucial level: the national governments, embattled though they may be" (Haas 2004a: xvi). This perspective adds clarity in defining actors and their roles; it does not add explanatory elements. Haas defends the central roles that member state governments were attributed also in early neofunctionalism by claiming that "[i]t is not true that NF downplayed these actors in the interest of puffing up supranational organizations. But it is true that NF exaggerated the rate at which national governments were expected to lose out on them" (2004a: xvi). Arguing that multilevel and polycentric governance will always remain a feature of the EU and similar systems, the emphasis on member state governments as central actors is more pronounced than in earlier versions (Schmitter 2003: 49–52).

The relevance of the vertical and horizontal division of powers in the EU governance system is key for understanding the extension of action capacity. Authority is divided not only between different levels but also across EU institutions. It follows that any increased involvement of one organization, such as the Commission, affects the relative power of the other organizations, such as the European Parliament or the Councils. Institutionalization processes therefore affect both vertical relationships across the levels of governance and horizontal relationships among the supranational organizations. Moreover, formal decisions on the conferral of powers to the EU level remain a matter of interstate bargaining among the member states. The functional analysis focuses on the reasons why decision makers adapt their strategies to allow for more supranational authority, or to counteract the extension of steering capacities on the EU level. In order to understand the conditions under which the Commission acquires new capacities, we therefore need to consider the interplay of various actors, including member state governments that play a decisive part as gatekeepers for the extension of action capacity.

(4) Linking neofunctionalism to constructivist metatheoretical notions raises another central question, namely, the *agency/structure dilemma.* Underlining that his version of neofunctionalism "has no concern with structures at all, while that of Lindberg and Scheingold for example, does" (2001: 29), Haas emphasizes that he does *not* conceptualize institutions as structures. Instead he stresses that "agency is constrained by the actors' enmeshment in networks, formed by institutions and habit, not by structural forces. These constraints, however, do not predict the results of agency or action itself because PC [pragmatic constructivism] also assumes that actors adjust their later behavior in the light of the perceived failure or earlier behavior to realize the actors' perceived interests. Put differently, later choices are the result of unwanted and unforeseen consequences" (Haas 2004a: xxvi). The strong emphasis on the primacy of actors over institutions is essential. Relaxing it would render the approach inevitably teleological. Nonetheless, institutions are not the only outcomes. Once in place they constitute constraints and opportunities for future choices. On the side of the explanans, they do not cause change but set the context that affects actors. As pointed out before, they are not "empty," but are containers of ideas, preferences, and so on, and thus influence the choices made.

It follows that for the empirical analysis we need to control for stability of the background of institutions for the period under perspective. An adaptation of the institutional context implies different context variables that impact the dependent variable differently. It follows, moreover, that structure cannot be an overreaching general force, or even be *the* independent variable. The relevant features of an (institutional) structure are time and case dependent. Agency remains always the ultimate source for action and the creation of structure. The notion of intended and unintended consequences reflects this: if actors set up formal rules to bind each other, they do so consciously in order to constrain their future options; if an institution causes unforeseen side effects, actors might be forced to intervene, and so forth.

(5) The causal mechanism by which functional pressure leads to *spillover* resembles strongly the concept of path dependency. Notwithstanding similarities to Pierson's work on path dependency (1996, 2000), Haas highlights the conceptual differences between neofunctionalism and historical institutionalism. First, neofunctionalism similarly refers to irreversibility and lock-in effects, though not envisaging positive feedback as historical institutionalism does. "Instead of developing a notion of positive gains, the spillover was driven by a postulated fear by the actors of suffering losses *unless* further sectors were integrated" (Haas 2004a: xxiii, emphasis in the original). Although in both approaches preceding choices have a decisive impact on future actor strategies, they differ in that path dependency is concerned with costs that derive from changing previous choices while spillover—and for our propose spill-in—consider future costs of not integrating further.

Second, Haas sets apart the concept of *unintended consequences* from other theoretical explanations because "these perspectives are not congruent. Principal-agent theory, PD [path-dependency], and rational choice theory are not concerned with specific actor values and interests; NF, using the logic of unintended consequences, is" (2004a: xxiii). Both the neofunctional and path dependency logic conceptualize unintended consequences as a strong integration mechanisms since they force actors to improvise and devise new strategies when confronted with unpredicted difficulties. What distinguishes the approaches is that neofunctionalism is primarily concerned with what spills over or not and which consequences are unintended and unwanted. The "idea that different actors entertain different hierarchies of values and interests," which are "factored out" by the other approaches, "is the mainstay of research" (2004a: xxxiii). Thus, "the logic of unintended consequences is clearly different from spillover and path-dependency thinking. Making it the centerpiece in an explanation of major changes dispenses with the mechanical aspects of both. It moves the empirical scope of study well beyond the expansion of economic ties and networks, by making *any* concrete policy domain and *any* constitutional issue subject to its logic" (Haas 2004a: xxiv, emphasis in the original). The subsequent empirical analysis will illustrate these two distinctions from historical institutionalism. First, the logic of spill-in concerns the member state governments' expected future costs in case of (non)integration from the institutional subset to the acquis. Second, unintended consequences, where they occur, will explain especially nonintegrative strategies of actors who are faced with unwanted outcomes.

To apply neofunctionalism to institutional effects that the implementation of eastern enlargement has had on EU organizations, we need to extend the concept of spillover to capture the extension of policy capacities from the enlargement to the acquis framework.

EXTENDING THE MODEL TO ENLARGEMENT: INSTITUTIONAL SUBSETS AND SPIN-OFFS AS TRIGGERS FOR SPILL-IN

The five points summarized above suggest in essence three clarifications: the adaptation proper of the integration outcome (the dependent variable), the reformulation of earlier research questions against developments in other theoretical streams (multilevel, constructivism), and the distinction from other related approaches (path dependency, principal/agent). The explanatory mechanism remains the functional linkage between policies that generate pressure for actors to adapt their strategies to further integration.

In order to include enlargement into the model, Figure 2.1 introduces the concept of functional *spill-in*. The theoretical extension is not

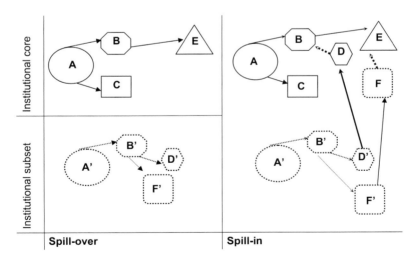

Figure 2.1   The concepts of Spillover and Spill-in
Source: own figure.

concerned with the question of why enlargement occurs. It does not offer a functional explanation to the phenomenon of widening but proposes a way to conceptualize the effect of institutional subsets and spin-offs on the course of integration. Under the Copenhagen pre-accession framework, enlargement was implemented in an institutionally distinct but acquis-dependent structure. It was a distinct institutional subset. Without creating genuinely new supranational competences, the Commission had extended powers that were limited to the pre-accession context. These are illustrated in the lower two boxes (policies A', B' . . .), in contrast to the formal competences that form part of the acquis, depicted in the upper part of the figure (policies A, B, . . .). On the left hand side, the concept of spillover is depicted both for the institutional core, say the EU acquis (upper cell), and an institutional subset, say the Copenhagen enlargement framework (lower cell). The logic is that integration of policy A will lead to integration of policies B and C, which again lead to integration of further policies.

The same dynamics may occur in the institutional subset. To illustrate this, the addition of administrative capacity building as accession precondition in the Madrid EU Council in 1995 was triggered by the perception that this was indispensable to achieve the pre-accession objectives set out earlier. Hence, a spillover into a related field occurred within the Copenhagen framework.

The right hand side of Figure 2.1 depicts the interaction between the two institutional systems. The innovation introduced is the jump of policies from the subset to the core. The underlying mechanism is that once established and exercised in a subset, pressure for integration proper rises and the likelihood for integration mounts. Should strong unintended consequences emerge, actors may, however, prevent a spill-in to be realized. The way in which I refer to neofunctionalism limits the explanation to the increased likelihood for integration. Whether F' will indeed be integrated as policy F depends on the microfoundational characteristics of the policy not fully captured by neofunctionalism.

In conclusion, what does the revised neofunctionalism contribute to analyzing the conditions under which new capacities are institutionalized on the supranational level? In contrast to the null hypothesis that capacities remain within the scope and temporal limits they were designed in, neofunctionalism hypothesizes that *policies newly established and successfully implemented in an institutional subsystem generate functional pressure for spill-in and thus raise the likelihood for supranational institutionalization.* (1) The underlying mechanism is *spill-in*. Policies are extended beyond the distinct institutional setting that they are restricted to by the original institutional design because political actors expect to suffer losses unless they move the policy from the institutional subsystem to the institutional core. (2) The dependent variable is newly *institutionalized capacities* on the supranational level as indicator for further integration of the multilevel and polycentered system. (3) The multilevel and polycentric nature of the EU implies that member states remain decisive political *actors* as regards proceeding supranational institutionalization. Member state governments' preferences and strategies and the adaptation of these are therefore the main focal point. (4) *Institutions* feature both on the side of the explanadum and explanans. On the one hand, an increase in supranational institutionalization is the currency to measure progress in integration. On the other hand, the institutional conditions influence actors' expectations and thereby constrain or facilitate—but do not determine—actor strategies. (5) The spill-in mechanism is based on member states' *expected costs* of nonintegration of policies originally created and exercised in an institutional subsystem. Unintended consequences may occur and lead actors to adapt their strategies. The first step of the model, building on neofunctionalism, thus explicates the necessary conditions for policy making to generate further supranational institutionalization. It does not capture the sufficient conditions under which a single policy is integrated.

ARENAS OF POWER: SUFFICIENT CONDITIONS AND MICROFOUNDATIONS

Whereas neofunctionalism spells out the necessary conditions for supranational institutionalization, it does not sufficiently account for the conditions under which action capacities over a single policy issue will be institutionalized. Sticking to a functionalist explanation, these conditions must be logically linked to the specificities of different policy types. Hence neofunctionalism is complemented with the *arenas of power approach* that distinguishes different modes of political interaction according to distinct types of policies. On the basis of the latter, the sufficient conditions for the integration of a particular policy are identified. Within the explanatory model, neofunctionalism and the policy typology complement each other. While Lowi's heuristic policy "model as it stands is a tool of microanalysis, but offers no theory of institutional change that can help us to integrate it into the analysis of systemic change" (Nicholson 2002: 170), neofunctionalism as it stands is a theory is a tool for macroanalysis, but offers no theory for institutional change that can help us to integrate it into the analysis of policy change.[5] Together the two approaches offer a comprehensive and coherent theoretical model to analyze the conditions under which supranational capacities become institutionalized.

Again, in order to explain the particular puzzle under perspective, the approach needs to be extended. Although the central notion of different arenas of power that imply specific actor relationships between policy makers and policy takers holds, the original approach neglects nonhierarchical forms, or new modes, of governance. Since these are of central relevance to supranational steering instruments in the multilevel EU polity, we need to stretch the arenas of power concepts to account for the full extension they have in EU policy making. Before doing so, I will introduce the basic approach by applying it to the policy framework of the EU.

Theodore J. Lowi first developed his typology of policies in the early 1960s and refined the approach throughout the 1970s and 1980s. Turning the prevailing understanding of political systems on its head, or "back on its feet" (Lowi 1988: xi), he claimed that it is actually policies that determine politics rather than the other way around. This implies that the structure of state-society interactions, the "political relationships," depends on the particular type of policy. The "general interpretative scheme" is based on the following argument: "(1) The types of relationships to be found are determined by their expectations—by what they hope to achieve or get from relating to others. (2) In politics, expectations are determined by governmental outputs or policies. (3) Therefore, a political relationship is determined by the type of policy at stake, so that for every policy there is likely to be a distinctive relationship" (Lowi 1964: 688). In other words, what is at stake shapes how policy makers and policy takers interact. Moreover, for the policies it is imperative that "these types are historically as well as functionally distinct," they correspond to real phenomena, and therefore "*these areas of policy or government activity constitute real arenas of power*. Each arena tends to develop its own characteristic, political structure, political processes, elites, and group relations" (Lowi 1964: 689–90, emphasis in the original).

In the early versions, Lowi referred to *coercion* as the defining characteristic of public policy, which encompasses positive or negative sanctions that are imposed intentionally on citizens (Lowi 1985: 70). The two dimensions of the typology refer to the ways in which a state exercises authority/coercion. The first is the likelihood of state power, which can be immediate or remote. The initial notion of immediate and remote coercion (1964) was in later versions replaced with the legalistic concepts of primary and secondary rule (1985), which clarified the concept in that it depicted better the role of political and social expectations that are endogenous to the formulation of a policy (Capano 1992: 562). While the former impose concrete obligations or positions, the latter refer to powers and privileges. The second dimension concerns the applicability of

state power. The respective units are individuals directly or their environments of conduct. Table 2.1 reproduces Lowi's revised typology, adding
examples of EU policies.

Why does this matter for the analysis of the European Union? The
EU has been described as "partial polity" (Wallace, W. 2005) because
its policy agenda is substantively incomplete. More pointedly, the EU
has formal authority and thus exists officially only where the Treaties
confer policy competences to it. In consequence the pattern of actual
policy competences remains patchy. Ergo, we can expect from the limited policy agenda that the EU's arenas of power and hence the political
relationships between citizens and supranational governance will show
a systematic bias. The following classification of EU policies may be
contested, not least because Lowi's typology itself can be criticized for
being too elusive to apply the types unambiguously empirically.[6] The
application is nonetheless considered relevant because it offers workable
heuristics to classify EU activities as to identify policy-specific institutional structures. Referring back to the empirical puzzle, this provides a
basis to formulate expectations on the effect of policy making on institutionalization processes. Beyond general concerns about the applicability
of the approach, the interpretation diverges from readings that underline
the overall redistributive nature of EU activities (see especially, Donahue
and Pollack 2001). In contrast, I strongly concur with writings by William
and Helen Wallace.[7]

As prominently argued by William Wallace the EU agenda incorporated form the outset regulatory and distributive issues. Even if "some
of the consequences were in practice redistributive . . . , neither the initial
compact nor the explicit policy prescriptions identified were fundamentally redistributive in purpose," while constituent issues were included
into the Treaties "largely in unspecific and conditional terms" (1983:
411–12). Although the issue range and scope of EU policy making have
considerably extended since, the bias for regulatory and distributive over
redistributive and constituent arenas still prevails. To illustrate this core
argument, I will briefly outline the main features of each arena and how
they play out in the EU context, including the latest institutional innovations of the Lisbon Treaty that took effect in December 2009. Beyond
Lowi's narrow legalistic definitions that assume hierarchical state-society
relationships, I will add illustrations of nonhierarchical relationships that
have come to play a central role in EU policy making. Special emphasis
will be put on the political relationships the arenas of power imply.

Regulatory policies, although rules stated in general terms, directly
impact individuals by raising costs and/or reducing or expanding alternative options. They are laws that focus on desired outcomes, imposing

Table 2.1 Lowi's policy typology

	Works through Individual Conduct	**Works through Environment of Conduct**
FORM OF EXPRESSED INTENTION / **FORM OF INDEPENDENT IMPACT**		
PRIMARY RULE imposes obligations or positions	**REGULATORY POLICIES:** Rules impose obligations; Rules of individual conduct, criminal in form **SYNONYMS:** police power, government intervention **EXAMPLES:** public health laws, industrial safety, traffic laws, antitrust **EXAMPLES EU:** Competition policy, Economic and Finance, Trade, Environment, Food Safety/Health/Consumer Affairs, Transport (open sky), Counterterrorism/Justice, Freedom and Security	**REDISTRIBUTIVE POLICIES:** Rules impose classification or status; rules categorizing activity **SYNONYMS:** Fiscal and monetary policy, overall budget policies **EXAMPLES:** income tax, Federal Reserve discount rates, Social Security **EXAMPLES EU:** Multi-annual Budget
SECONDARY RULE confers powers or privileges	**DISTRIBUTIVE POLICIES:** Rules confer facilities or privileges unconditionally **SYNONYMS:** patronage, subsidy, pork barrel **EXAMPLES:** public works, agricultural extension, land grants **EXAMPLES EU:** Common Agricultural Policy, Structural Policy, Cohesion Policy, Education, International Aid, Science & Technology/Research	**CONSTITUENT POLICIES:** *Rules* confer powers; rules about rules and about authority **SYNONYMS:** overhead, auxiliary, government organization **EXAMPLES:** agencies for budgetary and personnel policy, laws establishing judicial jurisdiction **EXAMPLES EU:** Intergovernmental agreements, Treaty reforms, Convention Method, expansive ECJ Treaty interpretation, EU accessions, principles of subsidiarity and proportionality

Source: Lowi 1964, 1985; extended by examples EU.

obligations and sanctions. Unlike distributive policies they cannot be disaggregated but create clear winners and losers. Accordingly, "[s]ince the
most stable lines of perceived common impact are the basic sectors of the
economy, regulatory decisions are cumulative largely along sectoral lines;
regulatory policies are usually disaggregable only down to the sector level"
(Lowi 1964: 691). As regards the mode of interaction, regulatory policies
evoke conflict between client groups with competing interests because
they imply the betterment of some at the expense of others. "Adjudi-
cation of conflicts depends primarily on technical and legal evaluations
of whether particular actions fall inside or outside the rules" (Wallace
1983: 412).

Regulatory policies are the main battleground of the EU, in fact the
polity has been characterized as a regulatory state per se (Majone 1996).
Examples of regulatory policies defined strictly in Lowi's terms are the
formally binding legal acts (regulations, directives, and decisions), which
leave limited or no leeway for interpretation to actors on the state level.
In cases of noncompliance, the Commission can appeal to the ECJ to
enforce law in the member states. Hard regulation in the EU concentrates predominantly on the economic sector, which comprises the core
competences of the Community assigned in the founding Treaties. The
heyday of the "EU regulatory mode" has been the development of the single market and the development of EU competition policy. To the extent
that the EU has industrial, social, and environmental policies, these build
mainly on regulatory measures (Wallace, H. 2005: 80–81). Beyond the
"ordinary" regulatory policies, the EU relies on less coercive instruments
that do not feature in Lowi's original typology. Complementing hard
regulation, the EU has a variety of tools, both in form of nonbinding
agreements among member states and as formalized regulation that leaves
considerable discretion to member states (especially recommendations,
framework decisions, and the instruments of the second and third pillar). In other words, the regular legislative procedures of the EU provide
for instruments that grant considerable discretion to the member states
on how to transpose regulatory policies. Still more discretionary is EU
soft law that has no binding effect but—in contrast to the redistributive
arena—can refer to a shadow of hierarchy because the regulatory arena
and the respective possibility for coercive steering is well established (Cini
2000; Héritier 2003; López-Santana 2006; Sisson and Marginson 2001;
Trubek and Trubek 2005).

The political relationships in the regulatory arena have evolved over
time. Rather than the emergence of strong EU parties, a form of plu-
ralist interest representation has increased with the widening of the
regulatory agenda. In particular in order to raise the legitimacy of EU

regulation, the EU Commission has promoted explicitly the consultation and participation of non-state actors since the publication of the white book on governance (Commission of the European Communities 2001). Although interest groups do not have direct influence on decision making, one can observe that decision making has developed well beyond intergovernmental cooperation in the regulatory arena. In the ordinary legislative procedures this is reflected in the strongly enhanced importance of the European Parliament. Accordingly, the most relevant changes to regulatory policies in progressive Treaty revisions have been innovations to the legislative process and the introduction of soft regulation as alternative forms of coordination that involve interest groups directly. The Lisbon Treaty does not introduce any substantial changes. Co-decision has become the ordinary legislative procedure and has been extended to a great number of existing policies. Although this further strengthens the potential role of the EP as direct representation of EU citizenship, especially the consistently sinking voter turnout indicates that the Treaty changes have not fundamentally altered the actual political relationships of the EU regulatory arena.

Distributive or *patronage* (Lowi 1988) policies are based on secondary rules (remote coercion) working through individual conduct without imposing obligations. Without regard of limited resources they confer privileges or facilities in a disaggregated manner. Privileges are allotted to small units or individuals that stand more or less in isolation from other units. Therefore distributive policies "are virtually no policies at all but are highly individualized decisions that only by accumulation can be called a policy" (Lowi 1964: 690). Political interaction is marked by mutual noninterference, instead of compromises on opposed interests. In the short term they are not perceived as zero-sum games because winners are disaggregated groups of beneficiaries, while losers are concealed. Decision making is characterized by logrolling and putting together in a "pork barrel" unrelated interests. In contrast to redistributive policies, it is not directly visible who is paying for the disaggregated benefits and group conflict is not evoked. In contrast to regulation, decision making "is thus a more politicized activity, but the absence from the process of policy-making of groups which are likely to be adversely affected limits the degree of politicization and the numbers of those involved" (Wallace 1983: 413).

Even though EU policies also entail redistributive effects, issues are predominantly framed as distributive. The very way in which Community money is dispersed creates patronage relationships with chosen groups of beneficiaries who are traded off by logrolling, rather than resembling conflict resolution typical for the redistributive arena. As the Commission states itself, "[u]nlike in the case of national budgets, where progressive taxation plays an important redistributive role, in the EU budget, contributions are proportional to the capacity to pay measured by nominal GNP at current exchange rates. Redistributive objectives, as noted above, are, therefore, pursued through expenditure alone" (Commission of the European Communities 2006g). Through "expenditure alone" no truly redistributive policy can be established. As regards individual recipients, policies will perforce have a tendency to turn distributive, thereby creating patronage relationships between certain clienteles that benefit from Union funding while grand redistributive conflicts remain matters of interstate bargaining.

Although overall limited in quantitative terms, distributive policies are of high importance for EU policy making and institutionalization dynamics. Benefits for specific groups were created mostly as side payments, either to create agreement for further integration or enlargement or to account for specific claims by newly entered states (van der Beek and Neal 2004). Instead of creating "EU classes" they establish patronage relationships because they are dispersed mostly to subnational units whose revision is explicitly not subject to broad ideological conflict. Thus, the EU's financial instruments confer privileges much rather than imposing societal positions. This is best reflected in the Common Agricultural Policy (CAP) (Wallace, H. 2005: 82–83). The CAP has created strong vested interests that grant its survival despite strong paradoxes, questionable outcomes, and massive external challenges, "creating a functionally segmented and politically insulated policy arena" (Rieger 2005: 188). More controversially, also *EU Regional Funds* have a strong distributional bias, despite their apparent redistributional objectives. With the creation of the Single Market in the mid-1980s distributional impacts of integration were first addressed in terms of social and economic divergence between regions and social groups. The creation of *Cohesion Policy* and *Structural Funds* "appeared to signal a shift from haphazard distribution of resources to a planned redistribution through designed transfers of resources" (Wallace, H. 2005: 83), as well as it ended central governments monopoly over EU policy making by drawing regional actors into "multilevel governance" (Marks, Hooghe et al. 1996). These apparent shifts have, however, not fully materialized. Policy formulation resembles still a pork-barrel, high-level bargaining process between member governments, whereas the Commission involves regional, subregional, or non-state actors in the multilevel system mainly in the implementation phase. Enlargement and recent institutional budgetary reforms have further strengthened the state influence rather than regional redistribution, and hence not cohesion but equity between member states was the underlying negotiation logic. In essence, this means that "the structural funds have been mainly used to *compensate* member states for both the 'widening' and the 'deepening' of European integration, and that this has been *rationalized* in terms of the EU objectives [such as economic growth, competitiveness, employment, sustainable development, subsidiarity, regionalism, and good governance, EGH]" (Allan 2005: 213–14, emphasis in the original). Furthermore, "[t]he idea of an EU distributional mode focused partially on deliberative redistribution is under attack for two other reasons: a shift toward the idea of collective goods and pressures for spending on external responsibilities" (Bache 1998: 133; Wallace, H. 2005: 84). In these areas, no inter-EU redistribution but genuine distributive spending emerges. In short, although in effect there is redistribution from richer to poorer member *states* that contribute differently to the budget, there is no clearly visible redistribution between *social groups*. There are therefore no EU classes but rather EU clients. The political groups involved remain issue stakeholders that defend their patronage claims. In the EU a "distributional mode" of policy making still prevails (Wallace, H. 2005: 82–85).

The stickiness of distributive policies in general makes these political relationships strongly patronage like. To regain some grip on the dispersion of funds, a number of safeguards exist in that the Commission controls and monitors the actual distribution of funds. With the introduction of Cohesion and Structural Policy "the EU began to acquire some scope for using financial incentives to influence policy developments within the member states" (Wallace, H. 2005: 83). Further, when, after the southern enlargement, the Mediterranean states pushed successfully for a substantial increase of regional policy funds, "the main contributing countries ('rich' countries) were only willing to accept this increase under the condition that the main recipient countries would submit to conditions about how to spend these resources" (van der Beek and Neal 2004: 591). Most importantly, Community assistance is based on co-financing by the recipient national body. The implementation principles comprise conditionality elements in distributive EU policies. Such conditionality contradicts Lowi's definition of relationships in the distributive arena as rules that "confer facilities or privileges unconditionally" (see Table 2.2). These safeguards do not only serve to achieve some control over spending on the ground, it also provides the Commission with means to direct national and subnational policy making through implementation principles. The Lisbon Treaty does not introduce major changes to the distributive arena. More relevant are trends over the passed years that strengthen member state vis-à-vis Commission influence in implementation, as outlined for Structural Policy above.

Redistributive policies, in contrast to distribution, are clear zero-sum games. They categorize activities in that they impose classifications or statutes under which individuals are subsumed involuntarily (Lowi 1985: 73). They affect social classes (property itself, equal possession, and the "being"), and their effects are not disaggregable as under distributive policies—winners and losers are openly conveyed. "Political issues become redistributive rather than distributive when those who are adversely affected by existing policies—or threatened by pending proposals—oppose those groups who benefit from them" (Wallace 1983: 413). State-society relationships therefore involve the major interest representations in order to channel strongly ideological positions. This entails that "politics is thus unavoidably played out on a wider stage, with a larger cast of actors: involving 'peak associations' rather than specific interest groups, parliaments and political parties rather than committees and spokesmen for particular interests, governments rather than ministries, the Commission rather than the Directorate Generals" (Wallace 1983: 413).

In terms of the EU policy agenda many authors have noted that "[o]f the five most salient issues in most west European democracies—health care provision, education, law and order, pension and social security policy, and taxation—none is primarily an EU competence" (Moravcsik 2002: 615). The logic EU integration was initially based on was that of increasing gains for all—thus not a zero- but a win-win game in which side payment were to mitigate adverse effects of overall gains. "While some of the consequences were in practice redistributive ..., neither the initial compact nor the explicit policy prescriptions identified were fundamentally redistributive in purpose" (Wallace 1983: 411–12). Instead of day-to-day policy making, the forum in which redistribution is directly addressed are the negotiations over the multi-annual budget plans in which member state governments decide on the ceiling (percentage of each national GNP) for contributions to the budget and the major budget lines. Because of the distributive mode of dispersing funds, the redistributive conflicts are formulated mainly as the distance between net contributing and receiving member states—not least because Regional and Structural Funds are open to beneficiaries from all states. Classifications or the imposition of social status remains to be defined within the states. Key redistributive policies expressed in zero-sum games between winning and losing social groups are precisely those that remain under the member states' authority. Crucial for this classification of EU policies is the multilevel nature of EU governance. Although in effect money is redistributed, political relationships are such that political responsibility and legitimacy to redistribute remain to be fought out in domestic processes.

Thus, the way political relationships play out on the EU level is influenced by this specific way that redistributive conflicts are dealt with between the member state governments. Although trade unions are organized on the EU level and despite the increased emphasis on the European Social Dialogue (ESD) since the Single European Act, what emerged is clearly not structures, political processes, elites, and especially no active group relations along broad ideological (class) conflict that are characteristic of the redistributive arena. From its very outset, it has been questioned whether the ESD could really create tripartite structures similar to those known from national settings (Goetschy 1999; Keller and Sörries 1999; Streeck 1994; Turner 1996). This early skepticism has been confirmed by empirical evidence (Keller and Sörries 1998; Leisink 2002). More so, viewed through the lens of policy-type specific interaction modes, it is striking that rather than establishing a platform for broad class conflict the social dialogue has evolved as an instrument to advance patronage interests. Analyses of the EDS in practice come to the "conclusion that the members of the European peak organizations have come to view the framework of the ESD as an alternative channel for lobbying" (de Boer et al. 2005: 62; likewise on drift into distributive arena: Gold et al. 2007). Short of substantive redistributive policies, both EU spending and political relationships with stakeholders drift into patterns that are characteristic of the distributive arena of power. To be explicit: in real effect EU policies do result in redistribution and especially the budgetary negotiations between member states are essentially about these redistributive effects. What matters for the identification of the policy arena is, however, that redistribution is generally framed in a way that no direct political relationships between individual citizens and the EU level evolve that would imply a real political spillover.

To substitute for formal competences, the Lisbon Strategy (Commission of the European Communities 2006e)[8] has created policy tools for nonhierarchical steering—again not theoretically conceptualized by Lowi. Working through means such as targeting, peer reviews, and the development of nonbinding standards voluntary adaptations of the domestic systems are to be promoted under the *open method of coordination* (OMC). In the absence of effective corporatist structures or compulsory negotiation networks between private actors, policy making remains dominated by member state governments (Mayntz 2008). It shows, therefore, that in the absence of a redistributive arena proper also nonhierarchical steering will be at best of limited effectiveness because success depends on the previously established structures, processes, and group relations of the arena of power. Without the backing of restrictive policy instruments underpinned by actual supranational authority, the effectiveness of these measures and their actual redistributive impact have been seriously questioned (Börzel 2008; de la Porte 2002; Héritier 2003;Idema and Kelemen 2006; Schäfer 2004; Scott and Trubek 2002) and the legitimacy of "new" modes of governance has become a matter of debate (Benz 2007). The Lisbon Treaty makes reference to the OMC as policy instrument explicitly in connection with the implementation of the Lisbon Strategy, for which no coercive instruments have been created. The strong resistance of the United Kingdom for any formalization of social policy during the constitutional convention was the most evident instance of opposition to more redistributive policies. Concerning budgetary rules and procedures, the major institutional innovations are the extended powers of the EP, which now co-decides on all expenditures of the annual budget and has to agree to the multi-annual financial frameworks. The definition of budget lines therefore becomes less susceptive to member state bargains, which is most likely to increase even further the importance of setting the ceiling of member state contributions and constrain the multi-annual budget plans in order to strike redistributive balances between member states. Most importantly, there are no novelties whatsoever that would mark moves toward fiscal federalism. Thus, the basic principles and biases of the budgetary system, and with it the redistributive arena, remain unchanged under the Lisbon Treaty. "Attempts by the Commission to refocus the EU budget toward European public goods and thus to reduce the redistributive emphasis within the existing 'EU distributional mode,' are hampered by the inflexibility of the current budgetary structure. Member states defend vested distributive interests, but are very critical of spending programs with benefits which cannot be attributed to member states" (Laffan and Lindner 2005: 211).

Constituent policies did not feature in Lowi's original model, but "a fourth category of policy *closed the logic of the scheme,* giving me a system of public policy and a method of characterizing and reasoning in comparisons of policies within a logical structure" (2008: 15, italics in original). Constituent rules are "referred to as rules about powers or rules about rules" (Lowi 1985: 74), that is, the monopoly to decide where and how to locate authority to coerce in a system of governance. In consolidated polities with questions about the framework and structure of the system occur less frequently than in less securely established ones or with major sources of instability. Thus, in the EU characterized as partial policy, "there is frequently an interaction between constituent issues and other categories of policy issue as arguments about relative economic or social advantage shade into problems of political power and influence" (Wallace 1983: 414).

The EU's constituent arena is marked by its hybrid constitutional character as a polity with features of both an intergovernmental regime and a supranational federation. According to the official regime character, the contracting member states remain the ultimate masters of the Treaties. This implies essentially that "in the long run" all EU policies are constituent because they are, at the end of the day, based on agreement between states that confer powers. In line with the principle of conferral, the EU formally only exists where competences have been shifted to the supranational level. Only some "[c]onstituent issues of authority in important areas of policy to a new level of government were there within the Treaties, but largely in unspecific and conditional terms" (Wallace 1983: 412). The ultimately constituent nature of EU law also features in the revised founding Treaties that lack an explicit hierarchy of law. Detailed rules on sectoral policies have the same status and are subject to the same revision procedures as rules of constitutional character and are thus also found in the Treaties themselves. In this vein, the architecture of the former intergovernmental second and third pillars guaranteed member states' ultimate authority over issues and excluded the respective policies from ECJ jurisdiction. Contrastingly, the ECJ has been a decisive actor in expanding Community competences. In short, lacking a general Kompetenzkompetenz, the competence to establish its own competences to create rules, the EU lacks constituent policies in the narrow sense of establishing rules about power proper. Room for maneuver exists only where the Treaties grant exclusive competences and where legislation based on this pushes the boundaries of formal competences. The lack of a genuine Kompetenzkompetenz does, however, not lead to a less, but rather a more prominent role of constituent issues: first, because each conferral of policy competences has a constituent dimension as it implies the reallocation of powers in the multilevel system, and second, because policy issues are often linked to basic constituent problems—as the EP has successfully done exploiting its budgetary competences to expand its institutional powers.

The peculiarities of the Union's constituent arena entail high hurdles for agreement on fundamental questions. Once established, formal rules are hard to amend (Farrell and Héritier 2007; Scharpf 1985, 2006). Because of the difficulty of changing rules, flexibility is often achieved through widening the room for interpretation in the Treaties, which increases the scope for informal institutional arrangements (Farrell and Héritier 2007: 228; Hix 2002). Beyond Lowi's definition, the EU relies systematically on underspecified constituent rules in order to evade the problems of readjusting rules about powers and rules about rules. This leads at the same time to the creation of a plethora of informal rules because "the 'remediability' of mistakes made by the member states depends on the decision rule that they adopt; and many mistakes will be difficult, or impossible, for them to remedy under the unanimity requirement for Treaty change" (Farrell and Héritier 2007: 230). The Lisbon Treaty has not fundamentally changed either the legal status of EU law or the rules for Treaty changes.[9] The member states' insistence on having the lengthy third part included into the Constitutional Treaty was to guarantee that all policy-relevant matters remained part and parcel of the body of basic treaties in order to prevent a hierarchy of law that might have led to legal interpretation that could have limited the member states' ultimate authority. New in the Lisbon Treaty is that the Convention method has been introduced as regular instrument for Treaty reform. Still, also in this procedure it is the national governments that have the last word over reforms, based on a proposal by a convention. In essence, the Lisbon Treaty does not change the hermaphroditic nature of the EU toward either of the sexes, but it reinforces the hybrid nature between regime and federation.

What does the classification of EU policies within the arenas of power framework add to our theoretical model? First, the illustration has shown that although the EU policy agenda has extended substantially, regulatory policies and a "distributive mode" still dominate over genuinely redistributive policies while constituent policies continue to fall short of a general Kompetenzkompetenz. Second, in consequence the political relationships between supranational rule and citizens is shaped in a peculiar manner that privileges the representation of certain client groups in regulatory and patronage relationships in the distributive arena and has not led to significant representation through peak organizations of political parties on the EU level, as well as the Constitutional process has strikingly failed to create a single European demos. Third, although these actor constellations put institutional constrains on actor choices, they do not explain the persistence of the limited policy agenda. Expected costs of further institutionalization matter and different policy types impose different costs on political decision makers. In the case of the EU, where the conferral of a policy to the EU implies also a shift of authority, costs include the redefinition of political relationships between national to supranational policy-makers. Forth, the illustration has also shown that beyond Lowi's definition of the arenas of power can be extended to capture all modes of EU governance, hierarchical and nonhierarchical. In the original approach replacing the notion of coercion with that of legal rule clarified that policy making is about actor expectations over outcomes. It also meant that "[p]ublic policy can be defined simply as an official expressed intention backed by sanction" (Lowi 1988: x). Most evidently in connection with the Lisbon Strategy, the EU has, however, extended the number of policies that are not backed by sanction. These are foremost soft regulation and new governance in the regulatory and redistributive arena. In terms of expected costs for national policy-makers, soft law and open coordination of domestic policies are advantageous because they offer a response to functional pressure without creating political relationships that might entail political spillover since the formal authority stays in the hands of member state governments. At the same time, also in contrast to Lowi's definition, distributive policies are normally linked to conditions, and a wide array of informal institutional rules has emerged to circumvent the pitfalls of the EU's constituent arena. To conceptualize the sufficient conditions for a policy to be institutionalized on the supranational level, we need to integrate these phenomena into the theoretical framework. Even with the extended arenas the EU system still shows a bias toward regulatory and distributive policies, while more recently soft law, new governance, and informal institutions have gained increasing relevance in supranational policy-making.

Mair pinpoints this situation as lack of politicization of EU policy making. The lack of "classical opposition" leads him to conclude that "we are afforded a right to participate at the European level, even if we may not choose to avail ourselves of that right less frequently; and we are afforded the right to be represented in Europe, even if it is sometimes difficult to work out when and how this representative link functions; but we are not afforded the right to organize opposition within the European polity" (Mair 2007: 15). The bottom line of the argumentation is that for classifying policies, not eventual effects but the policy mode during policy *formulation* and actors' *expectations* over policy outcomes matter. From this point of view, the redistributive and constituent arenas of power remain shortened on the EU level. Both the bias for regulatory and distributive arenas and new governance modes suggest that actor strategies of member state governments are open to functional spillover but restrictive when spillover is expected to turn political.

STEERING INSTRUMENTS: LINKING ARENAS OF POWER AND NEW MODES OF GOVERNANCE

Which expectations for the institutionalization of capacities on the EU level follow from these specificities of the EU's arenas of power? The dependent variable, institutionalized action capacity on the supranational level, has been operationalized as those steering instruments that the

European Commission has at its disposal. From the above discussion it follows that policy instruments are specific to the policy mode of each arena of power. Herein the degree of coerciveness can vary between formal/informal institutions and hierarchical steering/nonhierarchical coordination.[10] We therefore need to ask: what are the actual instruments by means of which coercion is exercised, say the action capacity of a policy-implementing authority?

In order to capture all modes of governance and policy instruments these comprise, we need to move conceptually beyond Lowi's concern with formal legal acts. A formal policy is defined as "a rule formulated by some governmental authority expressing an intention to influence the behavior of citizens, individually or collectively, by use of positive and negative sanctions" (Lowi 1985: 70). Informal governance in the EU is defined as "the operation of informal networks which link policy-makers to client groups as well as actors across the EU, national and sub-national institutions, and influence (or at least seek to influence) decision-making in the EU" (Christiansen and Piattoni 2003: 1). For each policy type both formal and informal modes of governance and the respective instruments can be identified in accordance with the EU policy arenas. I will briefly clarify the notion of informal governance for the four policy types: soft law (regulatory arena), certain new modes of governance (redistributive arena), recipient conditionality (distributive arena), and informal institutions (constitutive arena).

The various informal alternatives to "command and control" formal steering have been widely discussed in the literature on (new) governance (Kjær 2004). In essence, if "the 'modern governance' or 'new governance' perspective is adopted (Kooiman 1993; Rhodes 1997) then the question becomes one of how that centre of government interacts with society to reach mutually acceptable decision or whether society actually does more self-steering rather than depend upon guidance from government" (Peters 2000: 36). In terms of policy instruments, it is the turn from top-down hierarchical steering to the appreciation of the need to account for sector-specific structures that determine the ability of policy takers to oppose policies (Mayntz 2008: 44). In the context of the EU, new governance is thus defined as the departure from the classic community method, which grants the Commission the right to initiate legislation and is directed to create binding legislative and executive acts (Scott and Trubek 2002: 2).[11] Applying new governance instruments, the principles guiding political relationships are accordingly characterized by voluntarism (nonbinding targets, soft law), subsidiarity (measures decided by member states or private actors), and inclusion (the targeted groups participating in the decision-making process) (Héritier 2002: 106). In this vein, new modes of governance have been applied as a way toward cooperation in the Community framework without empowering it with sanctioning means and preempting the transfer of formal competences.

In the regulatory arena, *soft law* has primarily a complementary function to hard regulation. In contrast to formal regulation, soft law is not backed by hard sanctioning instruments and grants member states more flexibility when implementing policies. The definitions of soft law maintain in essence that "soft law is classified procedurally as rules that are not legally binding and that soft law comes in many variants" (Mörth 2004b: 5). In this sense, soft law is understood as "rules of conduct which, in principle, have no legally binding force but which nevertheless may have practical effects" (Snyder 1993, quoted in Mörth 2004b: 5). As mechanism of control, soft law may be a transitional phenomenon leading to hard regulation; yet equally, "soft law can be a more independent, and not a transitional form of regulation. In these cases, soft law is clearly linked to network governance" (Mörth 2004a: 193). Accordingly, political relationships are not determined by hierarchical structures and guided by a centralized authority but by looser and less formally organized coordination. In the EU, soft law frequently serves as a supplement to hard regulation, creating a mix of hard and soft regulation areas of traditional Community competence (Cini 2001; Senden 2004) or to complement and substitute hard regulation in areas with more restricted supranational powers (Falkner et al. 2005; Jacobsson 2004; López-Santana 2006). Soft law that is based on nonhierarchical means, therefore, extends the regulatory arena by instruments that grant more discretion in the transposition of member states than formal regulation.

Following up on this, new modes of governance have been most prominently promoted as an alternative tool in areas in which the EU has no formal powers. In particular in the redistributive arena, the open method of coordination has been introduced to encourage cooperation without harmonization. The intended mechanism is to foster mutual learning processes by formulating common guidelines in combination with periodic monitoring, evaluation, peer review, and identification of best practices. Borrás and Jacobsson identify seven points that differentiate the OMC from the related soft law approach. The OMC is intergovernmental as opposed to a supranational approach, political as opposed to administrative monitoring, and clear and iterative as opposed to weak, ad hoc procedures. Moreover, the OMC introduced previously absent systematic linkages across policy areas, explicit linkages of EU and domestic action; it promotes the participation of social actors, and aims explicitly at enhancing learning processes (Borrás and Jacobsson 2004: 188). Analyzing the efficiency of new modes of governance, Héritier argues that one of the explanatory factors is "the particular *policy problem* dealt with". Accordingly, new modes of governance only increase efficiency if applied to certain policies, and in this vein "[i]f redistributive problems are tackled with new modes of governance, political efficiency is unlikely to increase" (2003: 111; also: de la Porte 2002). The decisive difference is precisely the absence of potential credible option of hard regulation. In other words, without at least a short shadow of hierarchy, new governance seems rather ineffective, both theoretically and empirically (Börzel 2008; Idema and Kelemen 2006; Scharpf 2002). In consequence, the OMC creates instruments in the redistributive arena, which are, however, not fully backed by formal redistributive competences of the Union in the respective issue areas, which undermines both the effectiveness of the outcomes and the effective emergence of political relationships between supranational policy-makers and policy-takers since national governments remain the main mediating authority.

While new governance—as soft law or nonhierarchical cooperation through tools such as benchmarking—makes away with sanctioning instruments and increases discretion of policy takers, the distributive and constituent arenas are ideally defined as discretionary. While distribution that is normally free of conditions, constituent policies create powers and privileges. Once established, both privileges and powers conferred are hard to change because of the high decision-making hurdles in the EU. In both arenas, discretion is, however, reduced by informal means. In the distributive arena, the instruments for this have been increased conditions for beneficiaries of EU funding by which the Commission can gain influence on the domestic implementation of policies (van der Beek and Neal 2004: 591; Wallace, H. 2005: 83). In the constituent arena, informal institutions have been shown to play a decisive role in day-to-day decision-making processes (Eiseltet al. 2007; Farrell and Héritier 2003) but also in grand reform processes (Eiselt and Slominski 2006; Kietz and Maurer 2007).

Table 2.2 summarizes both "old" and "new" steering instruments according to policy type. The instruments are classified along two dimensions. These are the leeway granted to the recipient (framing of coercion) and the explicitness of the goals (framing of objectives). The former can be restrictive (leaving no opt-outs for the recipient), or it can be discretionary (relying on the voluntary receptiveness of the recipient).[12] The latter may be explicit (the policy instrument tries to directly promote a particular goal), or it is transmitted (the policy instrument tries promote certain goals implicitly) as captured by the terminology substantive and adjective rules.

Table 2.2 Steering instruments by arena of power

FRAMING OF OBJECTIVES FRAMING OF COERCION	SUBSTANTIVE (POLICY GOALS SPECIFIC)	ADJECTIVE (POLICY GOALS TRANSMITTED)
RESTRICTIVE (imposes obligations/positions)	**REGULATORY POLICIES** Rules imposing obligations, rules on individual conduct, criminal in form *Regulations, directives, decisions in: competition, economics/finance, trade, environment, food safety/health/consumer affairs, transport; in CFSP: joined actions.*	**REDISTRIBUTIVE POLICIES** Rules imposing status; categorizing activity *Intergovernmental budgetary negotiations*
Extending discretion/reducing restrictiveness softening coercion	Soft law *Nonbinding/flexible rules: Recommendations, framework decisions, conventions, nonbinding acquis; in CFSP: principles and general guidelines, common strategy, common positions (also JHA)*	Voluntary Cooperation *Open Method of Coordination, targeting, benchmarking*
Extending restrictions/limiting discretion/hardening coercion	Conditional privileges *Co-financing in Common Agricultural Policy, Structural Policy, Cohesion Policy; conditional targeting for fund, International Aid (ENP)*	Informal institutions *Informal institutions, inter-institutional procedures*
DISCRETIONARY (confers privileges/powers)	Rules conferring facilities or privileges unconditionally *Direct payments to farmers (CAP), Education, International Emergency Aid, Science & Technology/Research* **DISTRIBUTIVE POLICIES**	Rules confer powers; rules about rules and about authority *Treaty competences, principles of conferral, proportionality, subsidiarity* **CONSTITUENT POLICIES**

Source: own table.

In the *regulatory arena,* restrictive steering is the common mode of exercising coercion as defined by Lowi, namely, *binding legislative acts.* Examples in the EU are the formally binding legal acts (regulations, directives, and decisions) that leave at best limited leeway for interpretation to the member states. Still in the very same area, *soft law* is understood as regulatory policy, granting discretion to policy takers and thus reducing hard coercion while still formulating rules, which concretely spell out substantive policy goals. The EU has a variety of institutionalized tools besides nonbinding agreements among member states (especially recommendations, framework decisions, and the instruments that apply to decision making in the policies that formally constituted the second and third pillar).

Policy tools in the *distributive arena* guarantee by default more discretion to policy takers who receive *unconditional benefits.* While patronage policies established at the EU level have been shown to be very difficult to reform, let alone terminate, they have increasingly been bound to conditions. *Conditional privileges* increase the constraining control over recipients of funds. The patronage nature of political relationships is sustained, but the discretion of the policy takers is reduced, thereby granting the implementing body considerable leverage in evaluating compliance with the conditions. An example for unconditional distributive policy instruments is direct payments, say, in the Common Agricultural Policy. The main tool to impose conditions has for long been the co-financing principle in EU regional policy.

Although conditional patronage policies have redistributive effects, they remain distinct from policy instruments in the *redistributive arena.* In particular, the organization of political conflict along broad ideological divisions is not typical for the Union's "redistribution by distribution." Accordingly, the central instruments for redistribution remain *intergovernmental negotiations,* most prominently the European Council's budgetary negotiations. Increasing the discretionary scope of policy tools, especially in connection with the Lisbon Agenda, *new modes of governance* have been introduced to substitute for restrictive redistributive policies. Working through means such as targeting, peer reviews, and the development of nonbinding standards, adaptations of the national systems are to be promoted. Without the backing of restrictive policy instruments, the effectiveness of these measures and their actual redistributive impact have been brought into question.

The provisions of the founding Treaties, finally, are the basis for formal rules that are established through *intergovernmental negotiations* based on a proposal developed under the *Convention method,* which since the enforcement of the Lisbon Treaty are the instruments of ordinary *constituent policies*. In their pure form these policies are discretionary because they create powers for certain actors. Accordingly, the institutional rules, which make for constituent policies, are defined as enabling actors; in other words, they create discretion to coerce. *Informal institutions* further restrict these formal rules distributing authority, and the rules about rules. Following this reasoning, informal rules that adjust the power relations of actors increase the level of restrictiveness for those who *originally* hold the monopoly on authority. Informal institutions are thus understood as limiting those actors who are officially endowed with formalized powers.

CHAPTER 3

THE ANALYTICAL FRAMEWORK: DESIGN OF THE EMPIRICAL STUDY

The null hypothesis, challenged here, is that competences delegated to the Commission remain limited to the Copenhagen enlargement context as institutionally designed. The general hypothesis derived from the theoretical framework is that the successful implementation of policies in the Copenhagen framework creates functional pressure for further integration (necessary condition) but that only if member state governments do not expect political spillover to ensue, they will tolerate an extension of the Commission's action capacity (sufficient condition).

Whether political spillover is expected depends on two intervening variables: (a) the *policy type* at stake because different areas of power imply different political relationships between supranational policy-makers and citizens, and (b) the degree coerciveness because different *modes of governance* imply different degrees of hierarchy in the supranational/national relationships. It follows that if supranational action capacity is based on nonhierarchical steering instruments, the sufficient condition for spill-in is met. It also follows that if supranational action capacity is based on hierarchical steering instruments, spill-in may occur in the distributive or regulatory arena while action capacity based on hierarchical instruments will not occur if redistributive or constituent policies are at stake, which would create direct politicized links between citizens and the EU level and thus entail loyalty shifts in policy arenas that remain still nationally dominated. Since all policies under perspective were explicitly created in the Copenhagen framework outside the core *acquis,* it is actually expected that hard regulatory policies and unconditional distributive policies are unlikely to occur but that spill-in will be limited to soft regulation and distribution bound to certain conditions, for each arena of power follows a working hypothesis and respective empirical indicators that will be referred to in the empirical study.

A political response formulated in the *regulative arena* establishes rules constraining behavior of individuals (member states). The working hypothesis reads: *if contested regulatory issues are formulated in a soft way, they will spill in as hard regulation only if no alternative functional responses are not available.* The empirical indicators that confirm such hypothesis are new soft steering instruments (Commission capacities without tools to sanction member states); new hard legislation and a complete termination of monitoring at the moment of accession disconfirm the hypothesis.

A political response formulated in the *distributive arena* establishes distribution of resources perceived and negotiated as a win-win game. The working hypothesis reads: *if formulated as distributive policy, spill-in will most likely occur with safeguards to constrain redistributive effects or unconditionally for all member states (equal return).* Empirical indicators that confirm the hypothesis are safeguards to constrain redistributive effects (application of the principle of equal return/conditionality clauses); disconfirming are the dispersion of money among member state class lines and a complete termination of technical and financial assistance at the moment of accession.

A political response formulated in the *redistributive arena* establishes a reallocation of resources perceived and negotiated as a zero-sum game. The working hypothesis reads: *if formulated as redistributive conflict, member states preempt spill-in.* The confirming empirical indicator is that no such policy is formulated; the hypothesis is disconfirmed if conflicts are resolved along broad ideological lines and redistribution along lines of different "classes of member states" is introduced.

A political response formulated in the *constituent arena* establishes a reallocation of institutional power. The working hypothesis reads: *if formulated in the constituent arena, that is, as conflict over the vertical/horizontal allocation of institutional powers, member states will reject spill-in.* Confirming empirical evidence is the non-occurrence of new constituent policies; the reallocation of formal vertical or horizontal powers (new articles in the founding Treaties) disconfirms the hypothesis.

The problem-driven approach of the study, the limited number of cases available, and hence the backward-looking y-centered research design suggest a qualitative methodological approach. Tracing each case in detail is to provide in-depth information on the single cases. The results of the two clusters of cases will be confronted with each other in a most

similar case comparison in Part IV. The empirical analyses presented in
Part III cover all cases in which the Commission was delegated extended
competences in order to implement enlargement. None of these policies had been harmonized before 1993 in the way they were defined in
the Copenhagen framework. The policies newly assembled under the
Copenhagen accession criteria did not concern the traditional EU policies that were sufficiently covered by the accession negotiation chapters
derived from the acquis communautaire. In all five cases under perspective, functional pressure emerged to extend the Copenhagen capacities
to the wider acquis. This did not lead to a one-to-one copy of policies
from the Copenhagen framework to the acquis. Yet in all cases functional
pressure led to new cooperative arrangements to accommodate the most
pressing demands. While some of these extended the Commission's action
capacity, in other cases the member states actively prevented an extension of Community powers. Whereas in the former cases Commission
action capacity increased, in the latter the creation of functional responses
within the EU system of governance was sidestepped by fostering alternative albeit less efficient arrangements in other international forums that
exclude the Commission and hence preempt an extension of its institutionalized action capacity. The role of international organizations as
alternative settings to formal integration within the EU framework is foremost an empirical finding. It is linked to the nature of the policies that
were included in the Copenhagen criteria, namely, politically sensitive
questions of human rights, security, and internal state structures, which
above all the Council of Europe and the Organization for Economic
Cooperation and Development (OSCD) were involved in. Although one
may argue that overall functional pressure for EU involvement existed
even before enlargement, these sensitive policies had not been harmonized on the EU level. In contrast, they could be accommodated in the
Copenhagen framework that had no direct effects on the member states
but allowed a stricter scrutiny of the candidate states than the Council of
Europe or the OSCD provided for.

EMPIRICAL ANALYSIS

EXTENDING THE EUROPEAN COMMISSION'S ACTION CAPACITY: POLICY-GENERATED CHANGE

What we have learnt in enlargement are these very hands-on things, . . . okay, they speak of the Brussels bureaucrats but I think the least bureaucratic I have come across were the people that have worked on enlargement. And I think we have tried to bring this spirit also to the European Neighbourhood Policy because if you really have a bright idea, you can achieve something.

Official—European Commission[1]

The narratives on single cases are theory guided. The main propositions can be summarized along a set of questions that will guide the empirical chapters. (1) *What was the new competence in the Copenhagen framework, and to which degree was it extended beyond the existing competences (dependent variable)?* (2) *How was the mandate put into practice and actually implemented during the pre-accession phase ("functional value added")?* (3) *How was an extension of the Copenhagen policies framed (policy type/types)?* (4) *How did this new competence relate to existing capacities (institutional rules and expected constraints)?* (5) *What consequences did the member states expect in terms of future institutional constraints (expected institutionalized effect)?*

The first two questions take up the neofunctional contentions of the theoretical model. While the first question is about how much spill-in occurred, that is, the measurement of the dependent variable, the second question concerns the measurement of functional pressure in terms of success of the policy in the pre-accession framework. This is reflected by the way policies were created and implemented in the Copenhagen framework. It is expected that functional pressure will be observable in all cases, while not in all cases spill-in materialized. The third question leads over to the arenas of power. To identify which policy type the member states were faced with, we need to spell out into which arena of power a political problem would fall outside the Copenhagen framework. Additionally, question 4 on the institutional rules takes up the constraints that preexisting rules imposed for choosing one or another policy tool. Finally, the expected impact that the framing options and the respective institutional constraints surmount to will allow to hypothesize whether a single policy should spill in or not. Accordingly, the individual expectations for each case will be formulated at the beginning of each chapter.

Figure III. 1 recaps the theoretical expectations. The five questions will structure the illustration of each case study. The chapters are organized chronologically in order to trace the Commission's capacities in related policy fields. First, competences under the acquis at T1 in 1993 and relevant policy developments independent from enlargement are presented. Second, the dynamic phase T2 during which the pre-accession policy is implemented and policy tools are developed is scrutinized. Third, T3

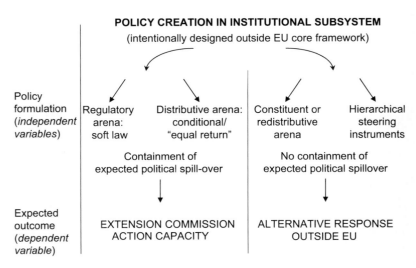

Figure III.1   Theoretical model and expectations
Source: own figure.

marks the point of measurement after the pre-accession phase to estimate the actual change on the dependent variable. Chapter 4–6 illustrate the three cases in which supranational capacities were clearly extended, and chapters 7 and 8 turn to the two cases in which the response to functional pressure did not lead to further institutionalization within the EU polity.

As pointed out before, the study is not designed to test competing explanations against each other but applies one theoretical model to the systematically selected cases. The main hypothesis is that policy making in the Copenhagen framework generates functional pressure. Thus, policy making is a vehicle for further EU integration and depends on the policy type at stake. Yet, implementing enlargement is an additional and not the only cause for the institutionalization. Therefore, reviewing the empirical cases and outcomes at T3 (point of measurement after the implementation of enlargement), we need to be aware of potential equifinal explanations. I will control the problem of equifinality conceptually and methodologically. Conceptually, all policies under perspective are contained to an institutional subset for which full integration was not intended in the first place. If there had been functional pressure for spillover (in the traditional sense) before enlargement, it was not effectuated but rejected for policy issues under perspective. However, related policies may be subject to other dynamics of integration. If spill-in occurs a linkage to these related fields is to be expected. Methodologically, I therefore include a discussion of related policies. This discussion does not elaborate on the causes for the integration of these related policies but simply depicts the as-is state at T1 (point of measurement before the implementation of enlargement) since they mark the relevant context variables (acquis communautaire) that set the conditions for spill-in. To control for equifinality regarding the outcomes at T3, the methodological approach is to carefully trace the actual development and application of policy tools during the implementation of enlargement (T2) to compare these with the tools applied outside the pre-accession framework (T3). The results are most conclusive where no spill-in materializes. In these cases in which capacities are not institutionalized because of the policy tools that would have been established, the explanation is rather unambiguous. Yet, also in the cases in which specific policy instruments exclusively developed in the institutional subsystem can be traced to have traveled beyond, the problem of equifinal explanations is controlled for in a pragmatic way by triangulating and tracing empirical evidence: (1) the identification of exclusive competences in the enlargement context based on reports by evaluating bodies, such as the Court of Auditors and the identification of related competences that the acquis comprises,

(2) primary sources by the European Commission that document the implementation process and thus the elaboration and application of action capacity in the Copenhagen framework, and (3) primary documents and interviews with Commission practitioners on Commission outside the enlargement framework.

INSTITUTIONAL CAPACITY BUILDING: EXTENDING CONDITIONAL DISTRIBUTIVE INSTRUMENTS

Institutional or *administrative capacity building* aims at improving national administrative systems. The capacity of national administrations was subject to monitoring during enlargement. The regulative elements were backed by financial and technical assistance from the EU. The Commission directed money into the candidate administrations in the conditionality-based pre-accession context and with reference to country-specific goal definitions negotiated in the *Accession Partnerships*. At the same time, the perception for administrative reforms of national bureaucracies was in ascent more widely. In this vein, some member states requested financial assistance from the Commission, which led to first pilot programs targeted at the cohesion countries. It was accordingly possible to frame the policy outside the Copenhagen framework either in the regulatory arena to harmonize national legislation along the lines of common standards or as soft regulation and more open coordination along these lines. Moreover, continuing the pre-accession assistance as financial and technical assistance in the distributive arena was feasible. This leads to the following expectations:

> If framed in terms of binding common administrative standards, no spill-in should be expected; spill-in should emerge if the standards developed

during the pre-accession phase are framed along the lines of soft regulation
or as a distributive policy offering financial or technical assistance.

Though there is little doubt about the integration process affecting
national administrative structures in various ways, "public administration . . . until now has remained strictly an area of national sovereignty,
there cannot be any European *policy* since there is no community *competence* in this area" (Mangenot 2005: 4, italics in original). Taking a wider
angle, the Community is limited to substantial competences with respect
to *services of general interest*. Besides this, administrative cooperation
between national civil services on a voluntary basis deserves mentioning.
In balance, formal competences under the acquis remained nonetheless
either limited to or derived from the Community's economic responsibilities, apart from some cautious interstate cooperation. In principle,
interference with the member states' administrative systems remains outside the Commission's sphere of influence, let alone any direct or indirect
say on the quality of institutions or even calls for institution building to
comply with the acquis.

It is quite to the contrary in enlargement policy. For the states aspiring
to join the Union, sufficient administrative capacities are a precondition
to accede. Although in the central and eastern European countries the
process of state and economic restructuring was a general objective in
the 1990s, a considerable role has been ascribed to EU conditionality
in advancing the reform of public administrations. Given the absence
of equivalent competences in the framework of the acquis, it does not
come as a surprise that the Commission had to newly establish standards
to define what makes an "efficient" and "effective" administration. This
happened step by step in the course of the pre-accession process in which
the notion of administrative capacity was first more narrowly limited to
sectoral matters of the acquis and the administrative and juridical ability
to apply it. In the later phases of the pre-accession strategy, the criterion was extended to general horizontal administrative capacities. The
respective policy tools that the Commission developed alongside were,
on the control side, monitoring starting with the initial *Opinions* and
refined in the *Regular Reports*. This was extended to the prescription of
specific national targets contained in the *Accession Partnerships*. On the
side of assistance, the financial resources were subsequently increased
within Phare. Moreover, specific programs were set up to prepare the
states for participation in the agricultural and structural policies of the
EU. Most markedly, a significant innovation regarding the main instrument for technical assistance was introduced with the establishment of
the *twinning* instrument in the framework of the Technical Assistance
and Information Exchange (TAIEX).

Outside enlargement policy, improving administrative efficiency and efficacy remains formally under the member states' sovereign auspices. Yet, since the accession of the ten states in 2004, this principle no longer applies perfectly in the areas most prone to incorporate the policy tools developed vis-à-vis the candidate states, namely, the cohesion and structural policies. As from the programming period 2007–2013 the distribution of financial assistance to the so-called *convergence regions* and *cohesion countries* within the European Social Fund (ESF) is made conditional on the integration of national administrative efficiency improvement into national programming plans. The conditionality element is thus extended to member states requesting EU funding in that recipient states have to prioritize administrative capacity building as one of their programming targets. The respective conditions are subject to bilateral negotiation between each state and the Commission. Moreover, the new principle of *transnationality* obliges states to include interstate exchange on technical matters, mirroring the twinning mechanism that had been developed as technical assistance tool in the Copenhagen framework. Inspired to a good degree by single initiatives for cohesion countries as from 2002 onwards, the tools integrated in the 2006 Council Regulations on the Social and Cohesion Fund take up the instruments exercised in the Copenhagen framework. They do not establish a genuine policy or competence of the Union since they apply only to states when requesting EU funds. The capacity to impact on national administrative systems is nested into the distributive arena; the Commission promotes individualized standards indirectly through conditions that recipient states have to comply with in order to receive funding. The inclusion of the so-called convergence criterion marks a decisive qualitative shift since it allows the Commission to judge on the national administrations' capacities to implement community goals and to negotiate the conditions that states have to meet with respect to their administrative structures. This marks the introduction of an additional conditional instrument in the distributive arena, tackling a core sphere of the state apparatuses, which has previously not been subject to EU interference. Against the expectation of pure distributive policies to emerge, the definition of a limited group of recipients and the conditionality element render the policy effectively redistributive in its outcomes. This notwithstanding, the policy is framed in the distributive arena as objective of the Social Funds, thus circumventing a debate along redistributive conflict lines. Moreover, as expected we see no extension of EU regulation toward more formal harmonization, but member states promote voluntary cooperative networks. The extended Commission action capacity is thus based on conditionality-bound distributive policy tools, with only limited additional steps toward soft regulation.

STATUS QUO ANTE: NATIONAL ADMINISTRATIONS AS NATIONAL BUSINESS

The question of the actual "administrative capacity" of member states remains outside the Commission's sphere of influence. Supranational actors have no say on the quality of member state institutions to comply with the acquis. A formal regulatory policy to harmonize national administrations remains unperceivable given the regime character of the EU. Supranational influence is limited to a few sketchy rules derived from ECJ case law, soft law, or distributive measures that support certain national reform efforts. Nonetheless, there are many indirect ways and related fields in which the supranational level affects national administrations. I will therefore start with a definition of the terminology and demarcate the concept from other related ones.

The term *institutional capacity* is usually used interchangeably with the term *administrative capacity*. Institutional capacity building is concerned with improving the efficiency and effectiveness of national administrations. It needs to be distinguished from processes of supranational impact on national structures by processes of Europeanization. The way it was defined in the Copenhagen framework, it was also distinct from a more global approach to "soft harmonization" through cooperative networks between member state administrations (D'Orta 2003; Mangenot 2005).

In the absence of an EU competence on national administrations, a very small body of binding rules has emerged from ECJ case law based on general administrative principles. Thus, "the jurisprudence of the Court is the main source of general, i.e. non-sectoral, administrative law in the Union" (Cardona 1999: 17). Two rulings are of particular relevance. The *Francovich* case (Court of Justice of the European Communities 1991: C-6/90 and C-9/90) established the principle of direct state liability for compliance with EC law and marked a shift away from domestic procedural autonomy in implementing EU legislation. This decision claimed uniformity across the levels of the EU concerning access to juridical review for citizens. This precedence for state liability marked a turning point because the "court has developed a law of administration which applies not only to the Commission, but also to national bureaucracies" (Bignami 2004: 5–6). The second case concerns employment in national administrations and has been referred to as a case in which "the Court has intervened to define the very concept of 'national public administration'" (Nizzo 2001: 3). The ruling forced member states to open up and reform their public administrations to comply with the basic principle of free movement of labor in the EU (for a comprehensive overview: Bossaert et al. 2001). Besides the ECJ case law, an adjacent but distinct field is a long-established Community competence regarding *services of general (economic) interest* (SGI/SGEI). SGEI were already enshrined in the Treaty of Rome. As a term for public services that cannot be equally well provided by private services, "the very concept of services of general interest was developed by the European Community" (Mangenot 2005: 4). Obviously, the authority to define what falls under national authority of SGEI or the Community's competition laws is crucial for the actual responsibilities of national public administrations in areas such as water management, telecommunications, or energy supply (services of general economic interest), but also security or education (services of general interest). For the Commission, SGI generally also includes social services (Commission of the European Communities 2006e). In essence, the delimitation of national SGEI/SGI by the Commission or the ECJ impacts not only the structure and practices of national administrations but their very functions to the extent that it implies the prohibition of public monopolies in certain areas. The Commission recognizes that the mission to fulfill a general interest takes precedent over the competition rules of the EC Treaties and that, in particular, many social and health services imply obligations that differ substantially from those offered on a commercial basis (Commission of the European Communities 2004g). This notwithstanding, short of a precise definition of the dividing line between SGEI/SGI and the EC founding principles of antitrust and competition, there is considerable scope to demark the actual functions of national public administrations. Similarly, in areas in which the Commission has exclusive competences that are administered directly from the EU level, national administrations are bound by more or less concrete ordinances on how to implement EU law (Ziller 2006). In addition, forms of shared or compound administration in which the Commission and national agencies or public administrations share authority and responsibilities have increased (Cassese 2004: 22; Trondal 2010). Against this background, both legal and political scientists have identified an emerging European Administrative Space (Hofmann and Türk 2006; Hofmann and Türk 2009; Trondal 2010), characterized as a compound system in which national specificities prevail under the umbrella of an increasingly integrated administration. Relevant to our context is that the channels through which the supranational and national levels interact in this emerging administrative space do not establish any EU competences to directly intervene in the administrative capacities of a member state (Heidbreder 2011).

Besides this, administrative cooperation between national civil services deserves mentioning since it has gained some more structured shape, most visibly in the framework of the European Public Administration Network

(EUPAN). EUPAN was founded in 1983 and has held biannual meetings at the ministerial level since 1991. Despite these incremental advances regarding national administrative systems of the EU member states, the EU's steering instruments on the member states' civil services remained either limited to or derived from the Community's economic responsibilities or restricted to the facilitation of interstate cooperation. Other than this, the matter of the general horizontal administrative capacity of member states was for a long time a non-issue.

The topic was touched upon in the framework of the Constitutional Convention. The innovations of the Lisbon Treaty will widen the legal basis for voluntary administrative cooperation. A novelty is the legal basis for adopting laws to improve member states' administrative capacity to implement Union law. Article 197 of the Treaty on the Functioning of the European Union (TFEU) establishes supranational supporting competences that "may include facilitating of information of civil servants as well as supporting schemes," but explicitly creates no obligations for the member states. Supportive competences do not imply any conferral of powers. This legal basis will only allow the adoption of EU legislation to assist the member states' efforts in improving their administrative systems. At the same time, harmonization in the field remains explicitly forbidden, which enables the member states alone to opt for or against Union support independent of the Commission's prerogatives (Verwilghen 2007: 740). Furthermore, the Treaty of Lisbon enforces a new general principle. The *Charter of Fundamental Rights and Freedoms,* which gained full legal power, introduces a "right to good administration" (Art. 14). To estimate the impact of this article can at date only be matter of speculation. It might become a door opener for future jurisprudence of the ECJ and could therefore lead to the positive formulation of administrative standards, although formally limited to areas that concern the national execution of EU law.

Institutional capacity building concentrates on reforms of national administrative structures to achieve particular policy goals or to improve civil services at large. This is either as a follow-up to legislative transposition, that is, to ensure that transposed EU legislation is indeed implemented, or it concerns the establishment and improvement of public service structures to achieve more general Community objectives. The latter has been linked to technical and financial assistance offered to national or regional units. Support to the improvement of national civil services—unlike general administrative cooperation—was initially applied in an ad hoc manner. Only with the programming period starting in 2007, a global strategy has been put in place that mainstreams "administrative efficiency" across the European Social Fund measures.

A qualitative novelty in this respect first occurred in the Union's structural policy with projects for Greece and Portugal. Projects for the overall modernization of public administration and a "completely new program—exclusively dedicated to the development of administrative capacity" (Commission of the European Communities 2006h: 11)—were set up in response to demands of these states for Community funding to support national administrative reforms in more general terms. Whereas the European Social Fund has since the 1994–1999 programming period offered technical assistance to support the implementation of the Fund's objectives (such as developing employment services, as well as education and training systems), the pilot projects for the two cohesion countries went beyond this scope in that "since the early 1990's, ESF has supported comprehensive reforms of the administrations in several Member States" (Commission of the European Communities 2006h: 11). The Portuguese program, which was introduced after the 2003 midterm review of the Social Funds programming period 2000–2007, served as a template for the further elaboration of a more general "institutional capacity priority," which I will turn to in the last section of this chapter.

In sum, the Union has no genuine competences on the structure and workings of member state administrations; efficiency and efficacy of national administrations remain exclusive state domains. Yet, from the 1990s onward, some punctual projects have been financially supported by the EU that mark the emergence of a distributive policy to promote wider goals in improving the efficiency of national administrations, especially in implementing the obligations of the acquis and the objectives of the Lisbon Agenda. Although there is no binding acquis laying down precise standards and benchmarks, a nascent distributive policy is emerging within the structural funds. Moreover, nonbinding links between the member states that are explicitly geared at improving administrative performance in general terms have been strengthened in the explicitly informal EUPAN framework.

PRE-ACCESSION PHASE: FOSTERING COMPLIANCE BY IMPROVEMENT OF NATIONAL IMPLEMENTATION STRUCTURES

Administrative capacity was the last accession criterion to be formulated. It was put down after 1993 against the background of the pre-accession strategy. The emphasis on administrative capacities increased steadily in the late 1990s. It was formally linked, on the one hand, to the demand on rule of law under the democracy criterion and, on the other, to the implementation of the acquis to comply with the obligations of membership. The European Council of Madrid introduced administrative capacity as an explicit criterion in 1995. On this basis it was included in the Commission's 1997 *Opinions,* which for the first time referred to "the criterion in its own right" (Verheijen 2000: 16). It gained additional weight in the preceding *Regular Reports.* Incrementally, the horizontal notion of administrative capacities replaced the narrower notion of sectoral capacities to cope with the adoption of specific obligations of the acquis. Whereas "sectoral capacity was linked to particular parts of the acquis, horizontal capacity, emerged as synonymous with administrative reforms" (Dimitrova 2005: 80).

This re-emphasis toward general horizontal capacities is reflected also in pre-accession assistance. The need for sectoral capacities featured already in the first Phare programming (December 1989, still only for Poland and Hungary). The initially project-focused and demand-driven program[2] was expanded stepwise. The European Council of Essen (1994) redefined Phare and its role as pre-accession instrument, including all candidate states besides the originally two targeted countries. The instrument was now to focus on providing knowhow and technical assistance and, where necessary, humanitarian aid. As progress was made, the demand for technical assistance declined in relative terms and the need for investment aid, particularly in areas such as infrastructure and environmental protection, increased considerably. In this vein, in 1999 the Council reformulated Phare's overall objective:

> Whereas the PHARE programme set up by Regulation (EEC) No 3906/89(6), will in future focus on the essential priorities linked to adoption of the acquis communautaire, i.e. building up the administrative and institutional capacities of the applicant countries and financing investments designed to help them comply with Community law as soon as possible.

Further amendments were made to the end that

> [f]or applicant countries with accession partnerships with the European Union, funding under the PHARE programme shall focus on the main priorities for the adoption of the acquis communautaire, i.e. building up the administrative and institutional capacities of the applicant States and investment, except for the type of investments financed in accordance with Regulations (EC) No 1267/1999(8) and (EC) No 1268/1999(9). PHARE funding may also be used to finance the measures in the fields of environment, transport and agricultural and rural development which form an incidental but indispensable part of integrated industrial reconstruction or regional development programmes.
>
> (Council of the European Communities 1999)

Likewise, *Agenda 2000* identified institution building as one of the two key areas of Phare, besides the access to EU programs. Further support was channeled through the preparatory instruments ISPA (Structural Funds) and SPARD (Common Agricultural Policy). Moreover, Phare provided a tentative definition of the term: "Institution building means adapting and strengthening democratic institutions, public administration and organisations so that, once adopted, EU legislation or the national equivalent is properly implemented and enforced. This requires development of the necessary structures, human resources and management skills" (Commission of the European Communities 1999).

Yet, in the absence of an acquis on horizontal administrative capacities, the Commission lacked standards to transpose the criterion into measurable benchmarks. In a first step toward the operationalization of the criterion, the Commission requested assistance from the member states in 1996. Input remained limited and came foremost from the United Kingdom. "According to a Commission source, 'we never found a way to judge administrative capacity among the existing member states. It was only in the case of the Central and Eastern European candidates knocking on our door that we erected the barrier of administrative capacity' " (Dimitrova 2002: 178). Nonetheless, no EU concept of administrative capacity was ever defined. Instead, the EU relied on external sources "as far as administrative capacity assessment is concerned, based on inputs provided by a new assessment tool: the SIGMA baseline assessment. This system is a response to the lack of specificity in horizontal administrative capacity assessment, combined with the perceived lack of accuracy by candidate states of previous assessments" (Verheijen 2000: 17). Cooperation with the Support for Improvement in Governance and Management (SIGMA) program, operating under the OCED Public Management Service (PUMA) and funded mainly through Phare provided the main tool for the assessment and support of administrative capacity in the candidate states. The SIGMA baseline criteria outlined for the first time minimum standards for horizontal administrative capacities (Verheijen 2000: 19). Regarding administrative capacities, the internal cooperation within the Commission was remarkably weak—if not completely absent. Thus, in DG Enlargement "the Commission sought expertise not from within the organisation (we certainly did not consult our Directorate General for Administration!) or from other EU organisations, but from a non-EU source, OECD's SIGMA" (official DG Enlargement, written exchange, September 2007).

As the main implementing tool, the Commission launched the *twinning program* in 1998. The wording of the twinning manual "reflected the Commission's eagerness not to repeat some of the mistakes which have tarnished the reputation of other Phare-funded projects in the past: namely, the vagueness of objectives, difficulties in monitoring progress and evaluation, and the reliance on expensive short-term western consultancy with few concrete results (Mayhew 1998: 138–50; Bailey and Propris 2004)" (Papadimitriou and Phinnemore 2004: 624). From 1999 onward, twinning was to support the capacity building for the implementation of the acquis, such as agriculture and fisheries, environment, structural funds, social policy, public finance and internal market, justice and home affairs, transport, energy, and telecom.

Criticized for relying too exclusively on twinning, the Commission came under attack by the Court of Auditors. "Institution-building is not equivalent to twinning. However, some representatives of the candidate countries criticised the Commission's tendency to over-emphasise twinning at the expense of other mechanisms directed towards institution-building that are eligible for support (general horizontal support to public service . . . ,private sector service contracts, participation in Community programmes)" (Court of Auditors 2003b: 31). This imbalance was in great part owing to the legal discrepancy of missing EU standards and benchmarks for efficient administrative structures. This especially hampered the promotion of de facto implementation beyond legal adoption of reforms that gained increasing attention as the pre-accession process drew to an end (Grabbe 2001: 1018–19).

The Court of Auditors underlined the same point in particular for the environmental sector. Criticizing that the Commission concentrated too much on the twinning instrument that was based on strong member state cooperation paired with a lack of measurable criteria to evaluate institution building, the Court stated: "The fact that there is no acquis in relation to institution-building means that the standards to be achieved by public administrations are not specified and the Commission has not established objective and measurable criteria to define the level of 'adequate' administrative capacity in the environmental sector although it has done this in other areas to the extent that the acquis enables it to do so" (2003a: 7). The Commission, in turn, defended the excessive use of twinning precisely with the lack of clear and measurable standards—and the fact that such benchmarks were impossible to create. Accordingly, the loose exchange of practices was defined more a virtue than a weakness in exploring ways to adapt the candidate states' administrative structures to some kind of shared standard of the member states:

> In the absence of any specific acquis as the Court observes and in the context of subsidiarity, the Commission has not established criteria to define overall levels of capacity that would uniformly apply to the diverse administrative cultures of member states. Consequently, it is not possible

to invent separate standards for candidate countries. This is precisely why twinning was so essential in exposing the candidate countries to existing practices, particularly given the fact that the Commission does not implement or manage the main body of the acquis but member states do. Thus, the Commission pioneered an unprecedented strategy in an area at the limit of its competence to transfer knowhow on complex technical issues from diverse administrative traditions to equally diverse candidate countries. Within this strategy the Regular Reports (on which the strategy papers and Accession Partnerships are based) tactically targeted the priorities and mobilized political will and resources in the candidate countries. The positive feedback from EU administrations engaged in twinning was essential in building the confidence that secured closure of the negotiations in Copenhagen. This evident success was one of the results undeniably delivered by twinning.

                                                    (Court of Auditors 2003a: par. 14)

Despite the weaknesses of the eclectically developed approach[3] and despite the underspecified definition of its standards, some observers have ascribed the Commission an important role in promoting administrative reforms. "The reform of the civil services in the candidate countries has taken place in recent years in no small measure due to the political pressure of the European Commission.... However, the criteria applied in assessing the efficiency and effectiveness of the civil service were not always clear" (Bossaert and Demmke 2003: 4). Also, for the shift in emphasis form reforms in the economic sector to institution building, EU conditionality was attributed a relevant role (2003: 6), and "[g]iven empirical evidence not only for rule adoption but also in some cases of a direct link between administrative reform legislation and the start of the respective candidate state's negotiation for membership, we can conclude that conditionality matters" (Dimitrova 2005: 89).

Nevertheless, there remained substantial doubts about the real success of administrative reform attempts. In absolute terms, the objective not only to transpose but to implement the full acquis on the ground could hardly be achieved before accession. Academic accounts like the Commission's Regular Reports concluded that although many announcements and drafts were produced, as far as effective implementation was concerned "there are strong indicators that progress in horizontal administrative capacity development has been limited at best" (Meyer-Sahling 2009; Verheijen 2000: 24–25). In retrospect, the evaluation of the actual impacts in terms of sustainable outcomes is thus at best ambivalent.

However, to conclude that the policy was dysfunctional because the ultimate goals were not fully achieved would be overly harsh. The Commission's increasing emphasis on administrative capacities found resonance and was therefore crucial, and—even if no silver bullet—twinning remained the best option available in the absence of uniform standards across the different states and the impossibility of harmonization on the EU level. This leads to the overall conclusion that, although "the European Union has played a significant role in this process . . . institution-building in the case of horizontal administrative reform has had mixed success in the post-Communist candidate states" (Dimitrova 2002: 172).

Throughout the pre-accession phase, the growing awareness of the problem in view of minimum standards—even if well contained as SIGMA baselines outside the EU framework—was coupled with the conviction that the challenges in the future member states would not be resolved before accession. This resulted in increased functional pressure for continued EU engagement. "Administrative capacity assessments have generally produced a picture of lack of progress, regardless of statements of intent, reform strategies and even adopted legislation," while it was seen that the "entry of a large group of new member states with inadequate administrative capacities can pose threats to the EU as political and administrative system, in particular to the decision-making system and the policy implementation system" (Verheijen 2000: 61). The very evaluation that administrative reforms had not fully achieved the desired outcome gave rise to the concern that insufficient administrative capacities in the new member states would affect the principle of mutual trust between member states and could negatively impact economic development in the respective states. Even though the effect of EU conditionality was disputed it remained the only available means to respond to functional pressure caused by the envisaged problems that related "both to participation in the EU decision-making process and to the ability to cope with the administrative workload generated by EU membership" (Verheijen 2000: 53).

In a nutshell, functional pressure derived from (a) demands by cohesion countries to continue Community support for administrative reforms and (b) the candidate states whose administrative capacities were arguably not yet fully capable of participating in EU policy making, and implementing and enforcing the full acquis. The latter had, moreover, the subtext that the new member states were to benefit from great amounts of EU funding, raising concerns about reliable administration of these common resources. We can assert functional pressure because, despite its fallbacks, the policy was extended instead of being abandoned within the pre-accession framework. Within the enlargement strategy, institution building and twinning were reflected as successful steering instruments. The need for action beyond this was furthered by concerns about the sustainability of the twinning results due to the high turnover in public administration staff and remaining weaknesses of the general framework for public administration and systemic failings of the systems (Court of Auditors 2003b: 28). The question of how to go beyond policy formulation and ensure actual implementation of the acquis, in both the new and some of the old member states, remained unresolved. Instruments to respond to these two target groups were needed, but there was only limited legal latitude for regulatory measures. What is more, some member states had asked for an instrument offering financial and technical assistance. At the same time but independently, voluntary cooperative structures between all member states further flourished. Although rising functional pressure triggered also new Commission tools inside the acquis, there is no evidence for unintended consequences during the pre-accession phase, because the pilot projects put in place were a response to demands by member states and therefore anything but outside the states' intentions.

STATUS QUO POST: CONDITIONAL DISTRIBUTIVE POLICIES AND VOLUNTARY COOPERATION

The main challenge for the period after enlargement was to create means to have an impact on the de facto implementation of the acquis and the administrative functioning beyond the mere transposition of legislation. Moreover, the improvement of civil services as such to ensure wider goals of stability and economic growth had moved up on the common agenda. A response has been accommodated in the revised regulations of the *European Social Fund* for the programming period 2007–2013.[4] Novel about these revised eligibility rules for the Social Fund are, first, the definition of goals for a specific *convergence objective*; second, the introduction of a *strategic framework* that each recipient state has to negotiate with the Commission alongside the objectives set out by the Council; and third, the extended policy tools that oblige the recipient states to include into their programming *interstate exchange* of the twinning type. These changes imply a substantial qualitative widening of ESF objectives. Referring to the obligation to implement the Lisbon Agenda, the ESF now recognizes explicitly that "[i]nstitutional and administrative capacity includes the ability of Member States and regions to contribute to the European Union's objectives and to fulfil the conditions and obligations arising from membership" and that to this end, "for the future programming period, the strengthening of institutional and administrative capacity will be generalised and will be one of the main ESF priorities" (Commission of the European Communities 2006h: 3–4).

As pointed out in the previous section, functional pressure augmented because administrative reforms in the entering states were not considered sufficient. As later studies confirm, even where administrative reforms had been implemented these had often a questionable effect in the mid-term (Meyer-Sahling 2001) or essential parts of reforms were even reversed at a later state (Meyer-Sahling 2009; Verheijen 2007; World Bank 2006). These effective outcomes create a dilemma for the EU: reforms introduced before accession had only limited lasting effect and increased the pressure to act, but the establishment of other more coercive instruments was and is to remain outside Community competences. The measures within the ESF do not establish a comprehensive new approach. The continuation of EU involvement is limited to the transfer of specific policy instruments from the Copenhagen framework to the ESF. In absence of pre-accession conditionality, the instruments, however, operate slightly differently.

Council Regulation 1083/2006 newly defined a *convergence objective* for the regions that correspond to the NUTS 2 level, that is, regions with a GDP below 75 percent of the Union average (Council of the European Union 2006a: art. 5(1)). Only for the regions that fall under this convergence objective, the national strategic reference framework needs to include "the action envisaged for reinforcing the Member State's administrative efficiency" (Council of the European Union 2006a: art. 27(4, f, i)).

For the period 2007–2013, these regions were all parts of the Central and Eastern European new member states, Eastern Germany, most regions of Southern Greece and Southern Italy, Western Spain, Wales and Cornwall (with some West and East German regions, the Italian Basilicata, some Greek and Spanish regions and Western Belgium and the Scottish Highlands still receiving funds but phasing out during this period).[5] The revised EP/Council Regulation on the Structural Fund defines further that for areas under the convergence objective the Fund should work toward

> strengthening institutional capacity and the efficiency of public administrations and public services at national, regional and local level and, where relevant, of the social partners and non-governmental organisations, with a view to reforms, better regulation and good governance especially in the economic, employment, education, social, environmental and judicial fields, in particular by promoting: (i) mechanisms to improve good policy and programme design, monitoring and evaluation, including through studies, statistics and expert advice, support for interdepartmental coordination and dialogue between relevant public and private bodies; (ii) capacity building in the delivery of policies and programmes

in the relevant fields, including with regard to the enforcement of legislation, especially through continuous managerial and staff training and specific support to key services, inspectorates and socio-economic actors including social and environmental partners, relevant non-governmental organisations and representative professional organisations.

(European Parliament and Council 2006b: art. 3(2)b)

Both monitoring and evaluation mechanisms are operationalized in the *National Strategic Frameworks* that define objectives and goals. As in the previous programming periods, Social and Cohesion Funds projects are appraised ex ante after a structured assessment of the social and economic situation, paying special attention to the environmental situation, equal opportunities, and the expected impact of measures. In the different programming periods this exercise was carried out first by independent evaluators, then by the Commission, and was eventually left to the member states (Bachtler and Wren 2006: 145–46). In contrast, for the 2007–2013 programming period, the Commission negotiated individual programs with the recipient states. Hence it goes beyond the previous strong concentration of evaluations on the project level (Florio 2006) by formulating more overreaching objectives to be achieved in a "strategic framework."

Concretely, states benefiting from the European Social Fund are obliged to respond to the *strategic guidelines* spelled out by the Council, including the objective of improving administrative efficiency. This has to be either through particular projects or inclusion of the objective into wider programs. This is subject to negotiations with the Commission that result in "national reference document" as framework for the operational programs (Council of the European Union 2006a: art 34). These *National Strategic Reference Frameworks* (NSRF) are a new tool that allows including ex-ante an additional conditional element to promote explicitly the objective of horizontal institution building, beyond the previously more narrowly defined assistance to implement the ESF itself. The NSRF is a tool similar to the individual *National Action Plans* introduced in the later stages of the pre-accession policy based on the *Accession Partnerships*.[6]

Continuity from the pre-accession implementation framework is visible in that the definition of efficient administrative capacities remains elusive. Instead, the Commission and each government define individual goals, which gives the Commission considerable discretion on how to operationalize the Council guidelines. Within the organization, there is coordination on different levels of the Commission.[7] The essential change of the new regulations is intentional and conditional extension to horizontal administrative capacities. This goes beyond the previously available

technical assistance that focused exclusively on the implementation of
ESF. As the Commission puts it, "the ESF will continue to finance actions
aiming at supporting the structures for the management and implementation of the Fund. This is financed with **Technical Assistance** and should
therefore be clearly distinguished from the activities under the institutional capacity priority. The objective of the institutional capacity priority
is to support the reform of the administrations irrespectively of their
role in Structural Funds' management and implementation" (Commission of the European Communities 2006h: 9, emphasis in the original).
The *Community Strategic Guidelines* for cohesion spell out the content of
the administrative and institutional capacity priorities for the 2007–2013
programming period. Going beyond the goal of an effective management
of EU funds the guidelines state that "effective administrative capacity
of public administrations and public services i.e. smart administration,
is a fundamental requirement for economic growth and jobs"; administrative capacity is framed in connection with the revised Lisbon Strategy
that "the Funds will support investment in the human capital of administrative and public services at all territorial levels" (Commission of the
European Communities 2005: 28). Linking the administrative capacity
goal to the Lisbon Strategy, the reform of public administrations and services are promoted in order to enhance sustainable economic growth and
to ensure good governance. Within the ESF the previous case-by-case support was hence generalized. Support within the ESF responds, therefore,
to the fact that "[a]fter accession, the Commission insisted on the need
not only to further invest in that area but also to extend the scope of
support" (Commission of the European Communities 2006f: 2).

As the introduction of individual national action plans showed, the
actual policy tools for technical assistance were drawn from the enlargement experience by adapting instruments developed in the pre-accession
context. The concept of *transnationality* has been introduced as a second element that recipient states are obliged to include in their national
strategies. This refers to the provision of technical assistance by national
administrations to promote the exchange of best practices. It draws not
least on the TAIEX networks established in the Copenhagen framework.
These networks are, however, opened up to exchange across member
states (instead of the previous "teacher/student" structure between old and
future member states). Considering that in twinning programs "the creation of an 'administrative market' (from where the applicant countries
could 'shop for' the most suitable solutions to their particular problems) has been one of the top priorities of the exercise" (Papadimitriou
and Phinnemore 2004: 625), transnationality is also an attempt to further profit from this market. "Twinning is another experience that we

wanted to incorporate in the future programming period, not only for this administrative capacity, and something like twinning can be done in transnationality . . . the transnationality *must* be promoted this is the requirement of the regulation, but it is the member states' choice if they do it across ALL policy areas that they get support for by ESF or if they chose some" (Interview 2007 DG EMPL).

In short, institutional/administrative capacity building has been incorporated into the European Social Fund for which the poorest regions of the EU are eligible, that is, the cohesion states and convergence regions. These funds have been made conditional in two respects. First, states need to make concrete propositions on how to improve their administrative structures for implementing the acquis, as well as the wider goals of the Lisbon Agenda. Second, in terms of policy tools, the recipient states have to get involved into direct exchanges with other member state administrations—a means to promote some harmonization in the absence of genuine standards and benchmarks. The Commission has wide discretion in the execution of the intuitional capacity priority since it negotiates, monitors, and evaluates the states' compliance with the individual strategic frameworks. Institutional capacity building is hence promoted through a distributive policy with re-enforced conditional elements under the umbrella of the European Social Fund. Though it is the Council that sets the general framework of objectives, the operationalization is incumbent upon the Commission that has considerable discretion to interpret the guidelines and control member states' compliance. In the light of continuous absence of genuine EU standards and competences, the actual effect of these steering instruments are likely to remain limited. Still, the new Social Funds regulations have offered a way to continue some Commission involvement in the consolidation of the new member states' administrative structures through raising the conditions on patronage policies by nesting demands on national administrative structures in the formally distributive policy.

SUMMARY: INSTITUTIONAL CAPACITY BUILDING

Functional pressure derived, foremost, from the need to respond to still insufficient implementation of the acquis in the new member states. Yet, similar shortcomings existed also in the EU-15. These two factors were reinforced by explicit demands for technical and financial support, based on positive experiences with EU-supported improvements of administrative services for citizens in Portugal. These projects took for the first time a horizontal perspective instead of focusing exclusively on the implementation of obligations linked to EU membership. The introduction of conditional assistance in member states parallel to the development of the policy tool in the Copenhagen framework was therefore no unintended consequence but an additional, intended, and strategic decision by national governments. The widening of the objectives to horizontal administrative capacities was, moreover, manifested in the revised ESF. The management and implementation of the Fund "is financed with **Technical Assistance** and should therefore be **clearly distinguished** from the activities financed under the institutional capacity priority. The objective of the institutional capacity priority is to support the reform of the administrations irrespective of their role in Structural Funds' management and implementation" (Commission of the European Communities 2006f: 8, emphasis in the original). General regulatory measures that could have been derived from the Copenhagen framework (in particular the SIGMA baseline criteria) remained out of question. Institutionalization beyond enlargement was limited to conditional distributive policies geared to the poorest states and regions in the EU.

The widened EU focus on horizontal administrative capacity building did not imply new hard competences for the Commission. The enlargement experience was, however, a forceful catalyst both for the recognition of the importance of national administrative capacities, and the awareness that further EU involvement in the future member states was needed. Although the SIGMA baseline criteria remained outside the EU framework, they established standards that have led to far-reaching suggestions for EU involvement. Thus, Verheijen even argues for the desirability and feasibility of an administrative acquis proper, "possibly based on the assessment criteria defined for the enlargement process" (2000: 56). Reckoning that to date member states would reject any such formalization, the author propagates that " 'soft law' or 'benchmarking' is probably the only acceptable form of interference in what will continue to be viewed as an exclusively national area. An administrative capacity charter . . . would be implemented through a mechanism of peer review, with related reporting requirements. It would constitute a logical follow-up to the definition of minimum requirements carried out in the enlargement process" (Verheijen 2000: 56).

The Commission itself has not even suggested a comprehensive instrument such as a charter, stressing rather the need to respond to individual national demands than proposing standardized harmonization. Apart from the Commission's prudence, as far as regulatory measures are concerned, the member states have driven forward some limited promotion of nonbinding coordination of national civil services outside the enlargement context. In 2000, the European Council adopted a *Common Assessment Framework* (CAF), guidelines for which were approved in 2001.

This "voluntary assessment framework aims to be 'an aid to public administrations in the EU' in the use of quality management techniques in public administration" (Dimitrova 2002: 182). This notwithstanding, these guidelines depend on the responsiveness of EU member states which leads to the conclusion that in a more binding way "none of the above SIGMA defined 'principles' can be identified as common EU norms or that they are in the process of negotiation in the EU itself and are not sufficiently specific yet" (Dimitrova 2002: 182). Notably, the way action capacity was framed outside the Copenhagen framework took account of the hurdles for hard regulation. It focused on the extension of capacities in the distributive realm—introducing standards through the backdoor of binding funds to conditions but evading member state resistance against new formal competences on administrative capacities.

By the same token, the innovations of the Lisbon Treaty widened the legal basis for EU involvement, although forbidding hard legislation. The Union's role is limited to supportive, coordinating, and complementary actions. Therefore, possible future measures are also likely to be contained to the distributive arena. The introduction of conditional spending that puts demands on administrative capacities of the recipient state is an important qualitative innovation. It marks a precedent for the organization of conditional patronage relationships in this area. Any further regulatory moves, in turn, should remain soft regulatory instruments such as benchmarking and the exchange of information. These are most likely to develop out of the *Common Assessment Frameworks* whose aim is "to assist public-sector organizations across Europe in using quality management techniques to improve performance" and—with also supportive functions—the *European Public Administration Network,* which serves as "platform for exchange of information concerning Europeanisation and facilitates dialogue between Public Administration teaching institutions in Europe."[8] The fact that the member states involve increasingly actively in establishing nonbinding cooperation by means of CAF and EUPAN took even more wind out of the Commission's sails to suggest harmonizing regulation.

While enlargement may have played a reinforcing role in the emerging stronger recognition of the need for strengthened EU capacities, implementing enlargement has surely been a crucial catalyst for the development of standards for soft regulatory means and the introduction of conditional distributive policies. It created strong functional pressure, while no serious unintended consequences emerged. Quite on the contrary, parallel to the policy development in the pre-accession context, member states raised claims for Community funding. Hence, framing the issue in the distributive realm suggested itself much rather than new formal regulatory claims. The latter were further weakened as voluntary cooperation between member states increased and extended the toolbox of nonbinding regulatory policy instruments.

Disconfirming expectations on straightforward distributive policies, funds are targeted clearly to the poorest member states and linked to conditions for the recipients. Although introduced as an additional distributive policy in the ESF (financial and technical assistance for regional units), the convergence and transnationality criteria create in the end redistributive effects. Instead of resulting from a broad debate on redistribution favoring the new member states, these changes were introduced as a reform of preexisting patronage policies. To contain these new patronage claims and to preserve a control tool targeted foremost at the new member states, funding is linked to conditions. Operationalizing and controlling these conditions in point of fact increases the Commission's capacities for impacting national administrations. The effect of these instruments can be expected weaker than the mechanisms of control used in the enlargement framework (backed by conditionality). Nonetheless, despite the questionable effects, the Commission enters the field of domestic administrative capacities that had previously been clearly outside the European Union's sphere of influence.

THE RESPECT FOR AND PROTECTION OF MINORITIES: EXPLOITING LEGAL GREY AREAS AND PATRONAGE POLICIES

"The respect for and protection of minorities" (European Council 1993) had strong regulatory features in the pre-accession monitoring scheme and was backed by conditional distributive policies.[1] Although in particular the responsibilities of the office of the OSCD *High Commissioner on National Minorities* (founded in 1992) overlap with those of the EU, both civil society and political actors alike attributed a distinct role and added value to the EU's promotion of minority rights in the central and eastern European states. This is not least reflected in manifold public calls that the end of the pre-accession policy would lead to a considerable gap in the effective protection of minorities.

Although the explicit focus on minorities was absolutely new in the Copenhagen context, strong links to the increasingly strengthened antidiscrimination acquis exist. Hence, a spill-in of minority competences to the formal acquis had to link up to the preexisting rules. However, a decisive difference impeded a one-to-one inclusion of pre-accession minority rights within related areas of the acquis. Unlike antidiscrimination, which establishes individual rights, the collective minority rights of the Copenhagen framework have a social redistributive element.[2]

The theoretical expectation for the spill-in of pre-accession steering instruments reads accordingly:

> If framed in terms of binding laws on minority protection, no spill-in should be expected; spill-in should emerge in if standards for the protection of minorities are framed nonbindingly in the regulatory arena and as distributive policy offering both financial and technical assistance.

The supranational level had no competences whatsoever in the field when minority protection was established as one of the core criteria for accession. Hence it has even been described as "a commonplace that the process of Eastern enlargement can be regarded as the primordial catalyst moving the protection of minorities onto the European Union's (EU) agenda" (Toggenburg 2006: 1). While formal competences on minorities proper remain absent, especially in the area of antidiscrimination a substantial acquis has been developed since. The emergence of this acquis was not directly caused by spill-in from enlargement policy. This body of new antidiscrimination acquis offered, however, a legal framework into which certain instruments developed in the pre-accession context could be embedded.

The formation of capacities in the Copenhagen framework was based on norms and standards defined by international instruments outside the EU. These applied implicitly to the EU by virtue of the member states' membership to key agreements. From these the Commission derived definitions and benchmarks to monitor and evaluate the criterion in the candidate states. The existence and successful application of these instruments lead to (a) a limited and implicit formal extension of the antidiscrimination acquis in the Treaty of Amsterdam and mentioning in the Treaty of Lisbon, (b) the informal extension of the Commission's capacities regarding the monitoring function—exercised by an agency with regard to all member states—and (c) financial support for minority programs focusing on Roma communities in all member states. In sum, the Commission could extend its action capacity in the field of minority protection informally. It continues both its monitoring and its assistance functions by legally linking these with the formally extended antidiscrimination acquis.

STATUS QUO ANTE: A STRONG CRITERION WITH WEAK LEGAL BASIS

In 1993, no competences regarding minority policy existed on the EU level. To assess which capacities were established after the pre-accession phase, some remarks on the EU's more general handling of human rights are required. Human rights have gained considerable importance in the EU's external action since the 1990s (Brandtner and Rosas 1998: 468). However, the Union is marked by a fundamental discrepancy between the internally and externally applied standards for evaluating respect for human rights (Williams 2000: 616). Overall, the EU suffers from "inconsistency, inherent in the CFSP, whereby the Union decries violations of human rights abroad yet has no voice with regard to human rights problems at home" (Clapham 1999: 639).

When the minority criterion was established for outsiders who wanted to join the Union, no equivalent regulations or standards existed inside the EU. This entailed normative and a practical problem. Conditionality exercised through the Copenhagen criteria draws its legitimacy essentially from the fact that the conditions imply necessary adaptations to the EU acquis, a justification hard to sustain for criteria that go beyond the acquis. This legitimacy problem of conditionality-based enlargement policy was inherent to the external demand for minority protection in absence of internal EU rules (see also Wiener and Schwellnus 2004: 2–4). Consequently, the rules monitored in the accession context could not be derived from established EU legislation.[3] Alternatively, the Commission filled the criterion with meaning derived from a set of international standards, most importantly the European Convention for the Protection of Human Rights and Fundamental Freedoms (ECHR, Council of Europe, 1950). The Commission did so despite the fact that the Union (the European Community respectively) itself has not joined the ECHR. The EC/EU's abstention from the ECHR has been strongly criticized, so Alston and Weiler state: "It appears to be highly anomalous, indeed unacceptable, that whilst membership of the Convention system is, appropriately, a prerequisite of accession to the Union, the Union itself—or at least the Community—remains outside that system. The negative symbolism is self-evident" (1999: 30), and Brandner and Rosas add that the fact that "the Community remains formally outside the written conventions, including the ECHR . . . is regrettable, as it means that the EC is not directly responsible for the execution of these conventions" (1998: 490).

This critique loses some bite considering that all EU member and applicant states have ratified the Convention. Moreover, the European Court of Justice has systematically taken direct reference to the convention as guideline for its jurisdiction. This practice has been strengthened by the introduction of Article F(2) in the Treaty of Maastricht as well as Article 6 in the Treaty of Amsterdam. Nonetheless, well into the 1990s the ECJ insisted that a Community accession to the convention was impossible without prior changes to the Treaty (European Court of Justice 1996).

Exposing the ECJ's and the member states' motives behind the long resistance to an EC accession to Convention, Gaja concludes that "what is at stake is the conservation by the Court of Justice of its present functions" (1996: 988). Accession to the ECHR would give the European Court of Human Rights in Strasbourg certain supervisory power over the ECJ. Hence, preventing an accession, "the Court has discouraged any external review of the way in which human rights are protected within the Community system" (Gaja 1996: 989). Likewise the proclamation of the *Charter of Fundamental Rights of the European Union*[4] (European Council 2000a) did not immediately change the legal situation within the EU. Although the general attorneys of the Court refer regularly to the Charter, it lacked formal legal status for almost ten years.

Against the background of this long-dominant opposition, the ratification of the Lisbon Treaty marked a decisive turning point because it gave the Charter legal force and set off the process for EU accession to the ECHR. As regards concrete minority rights, however, the Lisbon Treaty "astonishes in its strong symbolic pro-minority message but disappoints in its rather weak policy relevance" (Toggenburg 2006: 10). It will arguably have no substantive effect on the legal practice since it does not change the formal status of concrete minority rights in the EU.

Besides fundamental rights, on which antidiscrimination and minority rights are based, the Union's economic acquis is the second important legal basis that relates to minority protection. Both a substantial acquis as well as a nonbinding acquis exist on particular aspects.[5] While this acquis has extended—in the instrumental disguise of measures supporting the Common Market rather than promoting certain values—collective minority rights remain excluded and the principle of protection of individuals against discrimination prevails. Regarding individual antidiscrimination, the most important innovation was the introduction of an antidiscrimination acquis in the 1996 Treaty of Amsterdam (Article 13), on the basis of which antidiscrimination directives were passed in 2000.

The development of this new, wider antidiscrimination acquis was itself not caused by spill-in from enlargement. Geddes and Guiraudon analyze how the policy paradigm underlying the EU antidiscrimination policy changed and explain the emergence of the 2000 antidiscrimination directives as a "framing process" in which contrasting member state positions were molded. The authors point out that "the intergovernmental impetus to action came from state-level reaction against racist and xenophobic outrages early in the 1990s" (Geddes and Guiraudon 2004: 341–42). Very much in line with the theoretical model proposed in the current study, the expected effects for the member states were essential. For the two states under perspective, the low adaptional pressure was decisive in the case of the United Kingdom. In the case of France "[a]nti-discrimination had advantages since it cost little—much less than redistributive measures such as *politique de la ville* and shifted the blame to non-state actors, such as employers and nightclub owners" (Geddes and Guiraudon 2004: 345). In the policy formulation process "the two main factors that explain why an anti-discrimination Directive with a distinct Anglo-Dutch flavour was adopted are policy and ideational linkages to the fight against xenophobia and an equal opportunity frame inherited from the EU gender and equal treatment legislation. To the extent that our qualitative research design can 'measure' the respective importance of independent variables, policy linkage was key, because it accelerated the negotiations and silenced potential opposition from employers and national bureaucratic actors" (Geddes and Guiraudon 2004: 350). The directive was, however, much more quickly adopted than could be expected, and the "single factor most often mentioned to explain why the Race Directive was given priority and its negotiation accelerated is Jörg Haider" (Geddes and Guiraudon 2004: 346). This must again be seen in the context of the particular frames held by some member states in the face of the Haider's right-wing party entering government in Austria: "the success of Haider's party could act as an accelerator for EU negotiations only because for some key member states—France and Germany—anti-discrimination is synonymous with anti-racism and resonates with post-war attempts to fight the ideas of the extreme right" (Geddes and Guiraudon 2004: 347). The birth of the antidiscrimination directives happened independent from enlargement. This framework that emerged in parallel offered subsequently options to integrate specific instruments from the pre-accession context that specialized on minority issues. Just as policy linkage and the avoidance of openly redistributive policies had been essential for the establishment of the antidiscrimination acquis, these mechanisms were essential for the spill-in of instruments of minority protection.

In sum, at the time of mandating minority policy as one of the key areas regarding the Commission's approach toward the candidate states, human rights were only insufficiently institutionalized on the EU level— minority issues were completely absent. Moreover, while the definition of minority rights in the realm of enlargement marked a fundamental qualitative shift as it included the principle of collective rights, the incremental advances on the supranational level remained committed to the paradigm of individual rights protection. Hence, from its outset, minority policy in the enlargement context created strong functional pressure because of the double standards it evoked.

PRE-ACCESSION PHASE: DEVELOPING NEW STANDARDS
FOR MINORITY POLICIES[6]

The conferral of responsibilities on minority protection in the Copenhagen framework was by virtue of the Copenhagen criteria. Part of the political conditions to be met by the candidate states was "the respect for and protection of minorities" (European Council 1993). Along these lines, minority protection was given a twofold meaning. In addition to the protection from discrimination of individuals, the criterion implies the provision of special, also collective, minority rights (cf. Open Society Institute 2001: 16; Wiener and Schwellnus 2004: 8–9). The protection of individual rights already represented a generally accepted norm since the Helsinki Final Act (Conference for Security and Cooperation in Europe, 1975). Rights referring to minorities as groups were, on the contrary, formulated for the first time by the Organization for Security and Cooperation in Europe (OSCE) at the beginning of the 1990s (Hughes and Sasse 2003: 8). The phrasing and definition in the Copenhagen criterion conform to this turn toward the inclusion of collective rights. For the candidate states this entailed decisively higher requirements for norm adaptation than minority protection limited to individual antidiscrimination. Outside the Copenhagen framework, this normative reinterpretation remained limited mostly to a rhetorical meaning, and neither did the EU member states oblige themselves to the extension of minority protection to include collective rights. Even more so, the heavily diverging definitions of minority protection on the national levels in the various member states persisted and none of the EU Council Decisions extended beyond individual rights after the declaration of the Copenhagen criteria (Hughes and Sasse 2003: 4–10).

Faced with the discrepancy between a rather explicit external criterion and an internal legal blank, the Commission needed to set up standards and benchmarks on how to evaluate whether a candidate met the criterion—without having unambiguous reference points within the acquis to apply these "double standards" (see e.g., Amato and Batt 1998b). It was not obvious which standards and benchmarks should be used to enact the minority criterion applying the two tools it had at its disposal: monitoring and assistance. For both, operationalized benchmarks to measure compliance had to be found.

Deficient of clear-cut EU regulations on minority protection, the Commission drew mainly on international instruments. Accordingly, standards defined by other international organizations provided the tangible basis for what was to be monitored. Besides the *United Nations' Universal Declaration of Human Rights* (1949), the *ECHR* and the *Framework*

Convention for the Protection of National Minorities of the Council of Europe (1995) deserve mentioning here—disregarding the fact that not all of the EU-12, and later EU-15, member states had signed and ratified the last mentioned international instruments.[7] For the practical application of these established standards, the Commission drafted a catalog of items to be monitored in preparation of the Commission Opinions in 1997. In the form of a handbook, including concrete checklists, these practical guidelines were hardly adapted during the pre-accession phase and used at all levels involved in the annual reporting (Heidbreder and Carrasco 2003: 32). Even though this operationalization of the minority criterion is founded on international conventions, its specific contents are influenced by the particular conditions that the Commission considered of relevance in the candidate states, especially the situation of Roma as well as Russian-speaking communities (Heidbreder and Carrasco 2003: 33).

It is noteworthy that it was only because of pressure from key actors in the Commission that the EU approach embraced Roma minorities, too. The member states and parts of the Commission Services focused initially rather on "Estonia and Latvia whose Russian-speaking minorities were one of the main targets (not Roma!) that the authors of Copenhagen had in mind" (official DG Enlargement, written exchange September 2007). But also within the Commission, there was some resistance along these lines. "When it was suggested that we should leave them out of the analysis ('that's not what they meant at Copenhagen') I argued that one could not realistically exclude them in making an objective assessment of minorities" (official DG Enlargement, written exchange September 2007). From this disputed start, the concern for Roma minorities soon advanced as *the* focal point of EU minority policy.

For the practical operationalization of the monitoring task, the Commission developed a complex internal organization and an external network to assemble information for the regular reporting (Heidbreder and Carrasco 2003). The cooperation with other international organizations that play a role in European minority protection—the Council of Europe and the OSCE High Commissioner on National Minorities—had a privileged role in the process. Regarding Russian-speaking minorities, for example, more relevant than Commission's own services was the cooperation especially with the OECD's High Commissioner Max Van Der Stoel, who "rapidly became the authority on whose judgment the Commission relied [on], particularly in the case of Estonia and Latvia" (official DG Enlargement, written exchange, September 2007).

In spite of the intensive and extensive illustration of shortcomings in protecting minorities, the final evaluation on conformity with the criterion in the Regular Reports has, except for one case, always been positive.[8]

Whereas the system that the Commission set up within the Copenhagen framework may be judged an effective instrument to monitor minority protection at the national level, the eventual, less critical evaluations suggest that the judgments are not solely based on a strict application of the criterion. In terms of functional pressure, the dilemma was that the reporting was effective in spelling out shortcomings at the national level, while at the same time the scope for political responses was limited in the shadow of double standards—thus increasing policy-generated functional pressure as the monitoring process went on.

As regards the second means that the Commission had for achieving specific policy targets, from as early as 1989 the Commission offered support through the pre-enlargement programs Phare (main assistance program for the accession states), Phare LIEN (co-financing of projects initiated by nongovernmental organizations), as well as the ACCESS program (strengthening the Civil Society, in 1999 replacing LIEN Phare and partnership programs). Assistance to the central and eastern European countries focused foremost on Roma minority groups. Within Phare, as from 1998 DG Enlargement allocated significant resources primarily to Bulgaria, the Czech Republic, Hungary, Romania, and Slovakia. "Presumably, this funding was intended to support candidate states in addressing some of the problems identified in the Regular Reports. However, rather than dealing with minority protection or rights, 'most Phare programs were developed as socio-economic interventions designed to deal with some aspects of the social exclusion experienced by many Roma minority populations'" (European Commission Evaluation Unit, 2004, p. 1). A significant percentage of Phare funding supported equipment purchases or infrastructure development (particularly in isolated Romani communities) or 'social integration' (European Commission Evaluation Unit, 2004, pp. 63–4)" (Gugliemlo and Waters 2005: 771–72).

Supplementary to the Enlargement Directorate, the DG for External Relations was active with projects under the heading of the European Initiative for Democracy and Human Rights (EIDHR), which is preoccupied with the support for democracy and the rule of law in third countries. All budget lines dealing with human rights were pooled under this initiative in 1994, including also *PHARE democracy*. EIDHR supported microprojects that were managed by the Commission's delegations in the respective states. To ensure consistency across the various programs these projects were terminated for the accession states in 2001. For the budgetary period of 2002–2004 still a number of focus countries were financed with means from EIDHR as the fight against racism and xenophobia counts to the priorities of the initiative.

The reliance on double standards put a question mark on the actual agreement of the candidate countries to the validity of the criterion as such (Hughes and Sasse 2003: 24)[9] and reduced the leverage of conditionality as an instrument of enlargement policy (on this issue see also Checkel 2000; Grabbe 2001). As for all the cases analyzed, the closer accession moved the less was a strict application of conditionality feasible. In addition, external incongruence may be asserted, especially contradictions between the official compliance with the criterion measured against the improvement of the situation of minorities on the ground. However, it remains questionable whether the assessed states have and had even sufficient (financial) resources to implement the criterion to its full extent. Against this background Guy argues that the criterion, which does in principle also comprise a functioning implementation side, could be met in "merely formal terms in the foreseeable future, and certainly not by the time of accession" (Braham/Braham cited from Guy 2001: 16). Even if the assessment of real implementation makes up for a central part of the reporting, it thus seems plausible that the final assessments broadly ignore shortcomings in implementation and concentrate instead predominantly on the adaptation of formal legal structures.

Nonetheless, even if the actual outcomes of EU conditionality may remain sub-optimal because of a lack of credibility, the Commission's minority approach during the pre-accession phase was generally considered a valuable contribution, leading as it did to an open discussion fostered by civil society groups and politicians alike that called for continued EU involvement beyond the date of accession. The Open Society Institute offers one of the most explicit examples: "The EU should make it clear to aspiring members that assessment of basic human and minority rights will continue after accession; the best way to convey the seriousness of this message is to initiate a genuine and thorough assessment of all member States" (Open Society Institute 2002a: 64). Another example, more narrowly focused on Roma minorities, is the European Parliament, which continued to stress the "need to strengthen the system for monitoring such discrimination and to resolve the legal status of the Roma" (European Parliament 2005).[10]

Although other international organizations increased their involvement in minority policy, foremost the foundation of the office of the OSCD High Commissioner on National Minorities, throughout the pre-accession phase the Commission's role in the promotion of minority protection and rights was attributed a distinct and important function in the candidate states that would be lost with accession. For example, the legal advisor of the OSCE High Commissioner on National Minorities, John Packer, demurred in 1999: "we have serious concerns that if there is not an EU internal (human rights) assessment process and if there is not a continual annual reporting, new states which become EU members might feel less pressure to meet those human rights standards" (Report by

the EU Human Rights Forum (November 30-December 1, 1999), cited
in Tsilevich 2001). The Commission's monitoring system was generally
accepted as a well-functioning tool adding positive effects to the instruments of the Council of Europe and the OSCE (Vermeersch 2004). This
was argued especially pointing to the weak instrument the Council of
Europe Framework Convention offers in terms of enforcement.

Functional pressure surfaced above all because the reasons for tackling
the respect for and protection of minority rights persisted in the candidate
states and was increasingly perceived to exist also beyond enlargement
and the accession states. The perceived scope of the problem widened to
include also the territory of the old member states. Besides a concern for
the actual situation of the individuals belonging to a minority group, the
EU-15, moreover, increasingly perceived the Roma question in particular as a potential security problem affecting themselves. "Concerns about
migration, security and integration that surfaced at the beginning of the
accession process persist, but minority protection has decisively entered
European policy and Europe's self-image. It will become increasingly necessary to address Romani issues in a different register; in the light of this,
prudent policy will consider not if, but how, Roma will be integrated into
Europe as minorities" (Gugliemlo and Waters 2005: 764). Accordingly,
there was ample expression, either pointing to the future member states'
specific situation or by more generally reacting to calls to continue both
regulatory and distributive policies around minority matters in the EU.

This extension of the problem definition that defined minority protection and in particular questions on the Roma minorities as matters
concerning also the old member states indicates that the subsequent
extension of distributive policy tools was not an unintended consequence.
In stark contrast to this, the extension of collective minority rights as
created in the Copenhagen framework would have marked an unintended consequence—this, however, did not occur. Although individual
antidiscrimination rights developed parallel to the Copenhagen framework under the acquis umbrella, these did not undermine member state
intentions to contain the way in which minority rights were framed in the
enlargement context.

STATUS QUO POST: INFORMAL INSTITUTIONALIZATION
OF MINORITY POLICY

By tracing the evolution of EU minority policy in relation to enlargement,
some direct effects of implementing the minority criterion on the EU level
can be asserted. Foremost in order to maintain the potential impact on
minority protection in the new member states, some kind of continuation

beyond the Copenhagen framework had to be tolerated by the member states. First, the monitoring of minority rights, introduced as part of the regular reporting for the candidate states, is continued in a limited format in the framework of the European Monitoring Centre for Racism and Xenophobia (EUMC),[11] founded in Vienna in 1998. While the foundation of EUMC was not a direct response to enlargement, it nonetheless took on some of the monitoring tasks. Thus tasks could be responded to in the concurrently emerging institution. Moreover, the Commission considers itself to have an indirect oversight responsibility under Article 6 of the Treaty on the European Union that states fundamental human rights as basic principle of the Union. Second, assistance offered during the pre-accession phase—particularly regarding Roma minorities—has been extended to all EU member states. Third, the issue of explicit and collective minority rights has entered the supranational agenda not at least because of the expressed interests of one of the new member sates, Hungary. In sum, although the member states refrained from shifting further hard competences to the EU level, a process of informal institutionalization of the policy tools developed in the enlargement context can be observed.

First, the foundation of the EUMC, in connection with a Community Action Program (Council of the European Communities 2000), established a monitoring organization that deals with all old and new member states alike. While EUMC activities have been carried over to the Agency on Fundamental Rights (since 2007), the Action Programme has a follow-up in the Community Programme for Employment and Solidarity, PROGRESS (2007–2013).

One of the major tasks of the center/agency is the collection of reliable and comparable information and data on racism, xenophobia, islamophobia, and anti-Semitism in the EU. Drawing on this data it publishes analyses and strategies to fight these phenomena. The agency's Information Network on Racism and Xenophobia (RAXEN) contains national focal points that work along harmonized benchmarks, and, as part of that, also consider minority issues on the individual national level. Regular publications serve not only to draw public attention on states performing comparably badly but also to work indirectly toward an adaptation of standards.

Furthermore, actor networks in the field have been established. Reacting to a request by the European Parliament, the Commission has also established an expert network dealing, among other issues, with that of minorities. The European Union Network of Experts in Fundamental Rights has subsequently come up with a number of reports, including one outlining the "need for an EU Roma Integration Directive" (Commission of the European Communities 2004f: 44). Yet, the member states have not taken up calls for binding legislation on concrete minority groups' rights.

Apart from the agency's monitoring, based on soft enforcement tools in form of reporting, the Commission has developed the position that minority protection counts as one of its competences more generally. This interpretation creates considerable tension "with the simple fact that the words 'minority' and 'minority protection' do not appear anywhere in the EU and the EC Treaties. They are neither mentioned as being part of the values recognized by the European Union nor are they listed among the policy competences of the EU" (De Witte 2004: 110). Still, despite this apparently clear legal situation, parts of the Commission promote a more subtle self-understanding by referring candidly to the implementation of enlargement. While the first Regular Reports did not make a direct link between the Copenhagen criterion on minorities and Article 49(6) TEU,[12] the 2002 Reports referred explicitly to Article 6 TEU and stressed that "through the entry into force of the Treaty of Amsterdam, the political criteria defined at Copenhagen have been essentially enshrined as constitutional principle in the Treaty on the European Union" (quoted in Hoffmeister 2004: 88). This logic was also followed by the *Accession Partnerships,* as well as by the EP when issuing enlargement related resolutions. All this can be justified with reference to the Council of Europe Framework Convention on National Minorities (FCNM) that defines minority rights as an integral part of the protection of human rights (Council of Europe 1995: Article 1). "Hence, taking into account the latter text and unanimous practice by the EU institutions, Article 6(1) TEU could be interpreted widely, so as to encompass minority rights and the protection under the heading 'human rights'" (Hoffmeister 2004). From this perspective, Article 6 also provides the basis for some monitoring of the member states and the principles of Article 6(1) are "widely regarded as confirmation of the Copenhagen political criteria within the text of the TEU" (Nowak 1999: 692). Even more so, since Article 7 grants the Commission the right to request the suspension of membership rights in cases of serious breaches of Article 6 principles, one can read an implicit monitoring function also for minority issues into the TEU. This notwithstanding, since the only enforcement tool—the suspension of membership rights—is a means of last resort, the Commission has hardly any leeway to act. Given that initiating the procedure of suspending membership rights is too hard an instrument to be applied except for exceptional cases, the Commission actually lacks less coercive tools such as mentioning shortcomings in a regular reporting mechanism. Thus, oversight on minority protection in the member states is being exercised rather cautiously and remains little visible—but it is exercised and understood part of the Commission's responsibilities (Interview 2007 COM LS).

This interpretation of the EU's legal basis for minority protection is admittedly a balancing act and can be questioned from a number of angles. First, not all member states have ratified the FCNM, and neither has the European Community.[13] Second, the Amsterdam Treaty transposed basically all of the other accession criteria into primary legislation—apart from the criterion for minority protection. "The fact that the minority clause was kept separated appears to indicate that its inclusion—whereby it would have assumed a clear binding force and an internal dimension—was not desired" (Toggenburg 2000: 17). Consequently the official separation between the EU's acquis and the accession criterion has been sustained, "respect for democracy, the rule of law and human rights have been recognised as fundamental values in the European Union's internal development *and* for the purpose of its enlargement, whereas minority protection is *only* mentioned in the latter context" (De Witte 2000: 4, emphasis in original). Third, it seems that within the Commission's legal service different views exist. While some departments interpret their monitoring task to have officially ended with accession of the states, others promote the view outlined above (Interviews COM LS).

Despite all this, in the ongoing enlargement policy there is strong evidence for this latter, extensive interpretation, and what is more, the member states silently tolerate this extension of the Commission's capacities. Even though on a slightly dubious legal basis, minority protection has been moved from a pre-condition to open accession negotiations into chapter 23, *Judiciary and Fundamental Rights,* newly introduced in the revised enlargement strategies for Turkey and Croatia. Faced with the delay in the enforcement of the Constitutional and subsequently the Lisbon Treaty that strengthens the legal basis of fundamental rights, the Commission continued to refer to the basic rights references in the Treaties and the related international instruments. An argument of the Commission for turning minority protection into part of a negotiation chapter is that standards and criteria of measurement need to be clearer from the beginning of the process than they were for the Copenhagen criterion in order to raise transparency and credibility vis-à-vis the candidate states (Interview 2007 COM LS). At the same time, this clarification for the candidate states blurs the legal basis for EU involvement in the formally still national competence on a more genuine minority policy.[14]

The reasoning behind this argument further endorses a broad interpretation of Article 6 by linking the EU Treaty directly to the FCNM.

It suggests an implicit EU responsibility regarding minorities much more vividly than a narrow reading of the actual formal regulations. More than just tolerating this wide interpretation on arguably soft legal grounds,

> the Council and the European Council—and hence the representatives of the national governments—have substantially contributed to the development of second-generation conditionality. This might indicate that minority protection is no longer exclusively seen as a condition for becoming a member state of the Union but increasingly as an expression of being a EU member state. It seems as if the Council and the Heads of State and Government are aligning themselves with the legal position of the European Commission, which regularly holds that minority protection is part of the founding principles of the Union as outlined in Article 6 TEU.
> (Toggenburg 2006: 4–5)

As pointed out above, in the absence of any explicit legal basis this interpretation opens a vast legal grey area in which the Commission has de facto far-reaching additional capabilities.

The implementation of most initiatives directed at all member states relies on various soft implementation instruments, such as mainstreaming and impact assessments (Toggenburg 2006: 11–13), and also some closely related and relevant hard legislation has been passed. On the basis of Article 13 of the Amsterdam Treaty, the *Race Equality Directive* (Council of the European Union 2000b) establishes individual rights of members of societal minorities. Although limited to rights against individual discrimination, the directive includes the obligation to designate a body or bodies that promote "equal treatment of all persons without discrimination on the grounds of racial or ethnic origin" (Article 13). Alarmed by poor transposition by the majority of member states, the commissioner in charge issued formal requests to 14 member states in June 2007 for falling short of implementing rules banning discrimination on the grounds of race or ethnic origin (Commission of the European Communities 2007a), followed by more coercive legal steps. The Commission dropped the last infringement procedures that ensued in November 2009 after the laggards Spain, Slovakia, and Malta introduced the respective legal acts.

Moving to the second set, the continuation of assistance or distributive policies targeting minorities, a number of new tools have been established. The basis for this is primarily the antidiscrimination acquis. Measures are rather comprehensive, especially regarding the continuous concern with Roma minorities. The Commission developed policy programs during the enlargement phase, the bulk of which focused on Roma communities.

Initially placed within Phare, during the late stages of the pre-accession phase, a more global approach including candidate and existing member states was adopted. Thus, the *Support for Roma Communities in Central and Eastern Europe* (Commission of the European Communities 2003e) extended well beyond the enlargement context and involves different directorate generals of the Commission. Measures were accordingly not anymore limited to states outside the EU. In this vein the Commission stated: "However, there are Roma communities in EU Member States as well, and the EU has developed programmes to improve the situation—particularly in the educational field, and in combating racism and discrimination" (Commission of the European Communities 2003e: 6).

Nonetheless, at the moment of accession the perception that Roma were foremost an issue of the new member states persisted. The discourse on Roma as a minority of the central and eastern European states evolved as from the first half of the 1990s and was essentially interconnected with the establishment of the Union's enlargement policy (Simhandl 2006). Already for the programming period 2000–2006, support for Roma communities was given priority status by the EIDHR, DG Education, and DG Social Affairs as part of the mainstreamed aim to "fight off racism and xenophobia." Referring to the more general antidiscrimination law,[15] Roma programs have subsequently been fully integrated into the Commission's framework and have been placed in DG Employment, also running the above-mentioned PROGRESS program. Policy measures have been developed along the main conflict lines that were identified during pre-accession monitoring as indicators for discrimination on grounds of race and ethnic origin (Heidbreder and Carrasco 2003: 32–47). Accordingly, the main focal points of basically all initiatives that tackle minorities by approaching their particular problems from a wide interpretation of antidiscrimination are education, employment, and access to housing and medical care. In this, the Commission is going beyond assistance for Roma minorities. Following the same reasoning, minority issues have also found their way into the European Employment Strategy, more precisely the *Process of Social Inclusion* and *Migration/Integration Policy* (Toggenburg 2006: 14–19).[16]

The bulk of financial assistance outside enlargement policy is provided by the Social Funds. The Commission estimates that during the last seven years of the programming period, the contribution to various projects promoting the living conditions of Roma communities has amounted to some 300 million euros. An additional amount of three to four times higher was spent in other areas indirectly profiting Roma minorities in one way or another.

Especially in projects aiming to advance awareness creation and information campaigns, the Commission is collaborating strongly with various nongovernmental and international organizations. One prominent example is the *Roma Decade 2000–2015*, initiated by Gorge Soros together with the former head of the World Bank, James David Wolfensohn, and Commissioner Anna Diamantopoulou. Moreover, the Commission itself runs its own internship program hosting ten Roma interns a year, financed by the Soros Foundation. Furthermore, the EU has launched *European Year of Equal Opportunities for All* in 2007, with the declared aims to "make people more aware of their rights to enjoy equal treatment and a life free of discrimination—irrespective of sex, racial or ethnic origin, religion or belief, disability, age and sexual orientation, promote equal opportunities for all, launch a major debate on the benefits of diversity both for European societies and individuals."[17]

Finally, in order to develop more clearly a strategy for the future, the Commission has created a high-level group of experts under the auspice of the former president of the German Bundestag, Rita Süßmuth (Commission of the European Communities 2006c). The group produced a report in which it issued eight tangible recommendations and identified 14 major barriers to market inclusion of ethnic minorities (Süßmuth 2007).[18] The objective of the group was foremost to provide practical recommendations, including a practicable definition of minorities deducted from the antidiscrimination notion. In the words of a Commission official:

> It is clear, the members of the group are no professors, no ethnologists, we will not try to define that 'an ethnic minority is . . . in state A it is this group, in state B it is that . . . what we do is to go towards a pragmatic definition of the type: in every country there is a minority, and in every country there are spheres in which a part of society feels simply disadvantaged . . . we are not interested in the fact that . . . there is a Mr Öger in Hamburg, or a Mr Mitta in London. What we are interested in is the point of intersection, where the belonging to an ethnic group constitutes a social disadvantage.
>
> (Interview 2007: DG EMPL, my translation)

This definition underlines clearly the Commission's shift of interest and conceptualization from old minorities to new minorities (see also: Toggenburg 2006: 1), hand in glove with a limitation to individual antidiscrimination rights.

To wrap up, both in the monitoring/regulatory and in the assistance/distributive arena the Commission continues to be active. In the narrower legal definition this is based on the antidiscrimination acquis that developed since 1997. Yet, in the regulatory as the distributive arena the Commission stretches the narrower formal legal framework and pushes informally into further areas. Enlargement policy was key in this new emphasis on minorities in its various disguises. "The systematic, regular work with this topic was surely absent before all the enlargement activities, that is, before 1995" (Interview COM LS, own translation). Last but not least, a general sensitization and politicization regarding minority issues can be observed. This was apparent especially in the strong push by Hungary to make an explicit mentioning of minorities in the Treaty on a Constitution for Europe, which it eventually succeeded in against the reluctance of many member states (cf. Article I-2 The Union's Values, and Article II-81 Non-discrimination). Human and in particular minority rights have furthermore gained increasing attention against the background of the Yugoslav conflict, and the EU's enlargement policy directed to the western Balkans based on a "second generation conditionality" following "a so-called *graduated approach*" (Toggenburg 2006: 3–5) that reinforced the emphasis on minority protection as accession criterion. The expectation that formal accession of the new member states would internalize new demands on minority protection (regarding the issue persistence on the EU agenda, see also: Simhandl 2006: 97) has indeed led to an extension of the Commission's action capacity.[19] The sum of the related informal regulatory and supportive distributive policies "clearly demonstrates that the Union internalized its minority engagement. The enlargement experience did not only lead to an even more outspoken engagement of the Union in its relations towards current and potential candidate states but provoked a new EU-engagement for minorities within the EU territory. . . . This, however, corresponds to the fact that for questions of preservation the Member States will remain the primary responsible entities" (Toggenburg 2006: 27).

Moral pressure to legitimize the minority criterion existed from the start given the double standards of internal and external rules. This pressure amounted to increased functional pressure based on the positive evaluation of the Commission's performance in the Copenhagen framework and the extension of the problem definition in terms of territorial expansion to include also the EU-15. A push for spill-in occurred in both the regulatory and distributive arena. Unintended consequences did, however, not emerge because the official definition of minority protection was contained by (a) focusing on new minorities, and (b) limiting rights to those of individuals against antidiscrimination. Despite these formal restrictions member states silently tolerate a de facto much wider interpretation and application of minority policy in the ongoing enlargement process—and thus implicitly also with effect on themselves. Distributive policies have been extended to all member states and mainstreamed across EU policies. The main focus remains, however, on Roma communities that are defined as a special case, which again allows the containment of patronage claims by minority groups for collective rights.

SUMMARY: RESPECT FOR AND PROTECTION OF MINORITY RIGHTS

It is telling that extended minority policy in the EU was framed implicitly in the context of the European Employment Strategy, as well in Social Inclusion and Migration/Integration Policy, instead of moving toward a genuine minority policy derived from basic values. Capacities on minority policy were extended precisely because they were contained to single issues where these could be linked to the existing acquis on instrumental grounds. Thus, the inclusion into the Employment Strategy did not explicitly refer to minority rights "as a cultural phenomenon or a question of political participation but as an issue of inclusion in the employment market. Consequently, belonging to an ethnic minority is seen primarily as a 'particular risk factor' which enhances exclusion" (Toggenburg 2006: 15). This is as instrumental and exclusionary toward any shift to a fundamental rights value-based rationale as it can get. The same holds for the reasoning behind social inclusion and migrant policies, which are constructed as necessary responses to the challenges entailed by economic integration and not as genuine rights of individuals.

The underlying instrumental nature of EU policies renders also plausible that the increased attention on minorities and "the process of 'internalization' of the minority topic after enlargement went hand in hand with shifting the policy focus from old towards new minorities" (Toggenburg 2006: 19), the latter of whom base their definition as minorities on genuine rights to defend their "being different," which can hardly be defended on other than value-rational grounds. Moreover, it falls directly in line with the proposed theoretical explanation that these concerns are tackled with soft steering tools for which "new forms of governance apply such as employment policies, social policy and migration policy are characterized by the desire to include potentially segregated, disadvantaged, poor and discriminated groups into society" (Toggenburg 2006: 19). The way in which regulatory elements of minority protection were integrated was outspokenly reduced to an instrumental framing and attributed soft implementation instruments. In parallel, new hard coercive means were created in the field of individual antidiscrimination, which, however, continues to exclude collective minority rights. As illustrated, the expansion of the antidiscrimination acquis as such was not caused by enlargement, but minority protection as first introduced in the Copenhagen framework could be partially accommodated and reframed in the newly emerging antidiscrimination acquis.

In sum, the analysis gives support to Bruno de Witte's conclusion that "we are witnessing the gradual emergence of an EU minority protection system whose contours are blurred and whose treaty bases are largely implicit rather than explicit. What we see for *minority rights* is a replication, at a later state and at a much lower level, of the gradual emergence of a *human rights* system within the European Union" (De Witte 2004: 122). The evidence provided suggests that it is precisely this direction that the Commission is taking under a generously tolerant Council that allows the stretching of the acquis, in particular in the revised enlargement policy. It would be false to claim that the boost that the antidiscrimination acquis has seen since 1997 was all due to the prospect of enlargement. The inclusion of minorities as a focal point was, however, surely linked to the implementation of enlargement. It allowed transferring certain elements and tools to the EU level from which an increasing web of Community activities and capacities is evolving without the need to establish new formal Treaty competences for the Commission. Thus, new unconditional distributive policies from which all member states may profit have been extended, and strong calls for further EU funding have been raised most recently, without creating new institutional constraints that would impose new rules in an extremely sensitive area.

The trends observed in relation to the Copenhagen framework have been further carried forward since. Besides the elaboration of a more explicit Roma policy (Commission of the European Communities 2010a, b), especially the culmination of a dispute between the French government and the European Commission's Vice-President and Commissioner for Justice, Fundamental Rights and Citizenship, Viviane Reding, indicate that the conclusions drawn from the analysis of eastern enlargement are indeed supported by the later developments. Conflict escalated in September 2010 when the Commissioner threatened France with legal actions over the mass-expulsion of Roma with Romanian and Bulgarian citizenship. The legal grounds for such an action were primarily the improper application of the EU's free movement rules that must not be applied to a specific ethnic minority. Moreover, Reding referred to the Charter of Fundamental Rights. Earlier in August, she had already strongly criticized France and Italy over the states' Roma treatment outside the EU framework.[20] In a communication, the Commission's

Vice-President pointed out clearly that the Commission sees itself in the role of guardian of Roma rights:

> The European Commission is prepared to have a very open, frank and honest dialogue with all Member States on how best to take on—using the Treaties and the EU Charter of Fundamental Rights as the basis—our joint responsibility for the Roma. I call notably on the French authorities to engage in such a dialogue with all EU Member States. . . . National decision makers have an important role to play to ensure both public order and the social integration of all Europeans who choose to live within their territory. Because Europe is not just a common market—it is at the same time a Community of values and fundamental rights. The European Commission will watch over this.
>
> (Commission of the European Communities 2010c)

Further spurred by a nazi comparison drawn by the Commissioner, the junior minister for EU affairs furiously replied that "This is not how you speak to a major power like France, which is the mother of human rights,"[21] followed by an open exchange of blows between French president Nicolas Sarkozy and Commission President José Manuel Barroso[22] in which the latter gave Reding full backing emphasizing the Commission's role as guardian of the treaties. Although in the end France took measures that were considered sufficient by the Commissioner to refrain from taking France before the ECJ, the incidence showed unmistakably that power on the issue had shifted to the Commission which, if politically willing to do so, could take action and left no room even for big member states to escape from Brussel's reprehension. It also showed the surprise, if not shock by France that had not expected the Commission to intervene and unsuccessfully neglected a EU responsibility in its attempt to escape from unintended consequences.

Relating back to the theoretical model, because of the double standards the minority criterion created, moral pressure to create a solid legal basis was inherent in the policy from the start. Functional pressure rose as the implementation went on and because pre-accession monitoring was judged a substantial value add—while the leverage of the instrument weakened in the persistent absence of a substantial acquis. Moreover, the notion that minority issues would be "internalized" to the Union once the candidates joined reinforced functional pressure and led to a widening of the problem definition beyond the scope of the central and eastern European states. Hence, the extension of Commission action capacity that followed was no unintended consequence of implementing enlargement but intentionally tolerated or even unofficially promoted by the member states. In contrast, member state governments successfully prevented the wider definition of collective minority rights of the Copenhagen framework to spill in. Although the Race Equality Directive grants the Commission new hard policy instruments, these do not sufficiently disconfirm the theoretical expectation that spill-in from the Copenhagen framework will not lead to hard regulation. The directive expressly includes both direct and indirect discrimination within the scope of prohibited action, but it is limited to individual rights. In addition, those policy tools targeted at genuine minority rights that include collective rights and claims of "old" minorities remain limited to soft regulation of two kinds: benchmarking, both through the Vienna Agency and pragmatic standards to be developed in expert groups, and the acceptance of a wide self-interpretation of the Commission's responsibilities in monitoring the member states. Although the Commission is acting in a legal grey area, the member states accepted this blurring of EU competences in order to grant some minimum credibility and to justify a stronger take in the accession process with Turkey, Croatia, and other foremost Balkan candidate states. Only the enforcement of the Lisbon Treaty in 2009 underpinned this second generation of conditionality legally by rendering the Charta of Fundamental Rights and Freedoms legally binding. Finally, genuine distributive policies have been extended to all member states. Recalling the widened problem perception, which seems to be ever more shifting to calls in favor of treating the matter as a "common problem," the assistance offered by the EU has no implicit redistributive features and is not bound to additional conditions increasing Community control.

CHAPTER 6

CROSS-BORDER COOPERATION: EXECUTING INTERGOVERNMENTAL COMPETENCES

Cross-border cooperation is a distributive policy that provides funds to the Union's border regions. It was founded as a distributive policy before and independently from enlargement policy and was subsequently integrated in the Copenhagen framework. In the enlargement context, the functional demands on cross-border cooperation differed, however, from the previous purpose of abolishing EU internal borders. This entailed a substantial redefinition of objectives and extended the Commission's action capacity into the realm of foreign policy. Although cross-border cooperation remains under the administrative responsibility of the Directorate General Regional Policy, the following analysis will not so much concentrate on the extension of EU regional policies. To capture the essential features of new Commission capacities in the sphere of foreign policy, the emphasis is on the European Neighborhood Policy (ENP). ENP is a crucial innovation in the EU's foreign policy repertoire, which draws heavily on the enlargement experience. Within ENP, cross-border cooperation served from the start as a consolidated instrument that granted substantive foreign policy action capacity to the Commission.

By nature of the political problems dealt with, cross-border cooperation is distributive because it offers direct assistance to border regions. Since it touches on crucial matters of state sovereignty, regulatory aspects are unequivocally excluded from local cross-border initiatives. Regulative objectives may, however, be nested in the distributive arena depending on the goals financial and technical assistance focus on.

> Cross-border cooperation has evolved within the EU legal framework as a distributive policy for which all member states are eligible; spill-in from the Copenhagen context should hence also be framed in distributive terms, and we should expect an extension of Commission responsibilities.

When first initiated at the European level in 1990, cross-border cooperation was aimed at overcoming internal borders among members of the Common Market by promoting cooperation in all spheres of life between regional and local authorities in border regions. Soon after, in 1994, the ends to which cross-border cooperation had been created were broadened. Beyond a tool to ease the effects of creating a common economic space among members of the European Community, cooperation across borders was promoted among candidate states. Cross-border cooperation was integrated into the pre-accession strategy for enlargement aligning future member states among each other and with the EU member states. Drawing on the experiences of these first two rounds of EU internal and pre-accession cross-border cooperation, and in particularly from experience with the candidate states, the policy instrument was further extended beyond future member states to third states without an EU membership perspective. While cross-border projects with future member states remained an instrument for integrating and (even if not immediately) lowering borders, applying the tool to states that would remain outside the EU signified a substantive shift in the ends cross-border cooperation served for, namely, stabilizing the Union's external frontiers.

Drawing on cross-border cooperation to pursue straightforward foreign policy goals, as first done under Tacis CBC and MEDA and refined in the *European Neighborhood and Partnership Instrument* (applicable since 2007), entrusts the Commission with broader foreign policy responsibilities under the cross-border heading. ENP is a new element in the Union's foreign policy, which is made up of a variety of sectoral instruments that amount to a fragmented policy whose coherence and consistency have been recognized as particularly challenging (Duke 1999). To counter the drawbacks of this fragmented foreign policy responsibilities in the EU, ENP was created explicitly to bridge the three pillars of the Union and to amalgamate the various foreign policy elements into one single instrument (Cremona and Hillion 2006). Both its objectives and methodology draw strongly from pre-accession policy (Kelley 2006). In particular the management by means of the accession partnerships within the Copenhagen framework is replicated in the ENP Action Plans for each partner state. This reproduces the Commission's "pivotal role in implementing the *Union* enlargement policy" in which it promoted the application of the EU's acqui*s* "well beyond its traditional role as 'guardian of the [EC] Treaty' vis-à-vis the current Member States" (Cremona and Hillion 2006: 10).

The Neighborhood Initiative stresses "the dual nature of the instrument (external policy and economic and social cohesion) when it comes to financing cross-border and transregional cooperation between partner countries and Member States" (Commission of the European Communities 2004b: Title I, Art. 4). Although formally focusing on cohesion in border regions, the underlying goals of cross-border cooperation with third states include core issues of foreign policy—such as security and migration. The objectives that cross-border cooperation is to serve in this new context have substantially upgraded the Commission's scope to reproduce the soft capacities first exercised during the pre-accession phase. Without an official transfer of new competences, the outspoken objective of the Neighborhood Instrument to bridge the pillar division widens the issues embraced, including not least the promotion of EU security interests (Aliboni 2005; Cremona 2004). As the implementing and coordinating agent, the Commission has considerable discretion in particular regarding cross-border initiatives. Cross-border cooperation in the ENP therefore extended the organization's action capacity to some vital aspects of foreign policy making.

STATUS QUO ANTE: CROSS-BORDER COOPERATION AS INTERNAL TOOL

Cross-border cooperation was first initiated outside the EU framework and diffused across various groups of states. Interstate initiatives were set up in the mid-1960s without any direct involvement or funding by the European Community. As from the early 1990s onward these initiatives continued parallel to, and increasingly interlinked with, the emerging Community program *Interreg*. Supplementing Structural Fund operations, cross-border cooperation initially focused on areas entitled to special structural funding. Fourteen pilot projects were funded under Article 10 of the European Regional Development Fund (EDRF) in 1989 (Council of the European Union 1988). The pilot initiatives of 1989 were followed by a first programming period of only three years (1990–1993) and subsequent six-year programming periods (1994–1999, 2000–2006, and 2007–2013). Covered by strand A of Interreg, cross-border cooperation is distinct from transnational and interregional cooperation (covered by the strands B and C). Under Interreg IIA, cross-border cooperation was extended to all border regions along inner and external EU borders, independent of their relative degree of development. Accordingly all zones along the Community's internal and external land borders as well as certain maritime areas and areas bordering these became eligible under strand A. In addition, strand B was to cover the whole of the EU and the neighboring regions for transnational cooperation (including Western Mediterranean, Alpine Space, Southwest Europe, Northwest Europe, North Sea Region, Baltic Sea Region, Northern Periphery, CADSES (Central, Adriatic, Danubian, and Southeast Europe), "Archimed," Atlantic Area and Outermost Regions, whereas the whole Community became eligible for strand C funding (interregional cooperation).

Cross-border cooperation has been subject to repeated evaluation and revision processes. After each programming period the initiative was reframed on the basis of various evaluation schemes (see Commission of the European Communities 2004e, in particular Title VI). Beyond this, the Commission issued comprehensive reports compiling different monitoring data (Commission of the European Communities 2002b). Other than the safeguards for policy evaluation and reformulation built into the institutional design of Interreg, *Interact* was set up in 2002, which "is designed to capitalise on the vast pool of experience accumulated through INTERREG in the areas of regional development, cross border cooperation, trans-national cooperation and interregional cooperation" (INTERACT Managing Transition 2005: 2; for a full description see INTERACT Programme Secretariat 2002). Furthermore, external organizations, such as the Council of Europe and the *Arbeitsgemeinschaft Europäischer Grenzregionen* (AEGR) issue reports in the field. AEGR, a nongovernmental association of border regions, also evaluates and brings forward policy proposals focusing explicitly on Interreg (see, e.g., Arbeitskreis Europäischer Grenzregionen [AGEG] 1997, 1999). Thus, cross-border cooperation has been developed in a framework with various inbuilt mechanisms for evaluation and revision that fed experiences back into each new programming period. These mechanisms have supported the development and expansion of the policy by integrating new experiences collected in the cooperation along the borders with the candidate states, however, without causing major revisions in the policy design.

Cross-border cooperation among European states first started along the Dutch-German frontier as early as 1965, best known under the acronym EUREGIO (or Euroregion).[1] These "first cross-border initiatives were internal arrangements between contiguous regions of the founding members of the Union, most notably the Dutch and the Germans" (Kennard 2002: 188). Already in the 1960s further initiatives along Franco-German borders and the Franco-Swiss-German borders, as well as among the Benelux countries, followed. These initiatives established former collaboration between municipalities giving cooperation a formalized framework with a council, presidency, secretariat, and specialized working groups on relevant contents (Perkmann 1999: 658). The early EUREGIO initiatives were followed by initiatives of the Nordic states as from the first half of the 1960s and further to southern states as from the late 1970s. More than 70 networks were established by a multilateral approach at local level until 1999, that is, before the elaboration and promotion of EU objectives through Interreg or other Community initiatives.

A number of steps institutionalizing these early, little centralized initiatives followed suit. Encouraged by the Council of Europe, border regions started common initiatives in the end of the 1960s. This cooperation was bundled in the Association of European Border Regions (AEBR) in 1971.[2] Also the Council of Europe has been an important international actor promoting cross-border initiatives across Europe, yet with a slightly different focus than the one pursued by the EU. While the Council of Europe was relevant mainly for creating legal foundations to accommodate local cooperation across borders—that touched in principle on areas of central state authority—the European Union's involvement took mainly the form of financial assistance. Over the years, cross-border cooperation makes a substantial share of Community spending, which was scattered over different Community projects.[3]

The formalization of EU assistance in a single-standing instrument was first realized in form of the Interreg Community Initiative, introduced in 1990. Although part of Structural Funds, the Community Initiative enjoys more managerial autonomy than other regional policies (Perkmann 1999: 659). As regards the underlying objectives behind the increased spending, "[t]he Interreg Community Initiative, which was adopted in 1990, was intended to prepare border areas for a Community without internal frontiers" (INTERREG II 1994–1999).

Legally, cross-border actions potentially challenge existing divisions of competences between regions and central governments regarding the interaction beyond national borders. Initially, there was no formal legal basis for cross-border cooperation in public law and "[t]he first CBC initiatives were based on agreements with varying degrees of formality and mostly relied on good will" (Perkmann 1999: 658). Correspondingly, the *European Outline Convention on Transfrontier Cooperation between Territorial Authorities*, the so-called *Madrid Convention* (May 21, 1980), marked an important step for institutionalizing and creating opportunities for increased cross-border cooperation. Initiated by the Council of Europe, the Convention provided the first steps to place cross-border cooperation under public law (Perkmann 1999: 659). Before 1987, 13 European states signed the Convention. Although the approach of the convention, namely, to advance local-level initiatives dealing with local-level issues, was copied by the first Interreg initiatives, the Madrid convention was not organizationally linked to Community initiatives. This is reflected in the fact that a number of EU member states and current candidate states—for example, Greece, Serbia, and the United Kingdom—are not signatories of the Convention, even if they are beneficiaries of prominent cross-border programs such as the PEACE program between the United Kingdom and Ireland.[4]

Given the fact that the implementation of cross-border cooperation is strongly dependent on the local level but touches on some of the core responsibilities of central governments, the operational level deserves some attention. To balance interests and competences across the various levels of EU governance, an interlinked system of cooperation has been created. Formally, *Operational Programmes* are drafted between the respective central member state governments and the Commission. "This means that European funds are granted to Member States and not directly to Euroregions or similar cross-border bodies themselves" (Perkmann 1999: 659). Nonetheless, for the implementation of cross-border programs, the Commission relies on partners on the local or district level, such as support by AEBR on a trans-European level (Perkmann 1999: 664). The operational features of cross-border cooperation underline the disaggregated way in which benefits are dispersed and hence the strong distributive traits of the policy. Moreover, it reflects how formal authority remains with the member state governments despite the actual implementation privilege of local authorities and civil society.

Noteworthy about the early steps in institutionalizing cross-border cooperation within the Council of Europe and the EU was the careful design of rules to prevent conflicts between cross-border cooperation and competences of the central state authorities. Consequently, initiatives concentrated merely on very specific objectives of local cross-border collaboration. This could, however, not fully resolve the problem that "[f]or local and regional authorities, co-operating across borders means they enter a field long reserved for central state actors" (Perkmann 1999: 658). The objectives of the Euroregions, for example, remained limited to local cooperation in order to promote sociocultural and socioeconomic development, advice in day-to-day border issues, support of intermunicipal cooperation, and participation in interregional cooperation.

For cross-border initiatives by the EU, the "overall aim of the Interreg initiatives has been, and remains, that national borders should not be a barrier to the balanced development and integration of the

European territory" (Commission of the European Communities 2004e: Article 3).[5] This purpose and the very concept of cross-border cooperation have been widened and redefined—if not upturned—as part of enlargement policy and beyond the pre-accession framework. In the same vein, pursuing actual security goals the European Neighborhood Policy is basically reversing the approach: the aim is no longer to smooth the barriers in border regions in order to dissolve them, but to stabilize external borders. As the next section will illustrate, although cross-border cooperation was not all new, its use in the Copenhagen framework promoted a substantial redefinition of the initially purely internal policy tool.

Summarizing the development of cross-border cooperation independent from enlargement, we see that the European Community started to take up an instrument that had developed outside its system in order to compensate underprivileged regions at the dawn of the Common Market. The philosophy pursued in the first Interreg initiatives enhanced the goal of upgrading peripheral regions and worked toward the abolition of internal borders within the Community. Early redistributive elements of cross-border cooperation disappeared as subsequently all EU border regions became eligible and cross-border cooperation took the clear traits of a distributive policy.

PRE-ACCESSION PHASE: EXPERIMENTAL DEVELOPMENT OF A POLICY TOOL

The inclusion of the instrument into enlargement policy was crucial for the development of cross-border cooperation in general. Cross-border initiatives within the external assistance programs Phare and Tacis overlapped organizationally with the Community programs, and measures were financed out of both sources. Interreg IIA (1994–1999) and IIIA (2000–2006) and Interreg IVA (2007–2013) were adjusted stepwise to foster cooperation with EU-external states. Phare CBC was added on to Interreg IIA in 1994, and Tacis CBC followed in 1999. Up to this point, the institutional foundations of Interreg A had not undergone much change. Assembling pre-accession and other assistance programs under one single umbrella allowed to go beyond the established policy objectives and to introduce also programs that served wider underlying aims. Although the formal rules stated in Phare CBC and Tacis CBC remained in line with those of Interreg A, the fact that they were aiming at EU external states implied a qualitative shift in the instrument's basic principles because cross-border initiatives became part of broader strategies toward third countries. This change went beyond cross-border cooperation with the already strongly associated states of the European

Free Trade Association (EFTA). In particular relating to the candidate states that were to join the EU, cross-border cooperation was applied as a pre-accession instrument and therefore as a means to prepare the integration of external regions into the EU and among themselves as regions.

Somewhat different to this, cross-border cooperation with states without an accession option was introduced as part of the EU assistance to the former Soviet Republics within the Tacis program. Although the narrower formal rules and goals continued to focus on social, cultural, and economic cohesion in border regions, the implicit principles shifted. Instead of overcoming and lowering borders, cross-border cooperation along the (future) external borders between the candidate states and their neighbors emerged as a tool to achieve precisely the opposite, namely, the stabilization of the Union's frontiers along the future fringes. The decisive strategic move by the Commission was to apply and adapt an existing instrument to the end that it would also deal with these new challenges. Accordingly, Tacis CBC was launched as well as CBC with the southern adjacent states as part of the MEDA initiative. The experiences collected with the candidate states in Phare CBC was crucial for these initiatives aimed at third states without accession perspective.

The way cross-border cooperation was extended to external states— with or without accession option—was inclusive to the development of the policy within Interreg. Thus, functional pressure did not arise in terms of institutional rules and whether the policy was located within or outside the acquis. Functional pressure regarded the redefinition of policy objectives. Once the goal definition was widened beyond "overcoming internal borders" and was successfully implemented along the borders with and among the candidate states, functional pressure rose to use the successful instrument also along external borders. Although giving the Commission capacities in an area that is formally under intergovernmental member state control, the expansion of Commission responsibilities into the foreign policy realm was no unintended consequence. Quite to the contrary, making use of policy tools that had been developed inside the Community and refined in the pre-accession context, the European Neighborhood Policy provided a way to delve into sensitive high politics while keeping these on the operational level and thus circumventing direct state-level confrontation.

STATUS QUO POST: CROSS-BORDER COOPERATION AS INSTRUMENT FOR EXTERNAL COERCION

The extension of action capacity in cross-border cooperation does not concern the very existence of the policy as much as it concerns the actual capabilities it comprises. Founded as a purely internal policy it was intended to cushion the effects of the internal market along the borders between member states. In the context of enlargement the tool was applied first along the external borders with future member states and subsequently further expanded to external borders with states without a membership prospect. Drawing directly from these experiences, cross-border cooperation was included in the ENP, which meant a substantive extension of the definitions and goals pursued. Thus, the Commission is executing programs that are implicitly concerned with foreign affairs. The development of the tool itself has hence created Commission activities far beyond the internal realm and its competences in economic external relations. The ENP builds on Community resources and tools, although the actual policy contents fall into intergovernmental foreign policy. It is therefore an example of the extensive use of adjective Community resources in order to pursue policy objectives on the EU level although authority remains formally on the member state level.

The first step toward the Neighborhood Policy was the Commission's so-called *Wider Europe* Communication (Commission of the European Communities 2003a). Cross-border cooperation was identified as a key tool recognized in the Commission's strategic planning. The Commission took the Wider Europe initiative as reference point for the following motives. "One of the elements of the Wider Europe Communication was the specific possibility of creating a new Neighborhood Instrument, which builds on the experience of promoting cross-border co-operation within the PHARE, Tacis and INTERREG programmes" and which could focus "on ensuring the smooth functioning and secure management of the future Eastern and Mediterranean borders, promoting sustainable economic and social development of the border regions and pursuing regional and transnational co-operation" (Commission of the European Communities 2003c: 3). Moreover, the new Instrument was to "help to avoid drawing new dividing lines in Europe and to promote stability and prosperity within and beyond the new borders of the Union," and hence the Communications emphasized "that cross-border cultural links gain additional importance in the context of proximity" (Commission of the European Communities 2003c: 3), drawing explicitly from the experience that cross-border cooperation had brought forth while implementing enlargement and trying to institutionalize the policy tool beyond this realm.

The Commission's Communication was followed up by a *Strategy Paper* on the establishment of ENP, published in 2004 (Commission of the European Communities 2004d). The Initiative's core aim is to create a more coherent approach across the various policies that the EU had developed with a view to benefiting its neighboring states. Cross-border cooperation was included into ENP as a tool to promote the reformulated objectives of the EU's approach. With respect to the organization of cross-border cooperation, ENP assembled all previously existing programs within a more comprehensive framework. Besides profiting from earlier experiences, the new institution allowed also for more fundamental adaptations in terms of policy goals. According to the objectives defined in *Wider Europe,* cross-border cooperation within the ENP is "to work with the partners to reduce poverty and create an area of shared prosperity and values based on deeper economic integration, intensified political and cultural relations, enhanced cross-border cooperation and shared responsibility for conflict prevention between the EU and its neighbours" (Commission of the European Communities 2003a: 9). The *European Neighborhood and Partnership Instrument* (ENPI), proposed in 2004, operationalizes these goals for the programming period 2007–2013. The issues listed in the ENPI that carry foreign policy functions can be subdivided into thee categories that enter into foreign policy and hence depart from the context cross-border cooperation was originally designed for (the following states the items according to the paragraph numbering in: Commission of the European Communities 2004b). In short, the crucial items comprise, first, issues that were part of the accession criteria but not the overall acquis and, second, particular security concerns regarding external states that were newly introduced. Noticeably, the matter of migration and border control was integrated into the objectives, which was not the official part—though arguably informal motivation—for Phare and Tacis CBC. Third, ENPI embraces items accommodating a broader alignment of external states to EU activities as such. In more detail, first, conditionality tools that have been directly imported from enlargement policy are stated in paragraphs: (a) promoting political dialogue and reform; (c) strengthening national institutions and bodies responsible for the elaboration and the effective implementation of policies in areas covered in association agreements, partnership and cooperation agreement, and other future comparable agreements; (i) promoting and protecting human rights and fundamental freedoms and supporting the democratization process, including through electoral observation and assistance; (j) fostering the development of civil society; and (k) promoting the development of a market economy, including measures to support the private sector, encourage investment, and promote global trade. The second group of tools more directly external tackle security concerns and are designed at (n) ensuring efficient and secure border management; (o) promoting cooperation in the field of justice and home affairs, including on issues such as asylum and migration and the fight against and prevention of terrorism tax fraud; (p) supporting administrative cooperation to improve transparency and the exchange of information in the area of taxation in order to combat tax avoidance and evasion; (w) providing support in postcrisis situations, including support to refugees and displaced persons, and assisting in conflict prevention and disaster preparedness. Third, the tools to align external states point to (q) promoting participation in Community research and innovation activities; (t) supporting participation of partner countries in Community programs and agencies; (x) encouraging communication and promoting exchange among the partners on the measures and activities financed under the programs; (y) addressing common thematic challenges in fields of mutual concern and any other objectives consistent with the scope of the very regulation. These wide-spanning set of objectives was complemented by policy tools developed during the pre-accession phase (Commission of the European Communities 2004b: 15–16).

Turning to the operational programs and project management, the Neighborhood Programs were considered a great step forward since they introduced the idea of launching joint calls for proposals, combining different sources of funding. Moreover, joint management structures are encouraged also for dealing with third countries. Thus, the role of central governments is effectively further reduced in favor of joined local management structures.

Moreover, during the pre-accession phase, funding was based on matching Interreg money with the various funds external states were eligible for, which created many difficulties and was considered "a less than ideal situation," especially in procedural terms. To this end, Phare CBC had been created as a first step toward genuine cross-border cooperation between member states and candidate states. A Phare CBC regulation issued in 1998 already introduced joint management structures and joint programming documents, involving regional and local authorities. With the accession of ten new member states on May 1, 2004, this became a priority all along EU external borders. Drawing from the Phare CBC experience, the 2003 Neighborhood Communication addressed these problems comprehensively and reinforced the approach in the ENPI as from 2007, which also harmonized asymmetries in the funding periods that existed before 2004 between the mirroring funds external cross-border cooperation drew from.

With respect to the formal rules and the actual policy contents promoted by cross-border cooperation, the former were basically kept unchanged. However, nesting assistance programs into the cross-borer initiative moved the goals beyond overcoming internal EU borders toward the objective of establishing more stable relations along the Union's new external borders. Phare and Tacis CBC were especially geared to fulfill these aims, remaining formally restricted to the local level and programming objectives established before. The scope of the policy contents widened effectively with the introduction of ENPI.

Besides these shifts in the underpinning goals and purpose the cross-border instrument, *Wider Europe* underlined the objective of further diffusing the incrementally extended cross-border cooperation. "The Northern Dimension currently provides the only regional framework in which the EU participates with its Eastern partners to address transnational and cross-border issues. But participation is restricted to Russia" (Commission of the European Communities 2003a: 8). Thus, although Tacis CBC and MEDA offered the opportunity for cross-border cooperation with third states, in real fact initiatives existed only with two states.[6] The experiences gathered in implementing enlargement proved decisive for the subsequent active promotion of further diffusion of cross-border programs. Accordingly the 2003 strategy emphasizes that

> the Commission will consider the possibility of creating a new Neighborhood Instrument which builds on the positive experiences of promoting cross-border cooperation within the Phare, Tacis and INTERREG programs. This instrument will focus on trans-border issues, promoting regional and sub-regional cooperation and sustainable development on the Eastern border. For the Mediterranean, consideration should be given to whether such a unified proximity instrument could also apply to shorter sea crossings (between the enlarged EU and a number of Barcelona partner countries).
>
> (Commission of the European Communities 2003a: 14)

Indeed, cross-border cooperation extended to cover not only all EU internal borders but also cooperation among Belarus, Moldavia, Morocco, Russia, Ukraine, Serbia and Montenegro, Switzerland, Turkey, and the former Yugoslav Republic of Macedonia (INTERREG IIIA 2000–2006).

First experiences with the implementation of the Neighborhood Policy highlight the strong influence that the lessons learned in the enlargement context had. The transfer of experiences was in many respects very direct, not least since a great number of staff moved from the downscaled DG Enlargement to ENP. Yet, the limits of applying the same tools one-to-one in ENP became soon apparent. The direct transfer of elements from enlargement policy concentrates on actual policy tools because the "ultimate carrot of accession" was not available in the ENP, which made it impossible to apply a strong conditionality logic. A further difference concerns the targeted states for which policies have to be much more strongly differentiated than under the logic of enlargement, which was based on the principle of equal treatment of all candidates. While still relying heavily on concrete tools developed in the Copenhagen framework, the Neighborhood Instrument has incrementally developed a more differentiated approach. The target states vehemently demanded more differentiation between states—in contrast to the member states' strong preference for a single global approach. In the actual policy implementation it was therefore recognized that "in the beginning one of the mistakes—if I dare to say—is that we have too much tried to apply the enlargement logic because it does not really work in the ENP—you can use certain elements but not the logic because the logic is completely different" (Interview 2007 COM DG External Relations).

Despite the need for a more differentiated approach to implementation than during enlargement, it is precisely the framing of the Neighborhood Instrument in terms of a new universal approach that has opened a window for the Commission to extend its policy means to implement the wider goals. Thus, "by putting our relationships with the different countries in a sort of global framework, we have been able to mobilize certain things which we would not have been able to mobilize without such a framework," among these the direct continuation of twinning/TAIEX activities; in the words of a Commission official:

> we have been able to send the same type of missions to Ukraine—I think for the moment only Ukraine but others will follow—that we sent to the accession countries, the same kind: with experts in all the fields, on how the judiciary works, on public prosecutor, how the border should be managed—this would have been inconceivable before but since we have developed this expertise and we had these people available and in the neighborhood framework we could say "you have finished in the acceding countries, now you should go to Ukraine." And they did, and this was very beneficial.
>
> (Interview 2007 COM DG External Relations)

Noteworthy about the ENP as "policy in the making" (Delcour 2007: 130) is the rather eclectic way in which the more abstract objectives are put into action. The experience from activities in the Copenhagen framework—established in a comparably incremental manner—appears to be particularly relevant for the traveling of ideas. Generally, proposals and implementation of concrete actions and single projects are often based on previous experiences in other contexts. One example is a project at the border between Ukraine and Moldova, in the Commission's view

> an extremely successful border assistance mission where we have around 100 seconded customs officials and border guards from our member states,

and we took the idea actually from something very small that we did in
Albania and we completely adapted it to the local conditions, and I think
it is one of the most successful things that we have ever done because it
meets several concerns: it does capacity building, it brings new concepts
to the customs borer guards in Ukraine and Moldova, for instance the
question of risk analysis. . . . so we have been able to apply something . . . we
have done capacity building, we have learnt new concepts.

(Interview 2007 COM DG External Relations)

Where this creeping extension of Commission activities meets the resistance of the member states, the actual successful implementation of pilot
projects appears to be a strategy of the Commission to widen its scope
for action. This is clearly expressed by the view that "we will have to convince member states that what we propose can be beneficial"; even more
explicitly the same official comments on how the Commission managed
to overcome the member states' reluctance:

and now it works and they love it, there have been articles in the Wall Street
Journal, in the Times, and people come to look what we are doing there
from very far, we had a good idea, we were convinced of it but it took a
long time to convince them—but now we know and member states want
to do the same thing, while in the beginning we had to plead with them
like crazy to convince them; so our role, I think, is to be inventive and
to understand which tools we can usefully use and which tools we should
just forget about because they do not work in that context to try to be
creative and not to spent too much time in going for a sort of "battle on
competences" but just to *prove* that it works. . . . It's all about soft capacities,
and using them in a convincing manner because that makes a difference.

(Interview 2007 COM DG External Relations)

The distributive nature of cross-border cooperation allowed the reframing of the underlying objectives without the formal conferral of new
competences. Interestingly, the Lisbon Reform Treaty places the ENP's
objectives—to account for the "special relationship with neighbouring
countries, aiming to establish an area of prosperity and good neighbourli-
ness" (Article 8, TEU)—among the "Common Provisions" and not in the
chapters on foreign policy. This stresses the symbolic relevance attributed
to the policy. At the same time it further blurs the division of formal
authority over foreign policy matters between the supranational and intergovernmental modes of governance. The case of cross-border cooperation
illustrates how the supranational level is effectively steering in substantial foreign policy matters, extending the Commission's action capacity
in substance but containing it to the distributive arena. Accordingly,

initial redistributive notions of the very first cross-border actions disappeared with making all EU border eligible, which allowed subsequently the extension of distributive measures to external states promoting new policy objectives.

SUMMARY: CROSS-BORDER COOPERATION AND THE NEW NEIGHBORHOOD INSTRUMENT

The development of cross-border cooperation from rather loosely coordinated bilateral initiatives to a structured EU policy is summarized in Figure 6.1. The upper boxes relate to the degree of diffusion of cross-border initiatives across states. These are linked to the different stages of organizational institutionalization that are indicated in the boxes at the bottom.

The division into phases conforms basically to programming periods of the Community Initiatives. The initial phase is from the 1950s till the end of Interreg I in 1993. It marks the period in which the core objectives for cross-border cooperation as EC internal policy tool were developed with only a limited degree of institutionalization. Although external borders with EFTA states were part of the Community policy already under Interreg I, these initiatives were still in accordance with the original format and content of cross-border cooperation to reduce border barriers. A substantive change occurred when cross-border headings were integrated into pre-accession assistance under Phare and assistance programs for the former Soviet Republics, Tacis, in addition to the elements of the Barcelona process that are the framework for the EU's relations with its Mediterranean neighbor states, MEDA. The redefinition

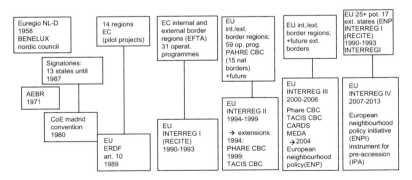

Figure 6.1   Evolution CBC in Europe
Source: own figure.

of cross-border cooperation as a distributive tool in foreign policy developed in connection with the integration of cross-border initiatives into the Copenhagen framework. The experiences collected during the implementation of enlargement crystallized the potential of the policy instrument with respect to third countries. In essence, we see a threefold shift away from the original design of cross-border cooperation that adapts the policy type (from announced redistributive trade-offs to a distributive framing), the scope of the policy (form a limited application to internal borders to external frontiers), and the underlying policy objectives (from integration and abolition of borders to the stabilization of external borders).

For the dynamics of change, it was highly relevant that cross-border cooperation was linked to enlargement policy in which the Commission had extraordinary discretion to develop the policy instrument. Integrating the variety of different programs for external relations in the European Neighborhood Policy, a further refinement of the policy instrument is reflected in additional programs for external cross-border cooperation for Interreg IV period (2007–2013) that are a direct continuation of the pre-accession policy. Research on the European Neighborhood Policy unanimously underlines that, both in terms of policy design and implementation tools, ENP is the continuation of enlargement policy (see, e.g., Balfour and Rotta 2005; Cremona 2004, 2006; Delcour 2007; Del Sarto and Schumacher 2005; Hillion 2005; Kelley 2006; Magen 2006; Marchetti 2007). This holds particularly true for the cross-border instrument for which in fact "the ENP programmes are to be inspired by the experience of cross-border cooperation between border regions within the EU, as well as between border regions laying along the EU's external border" (Sushko 2006: 44). Although in the absence of pre-accession conditionality the logic of ENP is decisively different from that of the Copenhagen framework, implementing tools were exported to the new post-accession policy. Overall, the most important import from enlargement policy was the inclusion of policy instruments developed in the Copenhagen framework. "This is the good thing about using expertise from enlargement, because we have really developed very, very detailed expertise that we have been able to test in reality and that we have been able to refine" (Interview 2007 COM DG External Relations). It is also by applying these tools that the Commission widens its capacities through actual policy making: "I think in general, in quite a lot of occasions we have been able to use a good idea from enlargement and adapted it, and we have been able to convince member states by doing that" (Interview 2007 COM DG External Relations).

The results therefore confirm the expectations that, if framed as a distributive policy, new capacities will spill in. In the case of cross-border cooperation this was not so much a matter of institutional incorporation, because EU internal and external actions were strongly linked from the outset and developed in parallel. The extension of capacities concerned the political agenda and how extended policy objectives were pursued with policy tools that traveled from enlargement policy to the EU's New Neighborhood Policy. The incorporation of cross-border cooperation into the ENP granted the Commission new steering capacities without establishing additional formal competences in an area that remains officially under intergovernmental control. Through the reframing of the policy objectives and the diffusion of the policy instrument, foreign policy goals were successfully nested within the formally purely distributive policy arena.

CHAPTER 7

NUCLEAR SAFETY: RESISTING UNINTENDED CONSEQUENCES

In the enlargement context, the definition of nuclear safety was substantially extended. This created high pressure for new formal regulation. In the Copenhagen framework some assistance was provided, in particular for the decommissioning of plants, but the main focus was on monitoring because of the regulatory nature of nuclear safety, which aims at controlling nuclear installations. Fostered by unintended consequences, namely, a ruling by the ECJ that confirmed formal Commission competences on the matter, the member states fiercely objected to any extension of Commission capacities. They succeeded against the expressed support by all EU institutions since the Euratom Treaty still operates on purely intergovernmental rules. Finally, a dominant non-state actor organization expressed heavy opposition. In so doing it represented an alternative response to binding EU rules in alliance with some decisive national governments. Given that a vast informal acquis already existed before enlargement, functional pressure pushed the Commission to go beyond the existing cooperation and left little option but to frame the policy in terms of hard regulatory policies, backed by the ECJ ruling confirming Commission competences.

> Nuclear safety was framed as regulatory policy, given the nature of the political problem to control nuclear installations; thus we should expect an extension of capacities as nonbinding rules or informal cooperation, but if nuclear safety was framed as a new binding regulation, member states should take action against spill-in.

In the field of nuclear safety, the Commission has been an independent regulatory authority since the first hours of European integration. As early as 1957, nuclear safety featured in the Euratom Treaty, which assigned the Commission a role in securing the separation of military and civilian uses of nuclear technology and safeguarding the attribution and distribution of radioactive material. Since then, what is commonly subsumed under the term "nuclear safety" has undergone a substantial extension and redefinition. This notwithstanding, the Euratom Treaty has not been adapted to these fundamental changes. Most relevantly, the safety of nuclear installations and waste disposal remain absent from supranational legislation.

In contrast, the Copenhagen framework applied a much wider definition of "western standards" of nuclear safety. During the pre-accession process "[f]or the first time in its history, the European Union started the process of carrying out an evaluation of nuclear safety in an independent State. In fact, in all the candidate countries" (De Esteban 2002: 5). The question, accordingly, is: did this wider definition of nuclear safety, which, for the first time, explicitly included safety of installations and waste disposal in civilian use of nuclear power, extend beyond enlargement policy?

Arguing that a general revision of the Euratom Treaty was overdue with respect to the changed use and challenges of nuclear technology, the Commission raised the explicit claim that the extended capacities exercised in the Copenhagen framework ought to apply to all member states. The respective legal proposals were bundled in the so-called *nuclear package* in 2002/2003. Disputed from the beginning, the package was strongly opposed by a number of member states. Despite pressure by all the supranational institutions, from the European Parliament to the Economic and Social Committee that supported the Commission's proposed path, and regardless of a judgment of the European Court of Justice, which granted that Euratom's safety objective covered also installations and waste management, the member states remained firm. A number of directives effectively passed are restricted to the applicability of safety standards in third states and the accession of the EC to an international agreement; in other words, Community capacities—and with it a more comprehensive definition of nuclear safety—were contained to application outside the EU, and any new instruments that affected the member states were pushed to alternative platforms outside the EU framework.

The bottom line is a strong support of the status quo before implementing enlargement. This means a continuation of safety controls on installations and waste management based on nonbinding international instruments instead of binding EU legislation. More so, the extension of

Commission capacities in tune with a modernized definition of nuclear safety was effectively blocked by the majority of member states, against the unison call in favor by EU institutions. Notably also, survey data on public opinion supported the call for more supranational regulation. However, such public views were hardly reflected in nongovernmental organizations that have traditionally raised their voice against nuclear power as such. Therefore, the promotion of nuclear safety is understood to be a contradiction to the more fundamental goal of abandoning nuclear energy in general. Quite the opposite, the power plant operators have built up a strong network that informally implements most of the proposed legislation to evade and to lobby against further hard EU regulation. In direct reaction to implementing enlargement, the member state governments actively blocked an extension of Commission action capacity against persistent functional pressure. After putting the initative for hard regulation to rest for some years, the Commission again took up its regulatory efforts and proposed a revised directive that took account of a stronger role of national administrators and reduced EU harmonization to general guidelines. This proposal was eventually adopted in 2009. In response to the reasons for which the initial regulatory package had failed, this revised regulation succeeded because it explicitly built on the subsidiarity principle and focused primarily on strengthening national agencies.

STATUS QUO ANTE: SIMPLY EURATOM

Nuclear safety has been on the political agenda since the very beginning of the European integration process. The *Treaty establishing the European Atomic Energy Community* (EAEC or Euratom Treaty) laid down the basis for the Community responsibility in 1957. In contrast to the *Treaty on the European Community* (TEC), together with which it was signed, the TEC expired after 50 years, while Euratom has indefinite validity. Another sharp and more relevant contrast is marked by the many adoptions to the TEC, whereas the Euratom Treaty has hardly been changed since entering into force. Also the Lisbon Treaty preserves the separate legal character of Euratom. Regarding safety issues, the Euratom Treaty has been interpreted from the start to give the Community responsibility in areas such as radiation protection of the work force and the pubic (Chapter III), supply of nuclear fissile materials for the developing nuclear power sector (Chapter VI), prevention of nuclear fissile materials usage for unauthorized military purposes (Chapter VII), and general aspects including research and dissemination of information.[1] However, the emphasis on safety issues "in the 1950s centred on ensuring that the separation of the civilian and military uses of the technologies was maintained [and responded to the need that] civilian uses of nuclear technology for electricity generation required secure access to the basic raw material of uranium" (Barnes 2003: 122). In this vein, the Euratom Supply Agency (ESA) and the Euratom Safeguards Office were established, while questions regarding the safety of nuclear installations remained of exclusive state concern.

Besides these formal Community competences in nuclear safety, a nonbinding acquis has emerged on the basis of a 1975 Council Resolution "on the technological problems of nuclear safety" (Council of the European Communities 1975). Given a substantial increase in numbers of reactors,[2] the member states agreed in the resolution to work toward the harmonization of safety requirements and criteria by closer cooperation between the national governments. Moreover, two expert groups were created to support this process: the Reactor Safety Working Group (RSWG) and the Nuclear Regulators Working Group (NRWG). The Council adopted a second resolution in 1992 in response to new concerns raised by the nuclear accidents in Three Mile Island in the United States (1979) and Chernobyl in the Ukraine (1986) (Council of the European Communities 1992). This resolution aimed at intensifying the harmonization of safety measures within the EU and to increase cooperation with the states of Central and Eastern Europe and the former Soviet Union.[3]

The stability of the Euratom legal framework in contrast to the broad extensions of the Treaty on the European Communities has, at times, demanded clarification on the relationship between the two documents. "Accordingly, Euratom competences have repeatedly given rise to litigation before the European Court of Justice. One set of cases concerned post-Chernobyl legislation on contaminated food, regarding which there is an overlap of EC legislative competences for common commercial policy and the internal market on the one hand and the Euratom competence for radiation protection on the other: there the ECJ decided as to the "correct" legal basis to be used on the basis of the "centre of gravity" of the individual acts. In doing so it accepted that, generally, EC legal bases could apply in the area of Euratom law as long as the relevant Euratom provisions were not conclusive" (Trüe 2006: 251).[4] Moreover, EC law on state aids raises questions regarding the applicability to member states' subsidies in the area of nuclear energy, which the Euratom Treaty explicitly promotes. Although Community law applies in general to nuclear energy and allows the Commission to intervene to prevent distortions of competition in the energy sector, the legal basis of the Euratom Treaty provides that state support on research and insurance contracts is admissible, which limits Community state aid control (Pechstein 2001: 311).

Finally, Euratom is a sectoral and not a framework treaty as the EC Treaty.[5] Unlike the legislative character of the latter, the former is mainly a sectoral limited administrative treaty. Thus, the Commission's legislative responsibilities under Euratom are in comparison very restricted. Furthermore, the legislative proposals are of highly technical nature because of which the drafting is to a great extent done by external experts (Grunwald 2007: 6). The two aspects leave the Commission relatively little scope to extend its competences by means of initiating legislation.

Outside the European Community framework, nuclear safety is regulated by a number of international instruments with which the Commission cooperates closely.[6] The most relevant ones are the United Nations' International Atomic and Energy Agency (IAEA), the OSCD Nuclear Energy Agency (NEA), and the association of 17 European nuclear regulators WENRA (see below, next section).[7] The IAEA has been active in all states with nuclear capacities since 1956, setting international standards and guidelines on nuclear safety and other areas, such as waste management. With respect to nuclear safety and waste management, the IAEA provides two conventions. First, the IAEA's *Convention on Nuclear Safety* was adopted in 1994 and entered into force in 1996. By setting international standards, it commits the participating states operating land-based nuclear power plants to maintain a high level of safety. As an incentive instrument, the Convention does not set legally binding obligations that could be enforced by control and sanctions but builds on a network of peer review reporting and trust in a common interest for nuclear safety. A Commission Decision of April 29, 2004,[8] laid the legal ground for Euratom to access the Convention on Nuclear Safety (see Commission of the European Communities 2004c). Second, the *Joint Convention for the Safety of Spent Fuel Management and the Safety of Radioactive Waste Management* was opened for signature in 1997 and entered into force in 2001. The EU played a decisive role in negotiating and defining the Convention: "we have been responsible for a lot of the work that had gone into safety standards in the IAEA, a lot of the IAEA safety standards and guidelines were based on work done by the EU" (Interview 2007 DG TREN). The obligations of the contracting parties include the establishment and maintenance of a legislative and regulatory framework to govern the safety of spent fuel and radioactive waste management as well as an adequate protection of individuals, society, and the environment against radiological and other hazards. The Commission has, furthermore, enacted resolutions on the transfer of information to support the IAEO's international security instruments (Grunwald 1998:

293). Euratom accessed the Convention in October 2005 (entry into force January 2, 2006).[9]

Within the OSCE, the NEA is an intergovernmental, semi-autonomous body with, currently, 18 members. It was created in 1985 as European Nuclear Energy agency "with 'the same spirit' as the Euratom Treaty (Q 664) although the NEA and Euratom operate completely separately" (House of Lords 2006b: 23). NEA operates as a think-tank trying to develop a common approach to nuclear energy issues on the basis of the exchange of best practices and feedback between its members. The Commission is a nonpaying member of NEA, and the IAEA acts as observer.

The Commission, in cooperation with and addition to other international organizations, has thus been active in certain fields of nuclear safety for decades. To some observers this stability, and in particular the continuous exclusion of safety, of nuclear installations—plants producing nuclear energy and waste disposal—is striking. "It is even surprising that the Euratom Treaty would not have undergone any significant alteration to date. Compared with the continuous process of evolution experienced by the (E)ECT, the Euratom Treaty has remained unchanged over the years, becoming *embedded* in a manner that is inconvenient for those who have unsuccessfully postulated its reform" (Prieto Serrano 2006: 13 emphasis in the original). Different claims for changes are made that range from challenging the underlying objectives of the text to the legitimacy of the decision-making processes it functions on. By the same token, critics of the current EU legal framework bring forward a number of shortcomings of Euratom: the inadequateness of the Treaty to respond to the changed definition of nuclear safety (lack of comprehensiveness and need for legally binding rules), a lack of democracy due to the exclusion of the EP, legal conflicts between the separate Euratom and the TEC, the general pro-nuclear approach of the document, and the negligence of the problem for nuclear waste disposal.

Interestingly enough, "[t]he 1957 European Atomic Energy Community (EAEC) EURATOM Treaty came at the time when there was great optimism about the peaceful use of nuclear technology. At the time negotiations for the [Euratom] Treaty began, the EAEC was regarded as perhaps having a greater integrative potential than the evolving European Economic Community. This was because it was originally perceived as non-threatening to major national interests" (Barnes 2003: 122). Yet, already during the negotiations, differences between France and Germany led to an unfalteringly more modest outcome, leaving the Treaty with relatively limited objectives while the Commission's control functions remained restricted.

Since then, the red threat in the evolution—respectively stability—of the Euratom Treaty is that "[i]t is in relation to the powers of the Commission vis-à-vis the Member States' nuclear activities that the Euratom Treaty has proved to be most contentious" (Scott 1996: 226). Pursuant to a reference for a preliminary ruling of an administrative tribunal in Strasbourg, in 1986 the ECJ gave a "purposive interpretation" backing the Commission under Article 37 Euratom according to which each state has to inform the Commission with data on any plan for disposal of nuclear waste. Similarly, Article 34 Euratom, establishing a member state's obligation to first obtain a Commission opinion before conducting "particularly dangerous experiments" that might affect the territory of another member state, was not respected during French nuclear tests in 1995; however, the Commission did not institute a case before the ECJ (Scott 1996: 226–28). These two examples underline the member states' consistent reluctance to accept too much Commission intervention under the Euratom Treaty, even in cases in which the Commission responsibility has been confirmed by a Court ruling, a pattern that we will see reemerging in an even more straightforward manner in response to the Commission's advances that evolved out of enlargement policy.

In short, when enlargement policy set in 1993, the legal framework of the Euratom Treaty provided the Commission with considerable discretion in producing efficient policy outputs within the limited definition of nuclear safety that neglected nuclear installations. Moreover, some expert groups and agencies, as well as a large body of informal rules on nuclear safety beyond radiation protection, were in place. Notwithstanding increased salience, in particular due to nuclear accidents and substantially more critical public opinion, the interpretation given to the definition of safety in the binding legal framework had not been extended to the safety of nuclear installations and waste disposal. Although indisputably part and parcel of an up-to-date nuclear safety agenda, the Commission remained without formal capacities. As a substitute for Community control, member states cooperated through a wide web of nonbinding acquis or through international agreements outside but with close links to the Community—not least by the fact that these instruments, foremost of the IAEA, have been drawn up in part on the basis of existing nonbinding Community standards. In policy terms, nuclear safety is handled purely as a regulatory policy. Regarding the existing institutional framework, the Euratom Treaty basically excluded the European Parliament from decision making, and the member states decide unanimously. Since its drafting, Euratom has undergone hardly any changes, which can be also attributed to its very loose formulations and extremely high flexibility to accommodate a wide range of different policies. This, in turn, lifts the hurdle for a consensus on changing parts of the Treaty even higher.[10] A major breakthrough that established a common binding legal framework emerged only in the aftermath of the failed nuclear package. The Council eventually passed a directive on June 25, 2009 (Council of the European Union 2009), well after the period examined here. This directive cannot be read as a direct effect of implementing enlargement, but it is relevant for the argument because it establishes hard supranational regulation—and thus apparently disconfirms the expectation formulated above in a more longitudinal perspective. A closer look at the regulation shows that the strong emphasis on the subsidiarity principle, the reference of WENRA, and strong flexibility for national transposition grant the persisting dominance of national regulatory agencies that are partially strengthened. Hence, the proposals for hard regulation that grew directly out of implementing enlargement were dropped. Taking a more long-term perspective we can, therefore, observe that hard regulation was eventually put in place that takes account of the imminent danger of political spillover by strengthening national regulators.

Nuclear safety has a long regulatory history under the Euratom Treaty. However, the safety of nuclear installations and waste disposal were excluded from the safety definition till 2009, and the Commission has accordingly not exercised any responsibilities over nuclear installations. By the nature of the problem, it has to be framed in the regulatory arena. Given the preexisting acquis, this would materialize in an extension of the definition of nuclear safety, which under Euratom rules demands unanimity of all member states.

PRE-ACCESSION PHASE: THE REINFORCEMENT OF FUNCTIONAL PRESSURE

The Commission became involved in matters of nuclear safety in the states of Central and Eastern Europe soon after the Soviet Union's breakup. Following a joint declaration that leveled the ground for bilateral relations between COMECOM states and the European Community in 1988, the European Economic Community and Euratom signed a trade agreement including nuclear material with the USSR in 1989 (see Council of the European Communities 1988 and Commission of the European Communities 1990). With Russia and the other predecessor states of the Soviet Union, a number of bilateral agreements on trading of nuclear materials were concluded (see Grunwald 1998: 302). Beyond this, the G7 meeting in Munich in 1992 entrusted the Commission to support the assurance of higher safety standards for Soviet-design reactors. Therefore, from the very beginning "[t]he Commission was put into a very unique position in the development of a strategy for nuclear safety in the States which at the beginning of the nineties were not Member States of the EU. Indeed at the time the work began they were not even candidate States for future membership" (Barnes 2003: 123–24).

Bilateral links with the central European states were further strengthened by the association agreements, concluded from 1991 onward. The Europe Agreements remained the formal legal basis on which the Commission developed its pre-accession policy in the area after 1993. The overall aim was to ensure safety standards comparable to those in the member states. A clear emphasis on nuclear safety in the enlargement process is traceable from the Commission's Agenda 2000 (Commission of the European Communities 1997a). The opinions on the potential candidate states included analyses of nuclear safety authorities. Monitoring continued in the Regular Reports as part of the requirements for accession, and the Commission reported additionally on the matter to the European Council of Cologne in 1999. The "twin approach" the Commission took was to, on the one hand, resolve the most urgent problems as the safe operating of nuclear installations and the establishment of competent safety operations. On the other hand, mid- and long-term incentives envisaged the closure of unsafe installations and the modernization of the most up-to-date plants, as well as the development of alternative energy sources to reduce the dependency on nuclear energy. A further refinement of the standards and benchmarks that the candidate states had to comply with was achieved through the assistance funds of the Phare and Tacis programs.

For the establishment of policy tools in the Copenhagen framework, it was essential that the Commission had to pin down a precise definition of "safety of installations," which subsequently led to the major disruption between the Commission and the member states' understanding of the wider responsibilities of the Community. As the Commission itself underlined, "[s]ince there are no prescriptive criteria in EU law governing the design or operation of nuclear facilities, the safety of the operating plants in the applicant countries has to be judged in relation to more subjective criteria, termed 'western standards' " (Commission of the European Communities 2007b). To gain the necessary legal basis the DG Environment, at the time responsible, claimed the need to accede to the IAEA convention to justify monitoring in the candidate states.

In response, the member states decided to withdraw the mandate from the Commission and moved the monitoring responsibility to the Council Services, which was partially even welcomed by the Commission, which

lacked the technical skills for inspections that could much better be provided by national regulator agencies (Interview 2007 DG TREN; on the
shortcomings of the Commission's human resources, see also Court of
Auditors 1999: 14). The formal ground for pre-accession assessment was
the Helsinki European Council of 1999, which had called on the Council
"to consider how to address the issue of nuclear safety in the framework
of the enlargement process in accordance with the relevant Council conclusions" (European Council 1999: I-7). In this the European Council
recalled "the importance of high standards of nuclear safety in Central and
Eastern Europe" as first expressed by the G7 in 1992 and subsequently
put into more concrete terms relating to the candidate states by the
Commission's Agenda 2000 (Commission of the European Communities 1997a). It followed an assessment by the Council's Atomic Questions
Group (AQG), which also set up an ad hoc Working Party on Nuclear
Safety (WPNS) in 2000/2001 that issued the "Report on the Evaluation
of Nuclear Safety in the Context of Enlargement,"[11] together with an
"Addendum" (Council of the European Union 2001) referring to inputs
by different sources.

Ascribing it an assisting role, the Commission was asked by the AQG's
presidency to draw up an inventory of the Community's nonbinding
acquis on nuclear installation safety, as well as the commitments the
candidate states had already taken on. The mandate was explicitly to concentrate only on installations' safety and directly related areas, foremost
that of spent fuel and radioactive waste (Commission of the European
Communities 2000a). This stocktaking was the first systematic inventory
of informal regulation, which turned out to produce a substantial body of
existing agreements between member states. It is worth quoting at length
how the nonbinding acquis was assembled, since it is telling for the status
and emergence of nonbinding EU legislation:

> All we had to do was to a large extent was to go to our cabinets and pull out
> one report after another that had been produced by our Nuclear Regulator
> Working Group and by the Reactor Safety Working Group, so we had the
> Reactor Safety Working Group and the Nuclear Regulators, and we had
> all these reports they had done, including common positions on safety, on
> pressure of water reactors and, and, and . . . this was the stuff, these were the
> reports that we used in reality to do guidelines from, and all we needed to
> do was to pull out all these things and say: "look, these are the things you
> agreed on in the past, you adopted as working group . . . ," and, of course,
> this is acquis, there is a big acquis, it's just not binding, but everybody
> agrees that these are common positions in the Community, it's a standard
> thing . . . it was a very extensive work that a lot of people that looked at and
> were amazed—how much work we had produced and how many reports

had actually been adopted, published, distributed, which they had never even thought about as being part of the acquis, but it clearly was.

(Interview 2007 DG TREN)

For the remaining parts, the Working Party's report was based on the nongovernmental organization WENRA's "Report on Nuclear Safety in the Candidate Countries" (Western European Nuclear Regulators' Association (WENRA) 2000). The very establishment of WENRA in 1999 was linked to this task, as its twofold mission reflects: "Firstly, nuclear safety was included in the European Union set of enlargement criteria and, secondly, national safety approaches have been developed from IAEA Safety Standards, the Convention on Nuclear Safety, but independently" (WENRA 1999). In other words, WENRA took the role that the member states did not want the Commission to exercise in order to preempt the creation of new supranational responsibilities for nuclear safety. More outspokenly, "WENRA was actually established in order to combat the Commission, to try and deflect any transfer of competence, or any competence being developed in the Commission, WENRA was being set up to say: 'look we still do all this, you do not need to rely on the Commission, you do not need a Community activity, we have a WENRA one' " (Interview DG TREN).

Accordingly, the objectives of WENRA comprised the development of a common approach to nuclear safety. Moreover, it acted as independent agency to examine nuclear safety in the EU candidate states. Requested by the member state governments, it conducted two studies in 1999 and 2000 for which the western operators relied on their bilateral links with their central and eastern European counterparts. Beyond being referred to by the Working Party on Nuclear Safety, the reports were used for the recommendations in the accession negotiations.

One of the limitations of mandating a EU external body with the monitoring task was that WENRA itself had no leverage on the candidate states but had to operate through the official institutions, which brought the Commission back in. "They produced a WENRA report, just as the Commission did . . . and both reports went into the Council, but the WENRA would have liked to have done it on their own—but then, whom could they give their report to? They had to send it to the Council and the Commission because otherwise it had no standing at all" (Interview DG TREN). Hence, although an EU external body conducted the monitoring on the ground, the Commission that drafted the Regular Reports and negotiated Accession Partnerships was indispensable to give affect the candidate states. The AQG/WPNS report issued in May 2001 was followed up by a decision of the Permanent

Representatives Committee in July approving the procedure for the monitoring of candidate countries' commitments with respect to the recommendations of the report. The mandate for peer reviews was subsequently implemented and completed with a peer review status report (Council of the European Union 2002b).[12]

A decisive difficulty in all this was the actual absence of the uniform "western safety standards" that the monitoring exercise officially referred to. The key problem is that among the western states regulation is dealt with following virtually opposite approaches. The most extreme differences can be asserted between the strong control-based German approach and the thoroughly liberal British model. The Commission, therefore, constructed a performance evaluation guideline "which focuses on important nuclear safety issues such as plant design and operation, the practice of performing safety assessments, and nuclear legislation and regulation, in particular the role of the national regulatory body" (Commission of the European Communities 2000b).[13] Given that these objectives and standards for safety levels to be met by the candidate states were actually first formulated in this context, "[t]he outcome of this approach has had an impact not only on the accession States but on the situation in the existing Member States of the EU in a number of ways" (Barnes 2003: 124). They did so in particular because they stood on somewhat muddy grounds. This guides us back to the Commission's initial response to the monitoring mandate.

While the Council tried to evade more Commission activity, the latter appealed to the ECJ arguing for the full accession of the European Community to the IAEA Convention on Nuclear Safety and asserted a Community competence in the field of nuclear safety (Articles 30–39 of the Euratom Treaty). The Commission reacted foremost to the member states' firm stand that it had no competences. This situation caused "frustration as much as anything else by the Commission, we were involved in the negotiation of the nuclear safety convention, just as we were involved in joining the convention for a *long* period of time . . . and it was just almost an insult I think, we felt restricted to kind of one and a half article of a convention we had negotiated." This created contradictions, and therefore "part of the driver was the increasing recognition that we were making statements about safety in the candidate countries, yet we had been told by the member states this is no competence" (Interview 2007 DG TREN). This legal dilemma, moreover, created practical difficulties in the implementation of assistance instruments. In a very critical report, the Court of Auditors took the Commission under attack regarding its activities under Phare and Tacis: "At the end of 1997, owing to the absence of a binding legal basis, there was still no formal consensus at the

European level concerning technical standards in the area of the design and operational safety of nuclear installations. The 25 basic nuclear-safety principles published by the IAEA are still implemented in accordance with each Member State's own technical standards and regulations, which has not facilitated the action the EU has been taking with regard to the safety authorities in the CEECs and the NIS" (Court of Auditors 1999: 10).

Therefore, "effectively, why we appealed to the Court was formally over the nuclear safety convention because we said that the member states restricted our competences too much in the context of the nuclear safety convention, but I suppose the main driver in many ways was the assessment of safety in the candidate countries which suddenly highlighted the fact that ten new member states are joining, several of them have nuclear power plants and the Community could not form a view on them formally—we *could* but in most member states said we had no legal basis" (Interview 2007: DG TREN).

In the Court ruling of 2002, it was decided that the Commission had competences on nuclear safety in the wider sense under Euratom (European Court of Justice 2002). "In relation to the Convention, the Court concluded that, in the light of points recognised in the previous judgments—including the superior overview of the Commission over the nuclear industry—it would not be proper to draw an artificial distinction between the protection of the health of the public and the safety of sources of ionising radiation" (True 2003: 673–75). The ECJ confirmed that no matter whether the Commission *or* the Council was active, Community competences existed. In its ruling the Court went beyond what the Commission had anticipated: "in fact we were surprised in the end that the Court gave us more competences than we had expected, purely because the member states were so active in this area as a Council—they kind of defeated their own objective by taking over the work from us" (Interview 2007 DG TREN).

Already before and independent of enlargement, technological and environmental changes raised functional pressure for a reinterpretation and extension of the traditional reading of nuclear safety in the Euratom Treaty. Applying a wider interpretation to the candidate states created double standards that increased the functional pressure. The member states changed their strategy and withdrew the pre-accession monitoring task from the Commission once the activities in the Copenhagen framework threatened to lead to new formal competences. Their attempt to avoid the extension of the safety concept failed, and with it the goal to prevent a new interpretation of Community competences under Euratom. More so, the ruling of the ECJ affirmed the opposite of what the member states tried to achieve by withdrawing the pre-accession monitoring mandate from the Commission. The unintended consequence pressuring for formalization, set off in connection with monitoring in the Copenhagen framework, was still elucidated by an ECJ judgment. Central for our analysis is that the functional pressure that increased because of unintended consequences left little options but to frame spill-in in terms of formalizing the preexisting nonbinding acquis on nuclear safety.

STATUS QUO POST: NUCLEAR SAFETY AS EX ANTE

After the ECJ judgment, the Commission drafted its so-called nuclear package in 2002/03. The package referred outspokenly to the new need to strengthen the supranational level in view of eastern enlargement, stressing that in the Copenhagen framework the EU, for the first time, was involved in nuclear safety control in independent states—and should continue to do so. The directives proposed have since been rejected by the Council (2002, adapted version 2005). Instead the Council promotes an extended consultation procedure to coordinate European nuclear safety standards. The package included two regulations on nuclear safety, one on the management of spent nuclear fuel and radioactive waste (*Waste Directive*) and one setting out basic obligations and general principles on the safety of nuclear installations (*Safety Directive*). Both directives would have set up legally binding rules for standards already widely recognized as part of the nonbinding acquis and the IAEA framework.

In this sense, especially the adoption of the *Waste Directive* appeared not to imply much of a change for the member states. It would have obliged them to report to the Commission and would in essence have replicated the IAEA reporting instrument. From the Commission's perspective such binding EU regulation "seems logical since I am more interested in what is happening in Spain than I would be interested about what is happening in Argentina for example, or in Australia, so it is a logical extension and a logical definition and . . . it doesn't impose anything dramatically different to what they already work with" (Interview 2007 DG TREN).[14]

Rendering the *Safety Directive* legally binding would have involved more severe concessions for the member states because of a clause on decommissioning funds. Although difficulties in passing a directive including decommissioning had been foreseeable, it was included to respond to a firm, yet nonbinding, request by the European Parliament, which Commissioner de Palacio (also responsible at the time for relations with the EP) decided to respond to. The shortcoming of the existing

Euratom regulations on decommission was that it only obliged operators to create sufficient financial backups to finance decommissioning when needed. This obligation was apparently well met with greatly sufficient resources declared for future expenses (and thus tax-freed). However, Euratom does not regulate how to handle these reserve funds, meaning that the reserves for decommissioning do not have to be kept in segregated accounts and are thus commonly used for other investments. The directive aimed precisely at this, prescribing the segregation of funds in a separate account—a substantial financial sacrifice for the operators from whom particularly strong resistance was raised.

The role of national regulators in maintaining strong member state opposition has been decisive. Not only have they created the alternative forum "WENRA" to take on functions the Commission claimed formal authority over, national regulators have also had a particularly strong influence on governmental positions because of two factors. First, regulators are usually placed within the public administration (even if acting widely independently) and have thus direct access to state officials. Second, and more relevantly, other societal groups taking an opposed position to that of the regulators' and lobbying in favor of more supranational involvement did not emerge. Rather, the vast majority of environmental nongovernmental organizations are in general opposed to nuclear energy, and they usually take a fundamentally negative standpoint against any atomic matters. Therefore, support for the creation of more binding legislation on power plants also remained off the agendas of organized societal groups, whereas those actively favoring nuclear energy without any Community interference exerted effective influence on political decision makers. Nonetheless, the Commission refers stoutly to public opinion surveys to stress that there is considerable the popular support for higher binding standards, as for instance reflected 2005 Eurobarometer Survey on Radioactive Waste (European Commission 2008). These references reflect a diffused notion of public opinion, and no organized nongovernmental voice in support of more harmonization has emerged.[15]

Similarly, a split between nuclear supporters and opponents existed among member states. States favoring nuclear energy rejected formal regulation because they feared that nonnuclear states could impose unwanted obligations on them. States rejecting nuclear energy were skeptical about an extension of Euratom capacities because they fear an upgrading of the positive approach toward nuclear energy the Community is understood to be propagating. This complex constellation hindered even further the achievement of the consensus required for any decision under Euratom. However, the same cleavages have led the European Parliament to vote

with and overwhelming majority in favor of the above-mentioned request
to the Commission for a proposal on decommissioning.

The split between member states blocked for a long time any moves
toward formal harmonization and member states limited their cooperation to informal arrangements. The pro-nuclear states actively promoted
WENRA to respond to functional pressure and to preempt more coercive
Community instruments. As a matter of fact, even the Commission sustained that to date WENRA is "mostly very much in line with what the
nuclear package did, but the nuclear package would have been binding,
whereas they want to do this work on a non-binding basis" (Interview 2007 DG TREN). The reasons for member states for rejecting the
nuclear package have been an alleged duplication of existing mechanisms
and, worse so, the retrenchments of necessary flexibility in implementing national safety policies. An elaborated report by the British House
of Lords offers a comprehensive overview of all the possible arguments
putting the effectiveness and legality of the two directives into question.
As a preferable alternative, this report openly supports "harmonisation
through WENRA" by holding that "[a]ny future EU action on nuclear
safety should be based on the work undertaken by WENRA" (House of
Lords 2006b: 33). Instead of a waste directive it is said that "the EU could
play a highly beneficial role in actively encouraging Member States to
prepare for long-term management" (House of Lords 2006b: 38), citing
Finland and Sweden as positive examples for national best practices. The
bottom line is thus that the member states continued to argue that the
instruments of the IAEA were sufficient or better suited to fulfill the necessary functions and that, where new pressure arose, WENRA was better
equipped to respond. As a Commission official paraphrased: "This is a
situation where basically the IAEA is doing a great job because it is nonbinding, whereas the Commission proposes exactly the same thing in a
more logical and limited area and we think it's wrong because it is binding! And, . . . it's just purely political, you know: 'we don't want to commit
ourselves.' . . . For me it's totally illogical—but as I say, the member states
see it as a kind of opening the door to community legislation, and they do
not want to give in even that little bit of stamp, even if it does not change
anything" (Interview 2007 DG TREN).

Despite the fact that the application of monitoring in the Copenhagen
framework created considerable unintended consequences and functional
pressure, the member states blocked new formal regulatory policies to
spill-in. This happened essentially by rejecting an extended updated definition of nuclear safety, as applied to the candidate states. In line with
the expectations derived from the theoretical model, the member states
preempted spill-in because the Commission had to frame the policy as

hard legislation. They did so by delegating both the pre-accession monitoring function and the execution of a broader interpretation of nuclear
safety—that could not be avoided—to an alternative less coercive forum
outside the EU and thus sourcing out the functional responses, which the
Commission had tried to answer with hard regulation.

SUMMARY: NUCLEAR SAFETY

In sum, the member state governments resisted successfully the direct
spill-in of capacities they attributed to, and subsequently withdrew again
from the Commission in the Copenhagen framework. Unintended consequences that emerged from the implementation of enlargement were side-
lined by referring responsibilities to existing international institutions or
new private organizations whose creation was actively supported outside
the Community framework. The vast body of preexisting informal acquis
was for the first time systematically summarized to provide standards for
pre-accession monitoring, which increased the pressure for formalization
of these rules while it closed the door for moving further into informal
regulatory policies within the EU framework. Functional pressure existed
already before enlargement because of the limited definition and outdated
reading of nuclear safety in the Euratom Treaty. Two causes increased
his pressure. First, the extended definition applied in the Copenhagen
framework created double standards because the call for compliance with
"western safety standards" was matched by a patchwork of very different
and even partially contradictory national approaches across the western
member states. Second, unintended consequences reinforced functional
pressure for spill-in because the ECJ confirmed the extended interpretation of nuclear safety policy to be comprised in the existing regulations
of Euratom. Given the preexisting substantial nonbinding acquis and the
new recognition of wider formal Community competences, spill-in could
only be framed in terms of new binding legislation, or more precisely
the formalization of existing informal institutions, as the only feasible
response to increased functional strains.

Decisive for the outcome was the involvement of the non-state actor
WENRA, which argued vehemently and very actively against further
supranationalization, offering, at the same time, alternative functional
solutions. Furthermore, the restrictive institutional rules of Euratom facilitated the member states' ability to reject proposed legislation that received
a generous backing by all supranational institutions (see also European
Economic and Social Committee 2003), although they remain excluded
from the unanimous decision making under the sectoral Treaty. Already
during the implementation of enlargement, the means of informal

governance were expanded. Referring to the "strong mediation between the national bureaucracy and interest groups" that the Commission relied on, Saurugger points out that this "form of informal governance delivers reliable policy-outcomes against the odds of a cumbersome, supermajoritarian decision-making system. Confronted with the high danger of unsafe power stations in Central and Eastern Europe, the Commission was looking for strategies developed by actors perceived as experts in the field, as they are confronted with similar questions on a daily basis" (2003: 224).[16] Short of sufficient supranational means, the Commission relied on and referred to national agents in the Copenhagen framework. The attempts to create more substantial own capacities in linking these to the enlargement instruments failed because of the hard regulatory and coercive nature of the nuclear package.

Hence, the theoretical expectations are met: the member states avoided the institutionalization of Community capacities in the area of nuclear safety because competences were framed as formal, hard legislation. Even more so, the member states have actively worked against the Commission to exercise its formal competences and propose binding legislation, and in the direct aftermath of accession the Commission was limited to some ad hoc own resources, especially making reference to statistical data in absence of actual monitoring functions. These activities did not amount to institutionalize new action capacity because they do not create any tools to directly adapt member states' behavior. Beyond the immediate impact of enlargement, the alternative functional responses offered by WENRA that informally took the role the Commission had foreseen for itself proved not sustainable in the midterm. In 2009 a regulation was eventually passed, which did establish hard regulation that acknowledged a much more central role for national agencies and made major concessions regarding all critical points that had previously evoked member state resistance.

CHAPTER 8

ANTICORRUPTION: OUTSOURCING RESPONSIBILITY

Anticorruption is a regulatory policy, and accordingly during the pre-accession phase the Commission focused on monitoring the candidate states and exerted pressure to pass and implement legislation to fight corruption. To this end, standards and benchmarks were established in the Copenhagen framework. At the EU level some related binding legislation existed, in particular on the protection of the Union's financial interests. As for the fight of corruption inside the member states, international instruments were launched parallel to the EU's efforts during the pre-accession phase. These international agreements established outside the EU framework took up the political problems for which the Commission had for considerable time tried to acquire Community competences. The pre-existing acquis and the creation and implementation of wider standards in the Copenhagen framework increased the pressure for spill-in in the form of harmonization with little scope for framing pre-accession competences as further nonbinding EU rules.

> Anticorruption is a regulatory policy, and thus we should expect an extension of capacities as nonbinding rules or informal cooperation, but member states should block spill-in if it implies the creation of new binding regulation.

Anticorruption policy in the EU has three targets: the Community's financial interests, officials of the Community or of the member states, and private sector corruption. In all three areas legal instruments are in place, the protection of the EU financial interests being the longest established since 1995. The actual implementation record in the member states, however, remained unsatisfactory. In reaction, the Commission had pushed for higher EU norms for fighting corruption inside member states until 2003, when it eventually dropped its claims for further hard regulation. Within the Copenhagen framework the Commission went decisively beyond the pre-existing legal basis as far as corruption of officials in the candidate states was concerned. Drawing both from EU's own and from other international conventions, benchmarks and codes of conduct were developed and used in the monitoring process to evaluate the accession countries' regulatory measures.

A significant feature of anticorruption policy during the pre-accession phase was the strong cooperation with other international organizations. Joint programs aimed especially at promoting the implementation of anticorruption policies. Moreover, parallel to the development of instruments in the Copenhagen framework, a set of international instruments were ratified that the member states acceded instead of developing further measures within the EU. Generally, the awareness of corruption augmented. The increasing concern in various international forums explains part of the member states' reluctance to surge ahead with actions on the EU level. As alternative international instruments were realized, the Commission eventually also lowered its claims on genuine EU legislation recommending member states rather to accede to those instruments established by the UN, OSCD, and the Council of Europe. However, at the same time the Commission further refined standards and specified a checklist of what candidate states should fulfill before entering the Union. For the latest entrants only, Romania and Bulgaria, monitoring of internal state corruption continues even after accession. In contrast, "outsourcing" part of the anticorruption control to new instruments outside the EU was the less constraining option for member states, since it allowed the preempting of the creation of hard enforcement tools for the Commission. Other than nonbinding EU legislation the shift of responsibility to alternative forums also preempted the potential for unintended consequences that could eventually lead to binding legislation. Simultaneously, the Commission is moving in on the grey area of the existing competences, in particular through communication and exchange between the various DGs. In this vein, the awareness for corruption matters has risen and anticorruption clauses are promoted as part and parcel of various types of agreements, including also increased concern with public opinion and attempts to build direct links to societal perceptions of corruption in general. Nevertheless, these moves remain dependent on the interservice exchange within the Commission and are restricted to the legal basis the Commission has. They do not create any stable institutionalized action capacity for the Commission inside the EU, while the EU's anticorruption stands toward third states has been strengthened.

In sum, in anticorruption no major unintended consequences emerged; quite to the contrary, the Commission successfully exerted high pressure on the candidate states. A spill-in that would have led to binding legislation for all member states could be prevented because new international instruments with congruent objectives offered a sufficient response to functional pressure. Therefore, the member states could opt for these less costly alternatives under less formalized international law instead of more restrictive EU legislation. The Commission followed this trend and lowered its claims for more upfront EU capacities. It nonetheless actively continues to exploit in an ad hoc manner the means it has, in particular by promoting anticorruption standards across the various Directorate Generals. These activities do, however, not amount to institutionalized capacities that should produce an effect that persists over time because the member states do not sufficiently acknowledge the limited policy tools.

STATUS QUO ANTE: ANTICORRUPTION IN THE ACQUIS

Legal instruments on anticorruption can be either specialized legislation, or corruption is classified as a serious crime in any other piece of legislation, for example, related to the European Arrest Warrant or money laundering. Both need to be backed by practical facilities in terms of standards and implementing capacities, relevant in particular for law enforcement agencies such as the police, customs, and border guards. The fight against corruption can be understood as part of the broader promotion of the "rule of law." It can be further differentiated between high-level corruption, organized crime and corruption, and petty day-to-day corruption. The Commission's definition of corruption is wide, going beyond current EU legislation focusing on criminal liabilities (active or passive bribery); besides the narrow penal definition it embraces a socioeconomic definition aiming at corruption prevention in the context of "good governance" (Tivig and Maurer 2006: 6).

Anticorruption policy falls under the former third pillar (Freedom, Security and Justice, previously Justice and Home Affairs). It is an intergovernmentally organized policy; unanimity applies and member states have a monopoly on initiating further integration. The European Parliament takes note of events and has commented in particular on cases of erupting scandals—it has, however, no official powers. Moreover, the Parliamentary Committee on Civil Liberties, Justice and Home Affairs (LIBE) issues reports under the consultation procedure regarding the European Community's accession to the international instruments (European Parliament 2006). As for all intergovernmental policy areas, the Commission has no powers to initiate legislation other than being asked to act under the third pillar. Although the Lisbon Treaty formally dissolved the pillar structure of the EU and moved a number of policies to the ordinary decision-making procedure, for anticorruption policy the former third-pillar procedures continue to apply.

Beyond the arguably weak control of fraud through the Community's antifraud office OLAF,[1] which focuses on the Community's financial interests, a set of more comprehensive common standards and norms was laid down in the second half of the 1990s (Daams 1999: 9). These mark the first steps toward a more embracing EU anticorruption policy. The first agreement to emerge was the *Convention on the Protection of the European Communities' Financial Interests,* 1995, and its first two *Protocols* in 1996/97. Second, the *Convention on the Fight against Corruption Involving Officials of the European Communities or Officials of Member States of the European Union* from 1997 is the area of our narrower interest, that is, the EU's policy tools that have an impact on anticorruption policy inside the member states. These two agreements progressively extended the definition of corruption. The 1992 Convention was the first to take the definition of corruption beyond the realm of the Community's financial interests. Notably, both agreements on the EU level were not immediately implemented, but the majority of member states remained highly reluctant to ratify the 1995 Convention, which eventually entered into force in 2002.

All member states are "required to put the legislation in place but there is not the follow-up in terms of detailed implementation" (Interview Commission, DG JLF). As is usual practice for conventions among member states, compliance with the conventions is regulated by a reporting system according to which the member states inform the Commission and the Council on the situation of transposition in their respective country.[2] The Commission reviews the national laws in an interservice procedure that involves various Directorate Generals. The resulting report is passed on to the Council that decides how to further proceed in the issue area. Accordingly, for the 1995 Convention on the EU's financial interests, the member states issued their reports in 2004 and were supported by investigations carried out by OLAF. The entering into force of the Convention was followed by further steps toward concrete implementation, most important and recently the establishment of *Eurojust,* in 2002, to "fight serious crime" by enforcing the cooperation across member states at the national and EU level (Council of the European Union 2002a).[3] Moreover, the *Hercule* action program for the protection of the Community's financial interests was founded in 2004 (European Parliament and Council of the European Union 2004).

The EU has a competence on the protection of Community financial interests. This chapter focuses on the highly contested extension of the concept to include domestic anticorruption policies and corruption on the member states level more generally. The 1997 Convention, focusing on public officials, entered into force in September 2005. Responding to a draft proposal in the *Communication from the Commission to the Council, the European Parliament and the European Economic and Social Committee on a Comprehensive EU Policy against Corruption* (Commission of the European Communities 2003b) in March 2005, the Council rejected the establishment of further new Community instruments referring to other international instruments, but urged the states that had not done so to ratify the existing conventions (Council of the European Union 2005c). The long time lag in the ratification process has led to the conclusion that "[a]lthough one could say from a criminal law point of view that these instruments are getting more refined, this does not necessarily mean that it really contributes to the effectiveness of the fight against organised crime in general and corruption more specifically, especially since many of the provisions are formulated in a rather vague way" (Daams 1999: 10).

As will be argued below, part of the delays in the Community instruments has to be seen against the background of evolving international agreements with partially overlapping functions. Although these remain even further behind possible binding EU legislation with hard enforcement mechanisms against public officials' corruption, such alternatives were eventually the preferred option to answer to functional pressure. Despite the dismissal of the Santer Commission in 1999 due to fraud and corruption allegations against Commission officials, the actual instruments for criminal investigation for both Community and national public officials remain limited.[4] Warner claims that the fact that the member states have not set up "real administrative, monitoring and enforcement powers to supranational institutions could imply that the concern of the member states is that the agents would be too effective in monitoring the behavior of the principals. If the concern of the member states were that other states would be defecting form the treaties' obligations, then a supranational institution should have been better situated than each of them individually to monitor the behavior of other states. It appears that the states have made various agreements they do not really want to keep, and the best way to not keep them is to retain the bulk of administrative, monitoring and enforcement power" (Warner 2003: 70). In sum, it can be sustained that the 1997 Convention has created some legal framework on the EU level, whose impact and binding force, however, remain limited and informal regarding the de facto enforcement options that the Commission has at its disposal.

In the third area of anticorruption legislation, the fight against private sector corruption, a Danish initiative triggered first a *Joint Action* in 1998 (Council of the European Union 1998), which led to the *Council Framework Decision on Combating Corruption in the Private Sector* of 2003 (Council of the European Union 2003). On the basis of the member states' transposition reports from the majority of states, the Commission has issued its report to the Council. Since the issue could be linked up to the area of competition, a number of member states have been interested in promoting further measures already mentioned in the Joint Action, and one can speculate that "there is a requirement for the Council to consider whether to redo that capability to delegate or whether actually to put forward a proposal, to do that would be a major reform for everyone, and that would be by 2010" (Interview Commission, DG JLF). Yet, no such "major reform" has ensued.

Generally, anticorruption measures remain up to future intergovernmental member state decisions. As a clearly regulatory policy on the EU level, anticorruption remains in the informal realm—in that hard enforcement mechanisms and direct coercive tools are absent—and, as will be illustrated below, has moved even more into this direction by increasing cooperation outside the more constraining EU framework in response to increasing functional pressure. Following up on the Tampere Program, operational from 1999 to 2004, which laid down an action program for fighting corruption (European Council 1999), the European Council of Hague spelled out a new program for 2005–2010 (Council of the European Union 2005b). The Hague Program includes the creation of a scoreboard to annually review measures in the area of freedom, security, and justice and the creation of comparable statistics (Council of the European Union 2005d). This notwithstanding, for the time being the legal instruments existing at the EU level remain limited, and in the Commission "there is limited capacity to inquire on the situation on the ground in the member states" (Interview Commission, DG JLF), unlike the leverage that the Commission had in the pre-accession context. In contrast to the member states' reluctance, the European Parliament has called for extended powers of the Commission as the ideal agent to monitor the implementation of international instruments (European Parliament 2003) and, beyond that, to establish an EU prosecutor to improve the efficiency of EU internal anticorruption control (Tivig and Maurer 2006: 51). This responds to the main problem in the fight against corruption, namely, the shortcomings in the implementation of existing framework agreements. De facto implementation depends purely on the voluntary cooperation and responsiveness of the member states because the EU lacks mechanisms to monitor and control the harmonization of national penal law, the execution of passed measures, and the implementation of agreements (Tivig and Maurer 2006: 18).

PRE-ACCESSION PHASE: FIGHTING CORRUPTION IN THE CANDIDATE STATES

The 1993 Copenhagen Council did not explicitly mention corruption as an accession criterion. This notwithstanding, the issue was included into the Regular Reports with a prominent independent chapter in the section on political criteria (democracy and rule of law) in which it stands besides "institutional issues" (the executive, judiciary, and parliament). Generally, corruption was perceived a considerably important issue for the public administrations in the central and eastern European states because of their postsocialist heritage (Bossaert and Demmke 2003: 3–4; Goetz and Wollmann 2001: 868). The monitoring of corruption therefore cut across different chapters such as, for some states, Industrial Policy, Customs Union, External Policies—and foremost for all states the negotiation chapter 24 *Cooperation in the Field of Justice and Home Affairs*. The standards and benchmarks for monitoring were drawn from the internally mal-implemented Community Conventions and international instruments alike.

But the Commission went further in translating these agreements into more tangible standards and benchmarks. The most concrete incarnation is an annex to the Commission's 2003 *Communication on a Comprehensive Policy on Corruption* (Commission of the European Communities 2003b). In marked contrast to the more reluctant tone that the document takes on desirable measures in the member states, it offers a concise checklist on the desired policies to be implemented in the candidate states. The proposed measures go beyond criminal offences by promoting more generally a culture against corruption. The checklist summarizes what the Commission considered essential elements in the domestic fight against corruption. Some of the "Ten Principles for Improving the fight against Corruption in acceding, candidate and other third Countries" went well beyond its actual competences, for example, the call for clear rules on whistle blowing, the promotion of public intolerance to corruption by awareness-raising campaigns in the media and by training, or the need to establish transparent rules on party financing, and external financial control of political parties (Commission of the European Communities 2003b). Even more striking, the Commission has imposed a unique exception for the last two states that joined the Union in 2007, effectively continuing the double standards treatment between old and new member states. For Romania and Bulgaria, a post-accession monitoring scheme has been put in place and anticorruption monitoring by the EU continues, which includes scrutinizing these two states exclusively.

As part of the standard monitoring in the regular reporting that relied on information collected by the delegations in the countries, governmental reports, nongovernmental organizations, or other international organizations, formal missions of experts from member states visited the candidate states (on an approximately biannual basis) both before and after the enactment of legislation. As implementation proceeded these missions included visits, for example, to border posts or local police forces with member state practitioners and the participation of experts in these very bodies in the missions (Interview DG JLF).

Regarding assistance, the cooperation with other international organizations active in the field and region was very extensive. While standards were formulated separately from the EU acquis, the bulk of financial means was Phare money. The core areas were joint programs to assist capacity building to ensure compliance, namely, the SIGMA program (support for improvement in governance and management), which was set up in 1992 together with the OECD, and the OCTOPUS program run by the Commission and the Council of Europe. Especially the OCTOPUS program gained increasing relevance for compliance control. "The first phase of the project (1996–98) concentrated on analyzing measures taken by the participating countries and making specific recommendations for each country. The Octopus II program (1999–2000) put the emphasis on implementing those recommendations and assisting European Union applicant states" (Utstein Anti-Corruption Resource Centre 2005). The new member states continue to participate in the SIGMA program, which transformed in 2005 its "multi-country activity . . . into two activities, carried out by to SAI [Supreme Audit Institutions] Presidents of the ten New Member States and SAI Presidents of the Candidate Countries" (SIGMA—European Union and Council of Europe 2005). The OCTOPUS program was dissolved in 2000 with all candidate states becoming members of the newly established Group of States against Corruption (GRECO). Established in 1999, GRECO "was conceived as a flexible and efficient follow-up mechanism, called to monitor, through a process of mutual evaluation and peer pressure, the observance of the Twenty Guiding Principles in the Fight against Corruption and the implementation of international legal instruments adopted in pursuance of the Programme of Action against Corruption" (Utstein Anti-Corruption Resource Centre 2005).

In sum, the Commission's involvement in anticorruption policy has been considered a success, and the end of EU monitoring was consequently deplored. The Open Society Institute, therefore, concluded: "The EU accession process has had a major impact on legal and institutional frameworks that are involved in the fight against corruption. Commission pressure has led to important legislative changes, especially in the areas of public procurement legislation, criminal and civil procedure, anticorruption legislation, and civil service legal frameworks. The relative clarity of the EU approach in the area of enforcement of criminal law has led to important changes in candidate States, such as increased coordination between the various organs of enforcement, training of law enforcement officials and EU-assisted reform of the judiciary" (2002b: 71). Despite this positive evaluation, the NGO pinpointed also the limitations that derived from the imbalance between the Copenhagen and acquis frameworks that entailed shortcoming in the implementation of standards in the EU. "However in the area of anticorruption policy narrowly perceived ... the Commission has lacked the mandate or any standard of EU best practice in the areas of criminal investigation and proceedings that would allow it to pressure candidate States to take steps to ensure the freedom of institutions of prosecution enforcement from improper influence, for example in Poland and Romania" (Open Society Institute 2002b: 71–72). In comparison with the Commission's influence on member states, we can hence conclude that the pre-accession conditionality substantively increased its leverage. This enabled the Commission to change candidate state behavior even if, as for the member states, the Community has no competences for own criminal investigation proceedings.

Implementing enlargement did not create fully new functional pressure. It rather reinforced pressure for action that was an increasingly articulated theme across all European states and various international organizations. It did so foremost by the outspoken extension of EU monitoring of internal state corruption. The difference that the Copenhagen framework made was in particular the refinement of what the Community would consider genuinely good standards and desirable legislation. In the implementation structures and organization of the policy, a novelty that developed during the implementation of enlargement was the strong inter-DG cooperation within the Commission, which led to the elaboration of further alternative options to promote anticorruption policy by means of mainstreaming across different policy areas. Remarkably, the same turn that the Commission took in enlargement policy to overcome the weaknesses in its enforcement tools, namely, the strong reference to the GRECO network urging candidate states to accede to these extra-EU instruments, was eventually also recommended to the member states that successfully refused hard Community competences despite increased functional pressure.

Although the promotion of anticorruption policy in the candidate states was supported by EU assistance, the policy is essentially regulatory, aiming at corruption control. Given that the EU had already established anticorruption conventions, implementing enlargement increased functional pressure for formalization because standards developed in face of the candidate states' administrations were spelled out more clearly and were bound to more concrete demands on implementation and enforcement on the national level. Moreover, not all entering states were expected to have resolved their problems at the time of accession. Since the creation of different types of membership was treated a taboo, the only credible way to continue monitoring would have been to establish rules applicable to all member states. Despite this, the Commission did not pressure for more binding legislation within the Union framework. Instead, it even fell behind earlier claims for Community competences. Thus, no unintended consequences occurred, but the Commission stayed well within the boundaries of the Copenhagen framework, setting high standards for the entering but lowering demands on the existing member states in terms of EU means of control. However, obliging the latest two entrants to continued EU monitoring of their corruption records broke clearly with the principle of universal membership rights for all acceding states.

STATUS QUO POST: EXTERNALIZING ANTICORRUPTION ISSUES

The Commission's anticorruption policy strategy changed during the pre-accession period because of wider trends outside the EU and the particularly strong relevance corruption played in the central and eastern European transformation processes. First, relevant new legal instruments were created in international forums outside the EU. Second, parallel to the incremental changes in the Copenhagen framework in which the Commission developed concrete standards for the candidate states, the Commission made an important turn its approach toward member states. From 2003 the Commission encouraged member states to join GRECO and other international agreements instead of further pushing for solutions in the Community acquis. Third, informally, the links between different services within the Commission have increased aiming toward mainstreaming anticorruption measures across different policies. Fourth, although harmonization among member states based on binding regulation has been ruled out, two new member states are still subject to Commission monitoring so that the pre-accession system of double standards is effectively continued after widening.

First, how did the generally greater attention on anticorruption policies at the international level affect the EU policy agenda, and what impact did this have on the member states' choices regarding anticorruption policy within the EU? From the late 1990s, both on the European and the global level a number of agreements were established. The *United Nations Convention against Corruption* (UNCAC)[5] adopted on October 31, 2003, provides common standards for national policies and practices, and it enhances international cooperation to address cross-border crime. The parties also oblige themselves to assist each other in preventing and combating corruption through technical support, such as financial and human resources, training, and research. The UNCAC entered into force on December 14, 2005. Also the *United Nations Convention against Transnational Organized Crime* (UNTOC)[6] adopted on November 15, 2000, and in force since September 29, 2003, covers corruption, recognizing that it represents an integral component of transnational organized crime and must be addressed as part of efforts to combat organized crime.

In the European context the regional organizations have set up a number of conventions. The *OSCE Convention on Bribery of Foreign Public Officials in International Business Transactions,*[7] signed on November 21, 1997, and in force since February 15, 1999, focuses particularly on the supply side of bribery by binding the countries that account for the majority of global exports. A coordinated framework aims to criminalize the bribery of foreign public officials in international business transactions, against which the contracting parties have agreed to introduce criminal sanctions. The *Council of Europe Criminal Law Convention and Protocol on Corruption* was adopted on November 4, 1998, to enter into force on July 1, 2002. Unlike the OSCD convention, not all EU member states have ratified this agreement.[8] Moreover, the *Council of Europe Civil Law Convention on Corruption,* adopted on November 4, 1999, and in force since November 1, 2003, covers public sector and private sector (private-to-private) corruption. An *Additional Protocol to the Council of Europe Criminal Law on Corruption* followed in 2003.

This links to the second point, the emergence of alternative enforcement mechanisms that have been created in connection with the broader regional agreements. Most relevantly, the implementation of the Council of Europe Criminal Law Convention has brought forth its own network. GRECO, which started functioning on May 1, 1999, and to which to date all EU member states have acceded, is monitoring the Convention. Thus, the main focal points of the Convention, that is, the criminalization of a large number of corrupt practices, money laundering, provisions regarding the private sector, and international cooperation, are underpinned by monitoring through GRECO.

The delays to the ratification of the 1997 Community convention must be read against the background of this emerging network of international agreements. "In some ways, perhaps because of the fact that there was this cascade of conventions, actually almost slowed down the process... so looking back with hindsight it is probably not so surprising for countries looking at this developing: they waited until they could see what was going to come up" (Interview DG JLF). In other words, in particular as regards enforcement mechanisms of anticorruption agreements, the member state governments opted for institutionally less constraining—but regionally wider—options outside the Union. Moreover, an interesting shift in the Commission's approach can be noticed. Instead of establishing own resources, still proposed in its first Communication on anticorruption policy (Commission of the European Communities 1997b), in 2003 "the Commission holds the view that, at this stage of policy development, mainly those measures should be strengthened and supported at EU level, which are not already substantively covered, or not with the same degree of mandatory character as EU instruments, by international organizations. This goes in particular for initiatives of the United Nations, the OECD and the Council of Europe, where the EU has been playing a leading role and should continue to do so" (Commission of the European Communities 2003b: 5).

The change in approach by the Commission cannot be attributed only to the member states favoring alternative solutions outside the EU. It was also promoted by tensions on competences on overlapping responsibilities between the EU and other international organizations (Interview former member College 2007). From this, the GRECO network emerged as the main instrument for monitoring and enforcement. Only "[i]n case participation in GRECO will not be considered a viable option, the Commission would consider if a separate EU mutual evaluation and monitoring mechanism on the fight against corruption could be set up" (Commission of the European Communities 2003b: 9).

In fact, a group of seven member states put forward a proposal for a Council Decision to establish a European Anti-Corruption Network (EACN) of anticorruption bodies in the member states in late 2005 that was intended to promote cooperation among member states without harmonization. Even if remaining in the informal realm, some member states have reacted reluctantly to the proposal. They did not express general disagreement but laid down the condition that "before giving the proposal its full support, it will need to clarify the scope of the proposed network to ensure that it does not overlap with existing networks and organizations" (House of Lords 2006a). An interesting contrast to the developments in the Nuclear Safety is that in the latter a network of independent bodies was set up in the member states. In contrast to this, in anticorruption policy, the Commission's legislative proposals considered the alternative instruments offered by other international organizations insufficient. Thus, functional pressure for a response within the EU framework could more easily be redirected to forums outside the EU, thereby evading even attempts for nonbinding cooperative networks among member states.

Third, how did the Commission extend its activities within the legal framework established since the mid-1990s? Despite the more cautious take on hard enforcement and binding legislation since the 2003 Communication, the Commission did not retreat completely. Rather, there have been informal attempts to promote anticorruption matters within the limited means it has at its independent disposal. The tools developed in the enlargement context have not played the most decisive role in this case, but offered a platform to develop single elements. In addition to the inclusion of corruption as a serious crime into various tools of criminal law, such as the European Arrest Warrant or money laundering, the most relevant development has been the increased cooperation between different Directorate Generals inside the Commission. On the basis of the general directions indicated in the area of criminal law by the European Council, the Commission developed its wider strategy as published in its 2008 in a communication that proposed a discussion forum but has not been followed up by legal acts. Concerning anticorruption, the Communication reconfirmed the shift of the 2003 Communication and underlined the special role of GRECO (Commission of the European Communities 2008a: 6). A central new element in this has been to go beyond the narrow focus on criminal law, or in the words of a Commission official, "we will be looking at—I guess the jargon is 'mainstreaming'—and mainstreaming, thinking about corruption in a whole lot of other areas" (Interview 2007 DG JFS).

An example for this is the checklist annexed to the 2003 Communication that puts down concrete benchmarks to evaluate a state's legal and implantation apparatus. "It is a handy checklist for our colleagues, particularly in the external relations area, in the area of development aid . . . these are the areas, they will never be specialist on corruption, but if they have a quick checklist of what are the things that are signals that things are going well, or that things are potentially going to go badly" (Interview DG JLF). Along such lines, the links between the different services in the Commission have been strengthened over the last years in order to increase the consistency in bilateral agreements between the EU and third states. The informal interservice coordination has led to a stronger emphasis on corruption in the Union's external relations and is expected to be extended in future in agreements between the Union and states around the world.[9] Moreover, the Council raised the awareness for anticorruption in the EU's external relations (Council of the European Union 2005a) and strengthened the Commission's external capacities by making the fight against corruption one of the objectives of the European Neighborhood Policy (Tivig and Maurer 2006: 41).

In the same vein, for future enlargements some changes have been introduced, opening up a second generation of conditionality. On the one hand, the accession of most member states to UNTOC and UNCAC means that these conventions are also considered in the monitoring process of candidate states. On the other hand, anticorruption has been moved from chapter 24 to the new chapter 23, which puts it into the context of the judiciary and stresses less the aspect of organized crime. This change has significantly strengthened the leverage on anticorruption in current and future candidate states.[10]

While in the external realm and enlargement policy the Commission has been strengthened, capacities applying to the member states have remained limited. The only substantial change is that the Commission has started to make progress in approaching crime through the development of comparable statistics, not least to get a comparable and comprehensive overview on all member states within the boundaries of existing competences. Aiming to go beyond the currently most elaborated statistics on corruption, the Corruption Perception Index by the nongovernmental organization Transparency International, the EU agency Eurostat gathers more focused information on the member states, and corruption has been chosen a pilot area for the development of more sound statistical data in the criminal area. Acting in this direction, on February 12, 2008, the Commission issued a "staff working document examining the links between organised crime and corruption. The paper draws together existing information to identify situations where Organised Crime uses corruption as a tool for infiltrating the public and private sectors. It reviews existing counter-measures and concludes that a better understanding of the links between organised crime and corruption is much needed. The Commission will therefore launch a study to examine what is an increasingly disturbing and largely unexplored phenomenon" (Commission of the European Communities 2008d). A first Special Eurobarometer Report on organized crime, cross-border crime, and corruption was published in 2006 (European Commission 2006), followed by Special Eurobarometer Reports on public opinion on corruption in the member states in 2008 and 2009 (European Commission 2009, 2008). The development of these comparable statistical data was intended to adjust the Commission's comparatively low knowledge about corruption in the member states compared to the candidate states. In the words of an official, standardized statistics were to lower the gap of "how much we watch and know in the member states as opposed to the countries that are acceding. This will help ourselves and the member states to be actually a bit clearer on what is going on across a whole range of crime areas, not just corruption" (Interview 2006 DG JFS). Yet, as indicated in Council draft document *European Policy Needs for Data on Crime and Criminal Justice: State of Play,* the Commission's initiatives on establishing comparative statistics are met by continuous disagreement among member states (General Secretariat of the Council 2007). The little support for relying on soft law underlines the argument that, in contrast to other policy areas such as administrative cooperation, the member states are reluctant to build up informal governance structures in the field of anticorruption. This undermines from the outset the potential impact of Commission initiatives such as comparative statistics that will lack effect for as long as the member states do not respond to them.

Fourth, post-accession monitoring was made a condition for the entry of Bulgaria and Romania, under the so-called *Cooperation and Verification Mechanism* established by a Commission Decision of December 13, 2006 (Commission of the European Communities 2006a, b) that includes safeguard mechanisms as means of last resort, which are triggered either to prevent or to remedy particular problems or threats to the functioning of the Union. The Bulgarian and Romanian accession Treaties list the areas to which these safeguard clauses apply. Furthermore, four concrete benchmarks for Romania and six for Bulgaria are listed in an annex (Commission of the European Communities 2007c). First Reports were published in June 2007 (Commission of the European Communities 2007e, d), followed by Action Programs on how to fulfill the benchmarks of the Cooperation and Verification Mechanism in October 2007 and Interim Reports in early 2008 (Commission of the European Communities 2008b, c).

In essence, the current position is the continued differentiated treatment of member states. New member states and external states are scrutinized by standards of limited reach, and the Commission has special capacities vis-à-vis these states. Despite the attempts to create comprehensive data on national anticorruption policies, under the general acquis the actual implementation and enforcement of measures still depends on the voluntary responsiveness of member states. The Commission's means fall short of institutionalized new action capacity because they lack sufficient leverage to indeed adapt to member state behavior, and the mechanisms of control remain without either hard mechanisms of control or sufficient receptiveness from policy takers to establish networks of informal governance. Member state reluctance is highlighted by the fact that member states refrain from informal cooperation based on peer reviews and the elaboration of nonbinding standards. Without such cooperation networks, comparable statistics will also lack a mechanism to exert forceful pressure on member states. In essence, functional pressure increased because of the extension of the notion of anticorruption in the Copenhagen framework and was subsequently redirected and responded to outside the EU framework. Not even the threat of internalizing corruption problems with the accession of new member states falling short of desired standards has led to a spill-in of pre-accession capacities. Instead, a different treatment for old and the newest member states has been successfully upheld in that monitoring applies exclusively to Romania and Bulgaria. This has led the Bulgarian minister R. Petrov to claim that "double standards are not to be tolerated. They are out of the question," and thus the need to elaborate comparative measures for corruption proposing "common standards" that would bring an "objective evaluation of every member state" (Europe.bg 2008). Effectively, the Commission's response has been no more than to refer to the creation of comparable statistics—which, as pointed out, does not create institutionalized new action capacity and thus cannot hide the fact that the Commission continues to apply different policy instruments short of formalized official competences. In contrast to the stricter EU pre-accession conditionality, post-accession studies that evaluate policy outcomes in the new member states are skeptical about the impact of the international instruments on actual performance on the ground (Batory 2010; Gadowska 2010; Wolf 2010). For Bulgaria and Rumania, the continued influence of the Commission is recognized, but the lack of support by domestic constituencies that support anticorruption measures substantially hampers progress, so that the states remain under constant critique by the Commission and European media alike (Ivanov 2010).

SUMMARY: ANTICORRUPTION

Implementing enlargement reinforced functional pressure rather than creating it. The perception that corruption was a serious problem in the candidate states gave the policy a prominent role in the pre-accession monitoring process, which has been re-enforced in second-generation conditionality in the ongoing enlargements. Yet, dealing with the issue in the Copenhagen framework it soon became apparent that corruption was not an isolated matter of concern in the were-to-be member states. "Since the Copenhagen criteria apply only to applicants, the assessments could not (officially) be applied to members, but the development of criteria inevitably led to comparisons with members. A striking example was corruption, where the only published source (practically the only systematic source) was Transparency International, which showed that some member states (such as Belgium) were placed below some of the applicants. I recall the frisson of embarrassment when I distributed these results to representatives of member states at a meeting of the Council's Enlargement Group" (official DG Enlargement, written exchange September 2007).

As a genuinely regulatory affair, and given that conventions existed on the EU level that member states, however, fell short of implementing effectively, formal regulation marked the only possible further response within the EU. Hence, spill-in would have led to new formal legislation. At the same time, corruption was tackled in various forums so that alternative and institutionally less costly options emerged for the member states in the form of international agreements in other international organizations. The Commission eventually gave in to the argument of member states and international organizations with overlapping responsibilities. The attempts to produce tools within the EU framework were given up in favor of promoting international instruments based on soft enforcement that provoked less member state resistance. Not even initiatives by some member states for ECAN as nonbinding network among member states have been realized so far. Instead, initiatives geared to inner-state corruption control have been redirected to bodies outside the EU framework. Standing out against this prudence are the continued post-accession competences since 2007. Accession of Romania and Bulgaria increased functional pressure for supranational capacities due to persisting shortcomings in the acceding states. This pressure did not lead to spill-in but gave the Commission sufficient backing to successfully push for continued post-accession monitoring in criminal matters and corruption, thereby sustaining the double standards in the post-accession system.

Nonetheless, there have been some attempts to informally expand the Commission's reach by mainstreaming anticorruption policy across the different services and by building up a more reliable set of information on the issue based on the elaboration of statistical methods to gather comparable data across all member states. Notably, these informal moves are not accompanied by soft steering instruments and are little welcomed by the member states—unlike the informal tools in the first three cases presented. Hence, these tools lack accompanying mechanisms to indeed have an impact on member states. Consequently, they do not establish new action capacity as defined for our purpose, because they rely on too limited actions by the Commission that are not institutionalized in the sense of guaranteed persistent policy tools because they are insufficiently recognized by member states.

The outcome does, therefore, support the theoretical expectations. Since a spill-in could only be framed in terms of hard legislation and in the absence of unintended consequences that could have strengthened functional demands for Commission capacities, no institutionalization in the wider EU framework occurred. Additionally, alternatives emerged outside the EU that allowed the member states to seek functional responses in other forums and to evade even more nonbinding cooperation within the Union framework. At the same time, conditionality for candidate states and even acceding states was increased and double standards sustained. In other words, member states successfully resisted functional pressure even against the credibility-threatening practice of granting the Commission monitoring capacities over two new member states only. This extension of pre-accession conditionality inside the EU framework goes beyond the theoretical expectations since it is not even "covered up" by nesting Commission capacities on national anticorruption control in other EU policies, such as in the case of administrative capacity building or minority protection, where specific regulatory goals are being pursued indirectly by distributive policies. Still, this does not establish disconfirming evidence but supports the line of argument beyond what we should have expected from the legally admissible perspective of a universally applicable system of rule of law.

CONCLUSIONS

THE IMPACT OF IMPLEMENTING EASTERN ENLARGEMENT: EFFECTS ON EUROPEAN INSTITUTIONALIZATION

> Whether it be the sweeping eagle in his flight or the open apple-blossom, the toiling work-horse, the blithe swan, the branching oak, the winding stream at its base, the drifting clouds, overall coursing sun, form ever follows function, and that is the law.
>
> Louis Sullivan, "The Tall Office Building Artistically Considered"[1]

CHAPTER 9

COMPARATIVE SUMMARY AND EMPIRICAL RESULTS

On the basis of a most similar case comparison, five policies that were formulated and implemented in the Copenhagen framework have been analyzed in order to identify the conditions under which policy making generates institutionalization processes. Regarding the necessary condition, in all cases under perspective, strong functional pressure was generated by the creation and use of new steering instruments in the Copenhagen framework. The formulation and implementation of policies—notwithstanding their restriction to external states before entering the Union—did not lead to the automatic termination of the policies as the design of the Copenhagen framework foresaw. Member state governments had to respond either by tolerating extended supranational capacities or by actively preempting them. Regarding the sufficient condition, the expected potential for political spillover proved decisive. Accordingly, if new supranational action capacity is limited to nonhierarchical steering instruments, spill-in occurs because it grants member state actors the politically dominant role. However, policies matter beyond the mode of governance because different arenas of power entail different political relationships and modes of conflict resolution. The EU's bias for regulatory and distributive policies is also reflected in the case studies. On the one hand, certain redistributive elements have been nested in the distributive arena. On the other hand, in one case in which a direct spill-in of hard regulation from the enlargement framework was rejected, functional pressure persisted and hard regulation that gave greater emphasis to the political role of national actors pursued a number of years later.

The decisive sufficient condition is hence the containment of political conflict on the supranational level. This is achieved by preempting strong redistributive or fundamental constituent policies and opting for nonhierarchical steering where possible. Moreover, across the case studies we can observe that in all cases, functional pressure leads to some response. In the cases in which the Commission could not expand its action capacity, EU external institutions attained less constraining capacities. Beyond the core period examined here, it shows that where EU external responses did not sufficiently respond to this functional pressure, new hard regulation inside the EU eventually pursued as well. Therefore both the policy type and the mode of governance are relevant to the extension of Commission action capacity that is void of potential for supranational political relationships with citizens.

COMPARATIVE SUMMARY OF THE EMPIRICAL FINDINGS: THE IMPACT OF IMPLEMENTING EASTERN ENLARGEMENT

The very manner in which the Commission framed its competences in the Copenhagen framework was decisive for the further institutionalization of steering capacities beyond the restricted mandate. Policy making generated functional pressure in all cases, yet spill-in depended further on the arena of power and the coerciveness of steering instruments. The way policies were exercised in the Copenhagen framework shaped actor expectations for institutionalization beyond this distinct setting. Against the background of the empirical results, the conclusion that policies matter in EU integration needs to be qualified in three respects. First, nonhierarchical steering instruments are crucial. These are not foreseen in Lowi's typology, which includes formal governmental policies exclusively. For the EU, however, nonbinding regulatory and conditional patronage policies are most likely integrated. Both soft regulation and conditional distribution lower the potential conflict over substantive policy issues in supranational decision-making processes. This has been argued prominently for soft regulation (Ahrne and Brunsson 2004; Schäfer 2006; Sisson and Marginson 2001; Trubek and Trubek 2005). In a similar vein, increases in regional policy resources that were introduced in connection to previous enlargements were tied to conditions; "the main contributing countries ('rich' countries) were only willing to accept this increase under the condition that the main recipient countries would submit to conditions about how to spend these resources" (van der Beek and Neal 2004: 591). The case of administrative capacity building falls into this trend and takes the usage of conditional patronage policies to a new qualitative level. Second and linked to this, nesting regulatory and redistributive policy objectives in the distributive arena emerges as a reoccurring pattern. Policies are framed as being distributive on the EU level, mostly in the European Regional and Social Funds, but are linked to conditions that produce regulatory or redistributive implications for the member states. Third, throughout the cases we can observe the important role of other international organizations, as well as networks of private actors as alternative forums that offer less coercive cooperation outside the EU. In all cases, the member state governments responded in one way or another to functional pressure. In the cases in which a response inside the EU could be expected to create new political relationships and, hence, create a move of not only functional policies but substantive political problems to the supranational level, alternative forums outside the EU were opted for to preempt the emergence of new political processes, structures, and relationships.

I will recap the five cases to summarize the results depicted in Table 9.1. The manner in which policies were framed in the Copenhagen framework was decisive; steering instruments that were institutionalized beyond enlargement were derived from those developed between 1993 and 2004.

Table 9.1   Framing of steering instruments in pre-accession phase and beyond

Policy Issue	Copenhagen Framework	Acquis Communautaire
Administrative Capacity	Regulatory Policy *monitoring SIGMA standards*	
	Distributive Policy *assistance, especially twinning*	Distributive Arena *nested regulatory & redistributive policies*
Cross-Border Cooperation	Distributive Policy *assistance lowering borders old/new & new/new member states*	Distributive Arena *all member states eligible*
Minority Protection	Regulatory Policy *monitoring internationally standards*	Regulatory Arena *nonhierarchical steering instruments*
	Distributive Policy *assistance focused esp. on Roma*	Distributive Arena *all member states eligible*
Nuclear Safety	Regulatory Policy *monitoring based on Euratom*	–
Anti-corruption	Regulatory Policy *monitoring based intended EU law*	–

Source: own table.

Notably, what is by and large considered to be the Commission's most powerful tool—the initiation of legal acts—was not available in the enlargement context. Instead, the Commission was restricted to monitoring compliance and offering assistance to support accession states to achieve desired policy goals. First, as basis for *monitoring* as a tool for compliance control, standards and benchmarks had to be set (van den Broek 1999). These could only partially be derived from the formal acquis. Transposing the Copenhagen criteria into concrete policies within the boundaries of limited treaty competences was congruent for all cases under perspective. The Commission drew foremost on international standards by other international organizations and those that were accepted by its member states. However, it occasionally demanded that the candidate states comply with agreements that not all member states were parties of.[2] Moreover, standards that had evolved on an informal basis had almost an obligatory meaning for the candidate states against the background of accession conditionality, which gave formally "soft" instruments a "hard" bearing (Wiener 2002). Given the limited human resources of the Commission to monitor on the ground, it established networks, including national administrations, governments, EU delegations, international organizations, and nongovernmental actors, to provide the relevant information for the Regular Reports. Later in the process, the Regular Reports were complemented by bilateral *Accession Partnerships,* in which the Commission defined goals to be achieved together with each single state. Backed by accession conditionality, the Regular Reports and Accession Partnerships were a forceful steering instrument to exercise coercion on the candidate states, at least in the earlier phases of the pre-accession period. In short, to realize the monitoring task, the Commission drafted rules, set benchmarks and defined standards of a regulatory nature, and, in collaboration with other international bodies, built up elaborate networks inside the candidate states to gather information on compliance.

Second, financial and technical *assistance* was given to support the candidate states in meeting the accession criteria. To prepare the candidate states for participation in the EU's Structural and Agricultural Policies, Phare, the main assistance program, was complemented by ISPA and SAPARD. Soon after its creation, after an initial period in which technical assistance was provided rather unsuccessfully by external agencies, *twinning* (delegation of member state officials to candidate state administrations) became the most important instrument. One of the Commission's major concerns that underpinned the distribution of both technical and financial assistance was preventing abuse of EU resources. Thus, disbursement of funds was partially conditional upon the implementation capacities of the recipient state, a reason for which SAPARD's disbursement was considerably delayed. In essence, while political problems that are prone to be framed in the regulatory arena featured strongly in the Commission's pre-accession monitoring, the distributive elements were developed in the pre-accession assistance programs. Backed by conditionality, distribution was linked to concrete commitments from the candidate states. Thus, by asking for legal and institutional adaptations in return for EU funding, policy objectives with regulatory implications on the state level were nested into the distributive arena.

To highlight the conditions that apply to the cases in which competences spill into the acquis, the distinguishing features of the two clusters of cases can be fleshed out recapitulating how monitoring and assistance were realized in the Copenhagen framework. Although tackling sensitive issues on minorities, external borders, and national public administrations, all three policies were framed inside the Copenhagen framework in such a manner that the Commission could further integrate policy tools because the level of potential political conflict was kept low. New supranational instruments were framed as nonbinding regulation, in legal grey areas or as distributive policies. Markedly, the regulatory rules that were the basis for monitoring minority policy and administrative capacities included in the Copenhagen framework remained distinct from the formalized competences of the acquis. In the case of administrative capacity building, the Commission relied on the so-called SIGMA baseline criteria to define monitoring benchmarks. Accordingly, the EU did not develop internal EU standards on what marks the efficiency and efficacy of national administrations (Court of Auditors 2003a: 7; Grabbe 2001). Instead, the Commission applied the standards developed externally in the joint program of the OECD and the EU, which was formally placed in the former but funded mostly by the latter. With respect to minority policy, the EU relied mostly on an internal handbook that had been drafted for this very purpose and that listed standards and benchmarks likewise derived from international agreements (Heidbreder and Carrasco 2003). Although a genuine antidiscrimination acquis was created in the Amsterdam Treaty (1996), no Community competences on collective minority rights were institutionalized, such as those considered in the accession criteria. Therefore, the double standards nature of the minority criterion persisted throughout (Amato and Batt 1998a; Open Society Institute 2002a; Wiener and Schwellnus 2004).

The closer accession drew, claims for creating formal competences to continue the monitoring that had been deemed successful were made both with respect to minority policy (European Parliament 2005; Open Society Institute 2002a) and national public administrations (Verheijen

2000: 56). However, the extension of rules to all member states was successful precisely because regulatory elements were framed without creating new treaty bases that would have formally moved sensitive issues to the EU level. Instead, the Commission silently stretched the meaning of existing rules with respect to its monitoring competences on the minority policies of all member states, thereby clearly moving into a legal grey area, given that explicit minority competences remain absent from the treaties (De Witte 2004: 110). Furthermore, some nonbinding regulatory policies emerged in connection with the creation of the European Monitoring Centre for Racism and Xenophobia (EUMC; since 2007, European Union's Fundamental Rights Agency). In turn, the standards and benchmarks of administrative performance remained external. The continuation of supranational steering into national public administration was achieved by keeping criteria within the SIGMA realm, while inside the EU, informal networks between governments and government agencies were strengthened to promote voluntary cooperation along nonbinding administrative standards. Most notably, the empirical analysis revealed the nesting of policies in less conflicting arenas of power. The distribution of financial assistance to the so-called *convergence regions* and *cohesion countries* (relatively poorest regions of the EU) within the European Social Fund was bound to obligations in enhancing national administrative efficiency (Council of the European Union 2006a, b; European Parliament and Council 2006a, b). Recipient states must prioritize administrative capacity building as one of their programming targets in order to benefit from EU funds. As previously seen in the Accession Partnerships, the precise conditions are bilaterally negotiated between each state and the Commission. Moreover, the new principle of *transnationality* obliges states to include interstate exchange on technical matters, basically copying and extending the *twinning* program. Since benefits are limited to the poorest member states, the effect is also redistributive in favor of the new member states, while general redistribution to the new member states was never seriously considered (Ivanova 2007: 351). Since benefits are bound to conditions, the Commission continues to have limited regulatory leverage on how the new member states organize their public administrations.

The distributive arena and the use of technical and financial assistance as instruments showed the further importance of the supranational steering of policies that were potentially politically contentious. Of the five cases that were looked at, cross-border cooperation in the Copenhagen framework was most strongly dominated by assistance. This is not very surprising given the highly political nature of the foreign policy issues that cross-border cooperation embraced, leaving no room for formulating pre-accession demands in regulatory terms. Accordingly, the tool—already used when cooperation within the Copenhagen framework was formulated and implemented—was to offer assistance that targeted particular objectives the EU was eager to promote. The vital extension of capacities derived from the redefinition of cross-border cooperation. From a purely interior policy to lower internal borders, it was transformed to an instrument to stabilize external borders. Although in fact, in dealing with sensitive foreign policy issues, the Commission could extend its capacities because cross-border policy was framed as a straightforward distributive policy that was generally open to all member states and external states along the growing periphery. Beyond enlargement, much of the staff that had developed the pre-accession cross-border program transferred to the European Neighborhood Policy and was successful in convincing the member states of the practical usefulness of applying the same formally distributive instruments in this new framework. Similarly, without creating substantive new supranational authority, the pre-accession assistance programs for minority groups, targeted especially at Roma minorities, were extended to benefit member states as well (Commission of the European Communities 2003e). As for cross-border initiatives, the funds have no special conditions, and all member states are eligible for them. The maintenance of distributive assistance instruments in administrative capacity building differed slightly from minority protection and cross-border cooperation. While in the first case, regulatory elements were nested into the distributive arena, thus allowing for a limited continuation of control over a restricted number of recipient states, in the second and third cases, distribution was open to all member states without special conditions. Yet, in all three cases, the substantive areas opened up new policy spheres that formally remain outside of the Commission's competences: national public administrations, foreign and security policy concerns in stabilizing external borders, and collective minority protection and rights in the member states. In a nutshell, the spill-in of steering capacities was successful because the potentially highly contentious politics linked to the substantive policy issues were circumvented by framing issues as low-key soft regulation or distribution. On the one hand, the regulatory elements developed to monitor the candidate states were not explicitly bound to new formal competences. The Commission acts upon external standards or a little noted reinterpretation of the treaties, arguing very much along practical or functional lines to achieve certain necessities and avoiding claims about new formal treaty competences. On the other hand, distributive policies were used to address sensitive issues not only by opening benefits to all member states, but also by linking assistance to conditions. Thus, the administrative functions in regional and social funds equip the Commission with certain powers to prescribe and control issues that are formally under national authority exclusively.

Contrastingly, in the two cases in which new supranational steering capacities were actively preempted, policies had already generated palpable potential for conflict over formal authority in the Copenhagen framework. The formulation of monitoring standards in the cases of nuclear safety and anticorruption was contentious because, from the outset, the Commission framed issues as broad regulatory concerns of general scope. Neither soft regulation nor nesting issues in the distributive arena were feasible, but institutionalization beyond the enlargement context inevitably resulted in new binding regulation and a formal extension of treaty competences. In the case of nuclear safety, open conflict had already erupted during the pre-accession phase. Faced with the task of monitoring nuclear installations in the candidate states, the Commission argued that *Euratom* included such a responsibility, although the treaty had never before been interpreted in this wide a meaning. In reaction, the Council withdrew the monitoring task from the Commission and delegated it to a newly founded agency of national operators, WENRA (Western European Nuclear Regulators' Association 2000). However, in a dispute over the accession to the International Atomic Entergy Agency (IAEA) Nuclear Safety Convention, the European Court of Justice backed the Commission's wide reading of Euratom (European Court of Justice 2002) and judged that also monitoring under the auspices of the Council confirmed the Community's competence. The Commission now pushed forward even further, proposing the *nuclear package,* a set of legal acts that would have formalized a large body of nonbinding acquis and would have enforced the legally binding interpretation of "nuclear safety" in the Euratom Treaty along the lines applied to the candidate states and confirmed by the ECJ (Commission of the European Communities 2004a). Yet, despite the ECJ judgment and calls by the European Parliament and other EU bodies (European Economic and Social Committee 2003), the Council blocked all initiatives to create binding legislation. Instead, WENRA and the IAEA were promoted as sufficient, if not better, alternatives to Community activity. The functional response of the less binding—and also, apparently less efficient—nature outside the EU was opted for to preempt a reinterpretation of Euratom that would have expanded the definition of "nuclear safety" significantly, even if into less politically sensitive fields than the already integrated competences on nuclear proliferation. There was no plausible option and evidently also no strategy in DG TREN to frame the matter as soft regulation or nest regulation in a distributive guise for two reasons. First, the Commission had, for the first time ever, drafted an inventory of the extensive nonbinding acquis in the policy field (Commission of the European Communities 2000a). It was therefore clear that an elaborate body of soft law already existed. Second, the fact that much of the soft law was referred to in the pre-accession context led to claims that these needed to be rendered binding for all member states. Although we can conclude that there was no direct spill-in of action capacity from the Copenhagen framework, hard regulation ensued in 2009. Two features about the regulation eventually passed that are decisive for this outcome. First, in contrast to the earlier draft regulations, the 2009 regulation strengthens national regulators in order to ensure the safety of nuclear installations. It therefore leaves the politically contentious matters to the member state level. Second, the weakness of the alternative international instruments did not provide a functional equivalent to the hardening of the EU's informal acquis, and thus, in the midterm, opting for EU external functional responses was not sufficient.

In this last point, it is relevant that the nuclear safety case differs from anticorruption policy, where other international organizations have so far provided sufficient functional responses. As a matter of fact, the Commission withdrew the initiatives before open conflict erupted, referring to solutions offered by other international organizations, although it had attempted to create binding anticorruption regulation for a considerable time before being called on to monitor the candidate states. Consequently, new steering capacities beyond the Copenhagen framework were framed in these terms. In 2003, though, the Commission inverted its approach of a more global anticorruption policy that had till then not been very successful. It changed its tune and argued for other international organization such as the Group of States against Corruption (GRECO), initiated in 1999 by the Council of Europe, to take a more prominent role, instead of further EU action, and listed quite the reverse concrete anticorruption measures in reference to the candidate states (Commission of the European Communities 2003b: 5). That the member states did not consider GRECO to be a *fully* effective substitute for regulation inside the EU is reflected by the fact that, for the two latest entrants, double standards are upheld even after accession. Without institutionalizing uniform regulatory policies, the Commission continues to monitor Romania and Bulgaria in criminal matters and corruption only, which thus offers a sufficient functional response to the political problem at stake. Neither in the nuclear safety nor in the anticorruption case was assistance put in the foreground or extended to the member states. Although the EU also invested funds in the areas of nuclear safety and anticorruption policies in the candidate states, the main thrust of the policies during the pre-accession phase was clearly regulatory, and hence institutionalization outside the

Copenhagen framework needed to be expected to be of a binding regulatory nature. The fact that the Commission framed these issues as policies that needed strongly binding Community regulation and could not be covered by external instruments—such as with administrative standards and minority rights—led to strong reactions by the member states. They successfully preempted new supranational steering instruments, even if a policy was of little political salience, could meet wide popular support, or could formally be derived from the treaties, despite considerable functional pressure at the moment of accession.

Table 9.2 maps out the necessary and sufficient conditions for spill-in. The necessary condition, functional pressure, was met in all cases. The sufficient condition, containment of expected political spillover, was met fully in the first three cases in which capacities were framed as nonhierarchical regulatory or distributive policies. Comparing this with the second group of cases brings to the fore that the expected institutionalization of binding regulatory policies could not satisfy the sufficient condition. Staying within the time frame of the immediate aftermath of eastern enlargement, the comparison of cases suggests that the nonhierarchical mode of governance was actually the decisive intervening variable. However, looking beyond the direct effect of implementing enlargement, in the nuclear safety case, hard regulation ensued in 2009. Moreover, the administrative capacity case showed that regulatory and redistributive objectives were nested in the distributive arena of power. This indicates that the policy type itself is relevant. We can therefore conclude that functional pressure is a necessary condition for the institutionalization of supranational steering capacities. Whether responses to functional pressure will emerge within or outside

Table 9.2 Necessary and sufficient conditions for Spill-in

	Necessary Condition	Sufficient Conditions	
	Functional Pressure	Nonhierarchical Instruments	Policy Type: Regulatory/Distributive
Administrative Capacity	X	X	Distributive
Minority Protection	X	X	Distributive
Cross-Border Cooperation	X	X	Distributive soft regulation
Nuclear Safety	X	–	(Hard regulation)
Anti-Corruption	X	–	–

Source: own table.

Table 9.3   Variance across policy issues and treaty bases

	Policy field	EU competence
Administrative Capacity	Internal state administration	No pillar
Minority Protection	Internal human rights	Third pillar
Cross-Border Cooperation	Foreign policy (border security, migration)	Second pillar
Nuclear Safety	Internal security	Euratom
Anti-Corruption	Internal affairs	Third pillar

Source: own table.

the EU acquis depends on the expected political relationships and thus the potential for political spillover that these new steering instruments imply. If nonhierarchical steering instruments are at stake, spill-in will generally ensue. If hierarchical steering instruments are at stake, the policy arena and the availability of satisfactory functional alternatives are decisive. Generally, the policy type and the political relationship these imply are decisive, not the policy issue in terms of high or low political salience.

Taking up the last point, Table 9.3 illustrates that whether a policy falls into an intergovernmental or a supranational EU pillar does not provide an alternative explanation. The population of cases does not allow for a systematic most different case comparison, but we can compare policies that concern different contentious political issues within and across the two groups of cases. The findings indicate, first, that all policy issues were outside the Commission's core competences and linked to treaty bases either in the second (foreign policy) or in the third (justice and home affairs) pillar, cannot be linked to any of the pillars, or fall under the equally intergovernmental Euratom Treaty. Second, within the group of cases in which action capacity was extended, the qualitative analysis did not show systematic differences between policies concerned with internal state organization, domestic human rights, and foreign policy. The cross-border cooperation case is particularly remarkable. Giving the Commission access to capacities on genuine foreign policy issues should, according to content, be one of the politically most contentious issues. Yet, the way in which the policy was framed as distributive made it one of the least contentious policies of the pre-accession framework and made the European Neighborhood Policy directly extend to it. Third, if we compare the two cases in which, at the moment of accession, no extended action capacity occurred, the fact that both cases fell under clearly intergovernmental EU rules seems, at first sight, to confirm the dominant role of member state governments in limiting the Commission's pre-accession competences to the initial boundaries. The nuclear safety case should have actually been of little political contention, since it was concerned with technical security matters that were even covered by Euratom. Again, the framing of the policy proved decisive since an extension of capacities as (at that point in time) pushed for by the Commission implied a significant disempowerment of national actors. The fact that anticorruption is a sensitive issue of internal politics that falls under the third pillar does not explain that integration was preempted by relying on agents external to the EU, since the same should apply for minority protection, a policy equally sensitive internally for which a number of alternative international agreements outside the EU could have been opted for instead. Even though the data do not provide a more elaborate comparison in a most different case design, the comparison within and across the two cluster of cases leads to the conclusion that the expected potential for political spillover clearly did not depend on the policy content but the policy type and mode of governance a policy was framed as.

ORGANIZATIONAL AND INSTITUTIONAL IMPLICATIONS: CHANGING THE COMMISSION'S CAPACITIES

The institutionalization of new action capacity has further institutional implications. The "creeping competence" extension of the Commission implies a vertical and horizontal calibration of powers in the polity. Moreover, capacities that spill in from the Copenhagen framework need to be integrated in the existing organizational structure and, hence, influence the organizational development of the Commission.

To account for the inter-organizational role of the Commission, simultaneous processes of reform and overriding change in the two dimensions need to be considered simultaneously. Overall, the effects of implementing enlargement fit the broader trends and directions into which the Commission kept extending its steering capacities. Most authors attest that the Commission has a less prominent role as an initiator of legislation (see for example: Jones 2000: 185; Rasmussen 2007) and the view prevails that it has been losing political weight in relation to the European Parliament and Councils (Bauer 2008: 627). Other authors sustain that rather than witnessing a decline in Commission power, the Commission's formal responsibilities have shifted and, "therefore, all four of the EU's major institutions play important roles that are reminiscent of those of legislatures (the Council and the Parliament), bureaucracies (the Commission), and legal systems (the Court) in national polities with bicameral legislatures (such as Germany)" (Tsebelis and Garrett 2001: 359). Peterson further finds "signs that the Commission has begun to accept that it must invest in assets that do not flow directly from its formal treaty powers, and that many of Europe's most important problems resist solutions through traditional Community legislation. . . . To illustrate the point, it was revealing that officials in the services learned, as a strategy for getting the College to back whatever project they were working on, to link it to the Lisbon agenda" (Peterson 2008: 774). These assessments are echoed clearly in the five case studies. The Commission keeps playing a vital role among the EU organizations by promoting less traditional Community legislation but exploiting the legal fringes offered by distributive or nonbinding policy instruments, which are predominantly instruments promoted by the Lisbon agenda. Widening reinforced this trend, so "there was no question but that the Commission showed a stronger predisposition toward non-traditional, non-legislative modes of regulating, not least in response to enlargement" (Peterson and Birdsall 2008: 72). Despite the fact that the stronger emphasis on subsidiarity and proportionality have made the Commission president Jacques Santer adopt "the slogan of doing less but doing it better" (Jones 2000: 185), it shows that for the actual policy delivery, functional pressure continues to lead to an increase in the Commission's capacities. As long as no apparent political stakes stay in the member states' realm, functional needs are responded to on the EU level, which makes its competences ever more "creeping."

Turning to impacts on the Commission's internal organization, for a capacity to spill in, it had to be placed into an existing Directorate General after enlargement. Implementing enlargement coincided with the most relevant organizational reform the Commission has seen so far: the Kinnock reform of 2000 (Balint, Bauer et al. 2008; Ellinas and Suleiman 2008; Kassim 2008; Kinnock 2004; Schön-Quinlivan 2008). This reform does not, however, play a relevant role in tracing the instruments that were developed in the enlargement context come across by other organizational units of the Commission. Since enlargement policy is horizontal in nature, basically every DG is involved and provides specialized knowledge under the coordinating leadership of DG Enlargement. Accordingly, sectoral responsibilities had already been established during the pre-accession phase and were integrated incrementally as they evolved.[3] The most eminent organizational change was the dominance of enlargement policy that emerged as the Commission's flagship policy. An independent DG took on the task previously dealt with by a unit located in DG1 External Relations. Since 1999, Günther Verheugen was the first Commissioner for the single-standing DG Enlargement into which DG 1A and the Task Force for Accession Negotiations (TFAN) were merged. Nugent and Saurugger point out that "[m]ost DG 1A officials were unhappy with the proposed new arrangement when it was announced, believing it amounted to a 'victory' for the TFAN over DG 1A in what had become a fierce internal struggle for control on the enlargement issue. However, there was nothing they could do to prevent the restructuring given the increased importance of enlargement on the EU's agenda and given also that Prodi saw the new DG as a key component element of his overall reform programme" (2002: 355–56). DG Enlargement rose to become one of the most influential units in the Commission under Günther Verheugen's leadership by attaining the responsibility for the Union's new Neighborhood Policy in 2003. Its importance was down-graded again with the accession of the bulk of candidate states in 2004, which reduced the DG's workload, if not in part because of its raison d'être as a single Directorate General, especially with the reinforced ENP having been reallocated to DG External Relations in 2004. In 2005, Olli Rehn was appointed Commissioner of the downsized DG Enlargement. A considerable number of officials who had been involved in enlargement have moved to other DGs. Officials working on all levels of the ENP have an especially strong enlargement policy background (Interviews DG External Relations 2007, see also: Kelley 2006: 32), which was of tangible importance for policy instruments to be transferred from the enlargement to the neighborhood policy. In sum, the reshuffling of personnel and responsibilities in the creation and downsizing of DG Enlargement had a sizable effect in the traveling of policy instruments in cross-border cooper-ation, while other capacities had already been developed in the respective sectoral DGs during the pre-accession phase.

Less persistently, some modest attempts to use horizontal structures—crucial for implementing enlargement—aimed at increasing interservice cooperation can be observed, foremost where the Commission could not realize any proper steering capacities. However, one cannot gen-erally sustain direct causal links between the organizational structures among Commission services and the extension of policy capacities. Nei-ther can the continuation of steering activities beyond the Copenhagen framework explain horizontal linkages across DGs, nor are inter-service networks a sufficient cause for the extension of a policy. Above all, the Commission's own resources are too limited to amount to institu-tionalized steering capacities as long as member states do not agree to some form of cooperation within the EU framework. In any instance, member state governments remain the most important actors for the allocation of political authority on the supranational level. Yet, it can be argued that the extensive involvement in the horizontal enlargement policy nurtured some attempts to strengthen links between Commission services. This finding is especially supported by the case on anticorruption policy in which interservice cooperation was upheld and further pro-moted by DG Justice, Freedom and Security. Unlike nuclear safety, for which DG *TREN*'s competence had already been curtailed during the implementation of enlargement, anticorruption policy was exercised and improved throughout the entire pre-accession phase. In contrast to the intensification of the supranational leverage within the Copenhagen framework, a decreasingly coercive approach toward member states crystallized. Notwithstanding the continuing absence of substantive steering instruments, the lead DG tried to continue promoting anticorruption issues in a less tangible way, namely, through attempts to mainstream anticorruption issues across the Commission services. In this vein, benchmarks developed as a pre-accession tool and were used to disperse anticorruption awareness across various DGs, the most promising field of application being EU external policies in the ENP framework (Interview DG JLF 2007), the legal thrust of which remains very restricted, however. Mainstreaming is equally applied but has more force in areas in which new steering capacities were integrated. For example, minority protection has been made a priority in social and educational programs, and "administrative efficiency" is mainstreamed across the European Social Funds.

Also, on the basis of its own resources, especially the matters for which it has no direct monitoring task, the Commission has promoted the development of comparable statistics. Corruption has been chosen as a pilot area for the development of more sound statistical data on public opinion in the criminal area (European Commission 2006, 2008, 2009). Such improved recording of statistical data as a tool to increase the Commission's knowledge on single policies in the member states can be observed in other areas as well. More than that, as in anticorruption policy, we see a tendency to refer to statistics strategically. Concerning minority policy and nuclear safety, references to public opinion are put forward as an argument in support of more Commission involvement in the regulatory arena. However, in the distributive policies—which are less susceptible to public opinion—there is no evidence that related data has been used to strategically promote the Commission's responsibilities. In short, the Commission's own resources to mainstream issues or address citizens directly by creating statistics in areas in which it has no monitoring task are very weak and do not amount to steering capacities of tangible meaning if not placed into the framework of at least voluntary cooperation between member states. Although the creation of DG Enlargement and the implementation of the horizontal enlargement policy had immediate organizational implications, it seems not to have altered the interservice cooperation more substantively, and the Commission's own resources to mainstream policy objectives or raise public awareness through comparable statistics appear insufficient to indeed create direct political relationships with citizens in the absence of more substantive steering capacities.

In addition to these ramifications that affect the Commission directly, the empirical studies underscore the significant role of other international organizations and private networks outside the EU. On the one hand, member states actively promote private networks and refer to less binding international instruments as alternatives to unwanted EU regulation. On the other hand, international organizations may be dealing with similar or overlapping issues. While in the case of anticorruption policy, this resulted in real conflicts over responsibilities, a more cooperative agreement emerged with respect to minority policy. In both cases, some kind of division of labor and responsibilities was defined. Because of the upcoming enlargement, the EU, for the first time, got deeply and openly involved in areas outside its core competences in economic matters that were tackled by the United Nations, the Council of Europe, and the OSCE for decades. Therefore, implementing enlargement was also a driver to distinguish the boundaries of EU responsibilities either by extending or by limiting capacities in relation to external actors. Besides the need to delineate EU responsibilities from other international organizations, a reason for the definition of the EU's legal boundaries was the sheer need to fill the accession criteria with meaning. The illusive initial mandate by the member states implied that the Commission had to derive clearly applicable rules from the incrementally grown body of EU primary and secondary law.[4] The *Common Market White Paper* (Commission of the European Communities 1995) is a key document in this respect because it was the first document in which the Commission offered a definition of the actual contents to the applicant states. Beyond this, the white paper has advanced to become a general point of reference to define and rank the constituent elements of the acquis. The broader institutional implications of implementing enlargement go therefore well beyond the internal organization of the Commission itself. Rather, they concern the inter-organizational balance in which enlargement strengthened more general trends of changing inter-institutional relationships, as well as Commission's role vis-à-vis external organizations that had to be defined more precisely as the EU entered policy fields previously dominated by other international organizations.

CHAPTER 10

CONCLUSION: POLICY-GENERATED INSTITUTIONALIZATION

Policies matter for the course of European integration. They matter because particular arenas of power and modes of governance imply specific political relationships and therefore different actor constellations and procedures to resolve political conflicts. Whether policy-making capacities are conferred to supranational agents depends on the expected political clout that will move to the EU level. Therefore, what primarily matters is not policies because of the eventual outcomes a single policy produces or the policy field it covers. Instead, policies matter depending on the policy type a single policy is famed in when formulated and accordingly the expectation policy makers attach to it. The EU continues to have a bias for regulatory and distributive over redistributive policies. This bias is reinforced by new modes of governance, which offer policy instruments that create common policies that avoid a shift in the political debate and substantive political contestation to the EU level in each of the four arenas of power. This reflects a perpetuation of what Schmidt has characterized as interest representation and governance for (and not by) the people, which "makes for *policy without politics* at the EU level" (2006: 156). Given an increasing number of policy problems that are dealt with commonly, national politicians must have an interest to hold on to politics in the domestic realm—the EU may provide action and policies; talk, legitimacy, and politics should stay national (cf. generally: Brunsson 1989). Analyzing conflict management in EU regulation, Mabbett and Schelkle explain in a similar vein that "EU regulatory processes solve policy problems formulated in terms of efficiency, they neglect problems that cannot be framed in this way" (2009: 712). While regulatory processes are generally political by nature, EU regulation is marked by "the paradox that it is essential for regulation that politics is suppressed. Regulatory decision-making aims for consensus rather than controversy; regulatory policy issues are framed as functional problems; regulatory venues exclude party-political representation and contestation" (Mabbett and Schelkle 2009: 700). Put in theoretical terms, member state governments do indeed react to functional pressure, but the condition to do so within the EU framework creates low expectations about a potential political spillover. Therefore, the choices of an arena of power and mode of governance are decisive for the extension of supranational capacities.

LEGITIMACY AND CONTESTATION: NORMATIVE IMPLICATIONS

The relevance of policy arenas explains why we can observe that certain policy objectives are framed in particular terms. These strategies raise normative questions about the accountability and legitimacy of EU policies. The framing of the regulatory objectives as nonbinding rules and in the guise of conditional patronage policies moves policy making to the fringes of formal competences. The evidence supports the conclusion that "subterfuge" in policy making "constitutes a structural feature of the European Union—given the diversity of its members and their inability to agree on the direction in which the polity should develop, with the exception that they are unwilling to relinquish sovereignty" (Héritier 1999: 97). Sharing the view that "the emergence of such escape routes has indeed become second nature to European policy-making in all its interlinked arenas" (Héritier 1999: 97) entails inevitable consequences for democracy and the rule of law. Disconnecting political contestation, at the national level, from actual policy-making capacities, on the EU level, by circumventing a formal conferral of powers, implies that third-party control by the European Court of Justice or European Parliament is discarded. Control is limited to direct oversight by the member states. Implementing enlargement has been another source to widen Community capacities without creating clear new formal powers. In consequence, authority does not only have to become more blurred regarding relationships between policy makers and policy takers. The nesting of policies into less contentious arenas of power on the EU level obscures part of the potentially affected societal conflicts to circumvent contestation and, at the same time, arenas for representation. In addition to the evident questions this nesting raises in terms of input legitimacy, questions may also be asked in terms of the output legitimacy of supranational steering instruments that are not linked to formalized competences and therefore lack the necessary shadow of hierarchy to produce tangible outcomes (Börzel 2008; Héritier and Lehmkuhl 2008; Idema and Kelemen 2006; Scharpf 1993). The empirical findings therefore pose two challenges to legitimacy. Besides familiar critiques of the legitimizing value of new modes of governance such as nonbinding regulation and voluntary cooperation (de la Porte 2002; Smismans 2006, 2008), circumventing political contestation by nesting political objectives into distributive EU policies is a new form of "subterfuge" that widens the structural gap in political relationships between EU policy-makers and individual citizens further.

CONDITIONS OF POLICY-GENERATED INSTITUTIONALIZATION

At the outset, the book raised three questions motivated by an empirical puzzle. First, why were some policies extended beyond the Copenhagen enlargement framework while others remained, as designed, restricted to the pre-accession policy? Tracing the formulation and implementation of five policies highlighted that the way a policy was framed in the Copenhagen pre-accession framework shaped the expectations for an extension of member state governments. In all cases, functional pressure emerged, yet, member states either tolerated a further involvement of the Commission or actively pushed for solutions outside the EU. The extension of action capacity does not automatically follow from functional pressure, but depends on strategic actor choices that are shaped by their expectations. Second, under which conditions does widening of the European Union cause deepening within the European Union? The conditions identified are functional pressure (necessary condition) and the containment of expected political spillover (sufficient condition). The sufficient condition has been operationalized by underpinning neofunctional theory with theoretically consistent microfoundations. Accordingly, assuming that policies determine politics, different policy types imply different political relationships and, correspondingly, different expectations on potential political spillover. In addition, the mode of governance is decisive because nonhierarchical steering grants more political leeway to the member states than hierarchical supranational rule. Framing a policy in a particular arena of power and applying a particular mode of governance therefore satisfies the sufficient conditions. Third, what effect does the implementing enlargement have on the European Union itself? Implementing enlargement has served as a catalyst for a further, creeping extension of the Commission's action capacity. The wider trends in the Commission's organizational development, namely, a more formally pronounced administration and executive rather than a controversial political entrepreneurial role, are supported by the results. The empirical study illustrated that actual policy making triggers further integration: the exercise of policies, even if designed to terminate automatically, creates functional pressure to incorporate steering instruments further and thus increases the likelihood of further supranational institutionalization. Conceptualizing the Copenhagen pre-accession framework as a distinct institutional setting suggests that we should expect similar dynamics from policy making in other institutional subsets that create rules of restricted applicability. The Lisbon Treaty increases the possibility of *enhanced cooperation* in order to offer more flexibility for cooperation in the enlarged Union. Hence, we might see more policy-generated institutionalization and ever more creeping competences in the years to come.

NOTES

CHAPTER 1

1. Quoted from Schattschneider 1975: v.
2. Founded by six member states, the European Community/Union enlarged in four waves: 1973 (northern enlargement) Denmark, Ireland, and the United Kingdom; 1981/86 (southern/Mediterranean round) Greece (1981), Portugal and Spain (1986); 1995 (EFTA states) Austria, Finland, and Sweden; 2004/07 (eastern enlargement) Cyprus, Czech Republic, Estonia, Hungary, Lithuania, Latvia, Malta, Poland, Slovakia, Slovenia (2004), Bulgaria and Romania (2007). Currently, Croatia, the former Yugoslav Republic of Macedonia, and Turkey have formal candidate state status; potential further candidate states are Albania, Bosnia and Herzegovina, Kosovo, Montenegro, and Serbia.
3. The explicit mention of the issue of administrative structures was essential to tackle the evident gap between a mere legal adaptation of EU laws without actual sufficient implementation, a consideration that gained increasing relevance in the later phases of the pre-accession period as repeatedly emphasised by the Commission: "While it is important that European Community legislation is transposed into national legislation, it is even more important that the legislation is implemented effectively through appropriate administrative and judicial structures. This is a prerequisite of the mutual trust required by EU membership" (Commission of the European Communities 2003d).
4. The Treaty of Lisbon clarified the status of supranational competences as exclusive (the Union can independently pass directives and conclude international agreements), shared (member states cannot exercise competences if the Union has done so), and supporting (the Union can support, coordinate, or supplement member states' actions). Under Title I (Article 2E) *Categories and Areas of Union Competence,* the Lisbon Treaty defines supportive competences of the EU in contrast to exclusive and shared competences.

CHAPTER 2

1. Quoted from Lowi (1988: xi).
2. I refer in particular to the following authors: Moe 1990, 1984; Epstein and O'Halloran 1994, 1999a, b; Banks and Weingast 1992; McCubbins et al. 1987.

3. To name but a few studies applying a principal-agent approach to the EU: Kelemen 2002; Kassim and Menon 2002; Thatcher 2002; Bradbury 2003; König and Junge 2006; Franchino 2005; Blom-hansen 2005; Pollack 2003; Kassim and Menon 2003; Hug 2003; Franchino and Rahming 2003; Wilks and Bartle 2002; Thatcher and Stone Sweet 2002; Tallberg 2002; Pollack 2002; Majone 2001a, b, 2002; Franchino 2001, 2000; Stone Sweet and Caporaso 1998; Pollack 1997, 1998.

4. Of the contributions not discussed but overall relevant for the development of neofunctionalism in its various variants, especially the work by Lindberg needs to be mentioned (Lindberg 1963, 1965, 1966, 1967; and in particular the edited volume Lindberg and Scheingold 1971).

5. In reverse, the arenas of power approach cannot explain why issues appear on the institutionalization agenda, but they can explain why issues will be further institutionalized or not once they are defined in an institutional sub-system and generate functional pressure; neofunctionalism cannot explain why a particular policy that comes under functional pressure will be integrated or not, yet it renders plausible when and why such functional pressure emerges in institutional subsystems and therefore raises the likelihood for integration. Given that the neofunctional proposition holds, i.e., the implementation of enlargement raises the functional pressure to integrate the competences the Commission had vis-à-vis the candidate states, the remaining question is why this functional pressure leads to institutionalization in one but not another case.

6. The most repeated criticisms in this respect are (1) the ambiguity of the typology in that the different types are not mutually exclusive (Greenberg et al. 1977: 71x; Wilson 1973: 328), and (2) the static nature of the categories while the political relationships are dynamic and adaptive (Heclo 1972: 105). Still, especially for the EU, in which the multidimensionality of policies is indeed often reduced to those elements that overlap with the Union's competences (most evidently in the division of foreign policy in "external relations" and "Common Foreign and Security Policy," but also social policy where only those elements linkable to economic concerns in the regulatory or distributive arena are communitarized), we can assert with Heckathorn and Maser that the "original appeal of the typology lay in its robust descriptiveness—most policies fit rather comfortably within the original typology's four cells" (Heckathorn and Master 1990: 1119).

7. See in particular their suggestively adapted argument as presented in the five editions of *Policy-Making in the European Union* (Wallace et al. 2005).

8. The Lisbon Agenda, also known as Lisbon Strategy or Lisbon Process, is an action and development plan for the European Union. Initiated by the European Council of Lisbon in 2000, the process aims at making the EU "the most dynamic and competitive knowledge-based economy in the world capable of sustainable economic growth with more and better jobs and greater social cohesion, and respect for the environment by 2010" (European Council 2000b: I.5).

9. Changing this by revising Article 48 TEU on Treaty revisions to allow an easier procedure, as proposed in the little lucky so-called "Penelope" proposal by R. Prodi (Commission of the European Communities 2002a). The idea was outwardly rejected in the Constitutional Convention by particularly one member state—yet on the basis of a more widespread agreement between member states that this would imply and undesirable weakening of the direct control by member states (De Witte 2007: 935).

10. Policy instruments are not an explicit focus of the approach (but see Hayes 1978). As pointed out before, the arenas of power approach is primarily concerned with policy formulation in the form of formal legislation, based on expectations about policy outcomes. This notwithstanding it is not the actual threat of sanctions that enforces a policy. "A great part of the ultimate success of a public policy may be attributable to the mere statement of the preferred future state of affairs. The purpose of good citizenship is to make public policies virtually self-executing. But most policies are accompanied by explicit means of imposing their intentions on their environments, and in all policies some techniques of control are inherent" (Lowi 1985: 69–70). It is precisely these "techniques of control" we are interested in when analyzing the Commission's action capacity.

11. The EU has shown particularly prone for new governance. Scott and Trubek distil six factors accounting for the increased use of new governance: increasing complexity and uncertainty of the issues on the agenda, irreducible diversity among the member states, general trends toward new approaches in public administration and law, the need to fill gaps of legal authority on the EU level (competence creep), the need to respond to claims for more legitimacy (through participation), and the need to respect the subsidiarity principle and therewith "to accept diversity, allow flexibility, and encourage decentralised experimentation" (2002: 8).

12. The definition of restrictive/discretionary policy instruments is similar to one of Hayes' dimensions (Hayes 1978: 145), which he calls "supply patterns," that have, however, three dimensions.

CHAPTER 4

1. Interview conducted in spring 2007, European Commission (Brussels).
2. The Phare objectives stated accordingly: "1. The aid shall be used primarily to support the process of reform in Poland and Hungary, in particular by financing or participating in the financing of projects aimed at economic restructuring. Such projects or cooperation measures should be undertaken in particular in the areas of agriculture, industry, investment, energy, training, environmental protection, trade and services; they should be aimed in particular at the private sector in Hungary and Poland" (Council of the European Communities 1989).
3. The Commission conducted a number of evaluations and subsequent improvements of the twinning instrument. See: Ad Hoc Report on Twinning

Instrument, OMAS Consortium (October 24, 2001); Commission of the European Communities 2000: *Report on the Assessment of the Twinning Instrument under PHARE* (July); and the subsequent revisions of the *Twinning Manual.*

4. The respective legal bases are Council of the European Union 2006a; European Parliament and Council 2006a, b, c; Council of the European Union 2006b, c.

5. The Commission's website on regional policy offers an overview: http://ec.europa.eu/regional_policy/atlas2007/index_en.htm (last accessed June 24, 2010).

6. All National Strategic Reference Frameworks are listed on the following page: http://www.central2013.eu/fileadmin/user_upload/Downloads/Document_Centre/OP_Resources/scoreboard17082007.pdf (accessed April 26, 2010).

7. At the lowest level are the desk officers responsible for the different states coordinate. On the next level up are the ESF managing authorities (national missions), topped by the ministerial level.

8. The EUPAN website offers information on CAF; see ttp://www.eupan.eu8 (accessed April 26, 2010).

<h2 style="text-align:center">CHAPTER 5</h2>

1. I will mostly use the term "minority protection" as shorthand for the two approaches to minority policy entailed in the criterion, i.e., the protection from discrimination and the respect for specific (collective) minority rights.

2. This holds especially for so-called old minorities, defined as national minorities, in contrast to immigrant ethnic groups, so-called new minorities (Kymlicka 2000; Kymlicka and Opalski 2002).

3. The Treaty of the European Union in its Maastricht version refers to human rights in the preamble, in Article J.1 and K.1, with regard to fundamental rights in the fields of Common Foreign and Security Policy and Justice and Home Affairs, as well as Article F(2), which relates to international instruments representing "the constitutional traditions of the Member States."

4. The EU Charter was solemnly proclaimed by the Council, the European Parliament and the European Commission on December 07, 2000 (OJ C364, December 18, 2000, pp. 1–22). It was originally included as the second part of the Treaty for a Constitution for Europe but eventually remained a single text outside the Treaty of Lisbon, which has no effect on the binding nature it gained with the ratification of the latter treaty (except for the reservation by the UK and Poland).

5. As soft law against racial discrimination are counted the following: *Joint Declaration on Fundamental Rights,* April 5, 1977 [1977] O.J. C103; *Joint Declaration against Racism and Xenophobia,* June 11, 1986 [1986] O.J. C185; *Council Resolution on the Fight against Racism and Xenophobia,* May 29,

1990 [1990] O.J. C157; Commission, *Joint Declaration on the Prevention of Racial Discrimination and Xenophobia and Promotion of Equal Treatment at the Workplace*; adopted by the Social Dialogue Summit October 21, 1995. Social Europe (1995); *Action Plan on the Fight against Racism* COM (98) 183 final of March 25, 1998 (McInerney 2002: 79).

6. For a detailed account of how the Commission applied the minority criterion vis-à-vis the CEEC, see Heidbreder and Carrasco 2003.

7. The only member state that has not signed the Framework Convention is France, whereas Belgium, Luxemburg, Greece, and the Netherlands have not ratified it yet. Among the new member states and remaining accession countries, only Latvia runs short of ratification. All candidate states were, moreover, explicitly called on to sign and ratify the Framework Convention for the Protection of Minority Languages, which has so far only been ratified by eight of the old member states.

8. The only state ever evaluated negatively is Slovakia. In the 1997 Opinion the state was judged not to meet the political accession criteria.

9. If we take into account that the French constitution rejects the principle of minorities altogether, the discrepancy is more than obvious if the 2002 Regular Report on Latvia states with reference to the Framework Convention for National Minorities that "Latvia is urged to ratify it" (p. 32). The acceptance of the Commission's reports is thereby undermined in principle.

10. More general claims, going beyond the direct responses to activities in the Copenhagen framework, were made by NGOs asking without success for a clause on positive minority rights in the drafting of the Charter of Fundamental Rights and Freedoms in 2000 and by the EP which called for a "Bill of Rights" on minorities as early as 1981 (De Witte 2004: 110).

11. Since 2007 the EUMC has been transformed in the Union's Fundamental Rights Agency, in the run-up to which some tensions regarding competences and the potential duplication of these emerged between the EU and the Council of Europe, which found resonance in a number of NGOs (see EUobserver March 1, 2007). These should eventually be resolved by the accession of the Community to the ECHR, which would formally underpin the primacy of the Council of Europe framework in human rights questions.

12. The numbering remains the same in the Treaty of Lisbon, Article 49, has, however, been extended beyond the conditions to enter the EU to include also the rules for a state to exit the Union.

13. Whereas all new member states were urged to accede and enact the Convention, Belgium, Greece, and Luxembourg have so far not ratified the FCNM. France has also not signed the Convention, given that the French Constitution does not recognize the existence of minorities. For a list of signatories/ratifications see http://conventions.coe.int/Treaty/Commun/ChercheSig.asp?NT=157&CM=8&DF=5/29/2007&CL=ENG (accessed April 26, 2010).

14. Hillion contests the Commission reasoning even more fiercely. "The legitimacy of the current enlargement process rests in part on the extent to which the conditions for accession are defined and applied in a predictable

manner. It is argued that the aforementioned conditions have been elaborated, strengthened, and sometimes applied in a different way, while new conditions have been added, notably during the process. Such a revision may have produced more detailed and sophisticated accession criteria, a necessary given—to use the Commission's terminology—the 'nature and number of candidates.' Nevertheless, it has paradoxically made enlargement appear more uncertain, especially from the candidate states' point of view; particularly because enlargement has also become subject to an obligation to be met by the Union itself" (2002: 407–08).

15. On the basis of Article 13 introduced in the Treaty of Amsterdam, this is in particular the Race Equality Directive (Council of the European Union 2000b), which was transposed in late 2006 by the last member state, the Employment Framework Directive (Council of the European Union 2000a), as well as antidiscrimination based on sex as provided for by the European Community Treaty and the some relevant case law on by the ECJ.

16. In November 2007, because of dramatic events in Italy that revealed missing instruments to tackle problems both in the member states and in the EU, the call for a stronger EU Roma policy has been raised vehemently, "Italian Prime Minister Romano Prodi and Romanian leader Calin Popescu-Tariceanu also called for a European strategy of inclusion for the Roma. On Thursday (15 November), EU lawmakers adopted a resolution suggesting that a network of organisations deal with the social inclusion of Roma as well as promote the rights and duties of the Roma community. The issue is expected to be discussed by a fundamental rights group in the commission, consisting of ten commissioner—Jose Manuel Barroso, Franco Frattini, Vladimir Spidla, Jan Figel, Margot Wallstrom, Benita Ferrero-Waldner, Olli Rehn, Luis Michel, Vivianne Reding and Sim Kallas. 'We hope the EU will play a facilitating role,' Andrew Wilkens from Open Society Institute told EUobserver, adding it should for example pay better attention to how the EU funds are targeted" (EUobserver.com November 22, 2007). However, no binding measures have ensued.

17. So the information provided on the Commission website, see http://ec.europa.eu/employment_social/eyeq/index.cfm?cat_id=EY (accessed May 29, 2007).

18. See also the Commission press release at http://europa.eu/rapid/press ReleasesAction.do?reference=IP/07/1833&format=HTML&aged=0& language=EN (accessed April 27, 2010).

19. The particular interests of the new member states, above all the Hungarian concern with national minorities outside the Hungarian territory, might play an additional role in future pushing to move from the informally emerging rules and actions to more explicit formalized regulation (Hughes et al. 2001 state a similar hypothesis). Moreover, it remains an open question as to how the ECJ will interpret the already formalized elements of the acquis relating to antidiscrimination and might thus work to a continued formalization of de facto rules.

20. See press report, Euractive (August 26, 2010): http://www.euractiv.com/en/justice/reding-criticises-france-italy-over-roma-treatment-news-497163 (accessed November 18, 2010).
21. See press report, EUobserver (September 15, 2010): http://euobserver.com/9/30806 (accessed November 18, 2010).
22. See press report, Spiegel Online (September 16, 2010): http://www.spiegel.de/politik/ausland/0,1518,717930,00.html (accessed November 18, 2010).

CHAPTER 6

1. The Council of Europe defined Euroregions, referring to AEBR, which

> sets the following criteria for the identification of Euroregions: An association of local and regional authorities on either side of the national border, sometimes with a parliamentary assembly; a transfrontier association with a permanent secretariat and a technical and administrative team with own resources; of private law nature, based on non-profit-making associations or foundations on either side of the border in accordance with the respective national law in force; of public law nature, based on interstate agreements, dealing among other things, with the participation of territorial authorities. It would appear that several "labels" are used which are categorised under "Euroregions." These include: Euregio, Euregion, Euroregion, Europaregion, Grand Region, Regio, Council. In some cases the label "Euroregion" is not used at all, such as the "Nova Raetia" which is composed of territorial communities of Switzerland, Italy and Austria. The terms "Regio" and "Euroregions" are also used for national border associations created by the municipalities and counties. This is the case with the Czech Klub Euroregion Labe, the German Euroregio Egrensis Arbeitsgemeinschaft Bayern and the German Inn-Salzach Euregio e.V. (association of Bavarian municipalities) and many others.
>
> (see http://www.coe.int/t/e/legal_affairs/local_and_regional_ democracy/areas_of_work/transfrontier_co-operation/euroregions/ WhatIs_Euroregion.asp, accessed April 19, 2008)

2. AEBR's first president, Alfred Mozer (1971–1975), was moreover a former Head of Cabinet at the European Commission, for further reference consult: http://www.aebr.net/ (Accessed June 13, 2006).
3. Other authors list the various EU financial assistance schemes:

> Since 1988, co-finance has been made available for such co-operative initiatives under Article 10 of the European Regional Development Fund (ERDF) particularly through RECITE (Regions and Cities of Europe), INTERREG (International Regions) and the EEP (Experience Exchange Programme) (Brenner 1993). In the early 1990s, RECITE alone supported 37 interregional cooperative networks (Williams 1996). INTERREG, in particular, has supported cross-border programmes. Whilst it is limited in financial terms, representing just under 1% of the Structural Operations

budget, it is politically significant. By 1994 it was the largest of 13 Community Initiatives which are programmes proposed by the EC on its own initiative to encourage Member States to tackle problems the EC has identified at the European scale (ibid.).

(Church and Reid 1999: 643–44)

4. The states that signed before 1987 were Austria, Belgium, France, Germany, Ireland, Italy, Lichtenstein, the Netherlands, Norway, Portugal, Spain, Sweden, and Switzerland. They were followed by Albania, Armenia, Azerbaijan, Bosnia and Herzegovina, Bulgaria, Croatia, the Czech Republic, Denmark, Finland, Georgia, Iceland (not ratified), Lithuania, Luxembourg, Malta (not ratified), Moldova, Monaco, Montenegro (not ratified), Poland, Rumania, Russia, Slovakia, Slovenia, the former Yugoslav Republic of Macedonia, Turkey, and Ukraine. EU member or candidate states that have not signed the Madrid Convention are Cyprus, Estonia, Greece, the former Yugoslav Republic of Macedonia, Serbia, and the United Kingdom; see http://conventions.coe.int/treaty/Commun/ChercheSig.asp?NT=106&CM=1&DF=&CL=ENG (Accessed June 23, 2010).

5. Strand A priority topics are "promoting urban, rural and coastal development; encouraging entrepreneurship and the development of small firms (including those in the tourism sector) and local employment initiatives; promoting the integration of the labour market and social inclusion; sharing human resources and facilities for research, technological development, education, culture, communications and health to increase productivity and help create sustainable jobs; encouraging the protection of the environment (local, global), the increase of energy efficiency and the promotion of renewable sources of energy; improving transport (particularly measures implementing more environmentally-friendly forms of transport), information and communication networks and services and water and energy systems; developing cooperation in the legal and administrative spheres to promote economic development and social cohesion; increasing human and institutional potential for cross-border cooperation to promote economic development and social cohesion" (Article 11) (Commission of the European Communities 2004e).

6. Morocco's initiatives are with Spain, and between the United Kingdom/Gibraltar-Morocco. For (ES/MA) Spain-Morocco (2000 CB 16 0 PC 007), whose main purpose is to "contribute to an integrated and sustainable development of the area. The programme seeks to increase the competitiveness of the production system, to speed up convergence with the most developed economies and to promote the economic cooperation between border regions."

CHAPTER 7

1. A number of Council Regulations have extended the Nuclear Safety acquis regarding the safety of workers in nuclear plants, of citizens in case of emergencies and in relation to the shipping of nuclear materials: Council

Directive 90/641/Euratom of December 4, 1990, on the operational protection of outside workers exposed to the risk of ionizing radiation during
their activities in controlled areas (OJ L 349, December 13, 1990, pp.
0021–0025); Council Directive 92/3/Euratom of February 3, 1992, regarding the
supervision and control of shipments of radioactive waste between Member
States and into and out of the Community (OJ L 35, February 12, 1992);
Council Regulation (Euratom) No. 1493/93 of June 8, 1993 on shipments
of radioactive substances between Member States (OJ L 148, June 19, 1993,
p. 1.); Council Directive 96/29/Euratom of May 13, 1996, laying down
basic safety standards for the protection of the health of workers and the
general public against the dangers arising from ionizing radiation (OJ L 159,
June 6, 1996, pp. 1–114). Moreover, in 2003 the Council passed on the
Control of radioactive sources: Council Directive 2003/122/EURATOM of
December 22, 2003, on the control of high-activity sealed radioactive sources
and orphan sources (OJ L 346, December 31, 2003, pp. 0057–0064).

2. Between 1964 and 1977 some 148 reactors were constructed and started
   operating in Western Europe (Belgium, United Kingdom, Finland, France,
   the Netherlands, Spain, Sweden, and Germany) (see Barnes 2003: 120).

3. The increased use of nuclear technology for the production of electricity
   marks the decisive change not foreseen by Euratom when drafted. "Increased
   levels of interest in nuclear electricity production and a dramatic rise in numbers of reactors under construction by the national governments during the
   1970s pointed to the need for some level of convergence of national safety
   practices in the nuclear installations" (Barnes 2003: 123).

4. The relevant case law regarding the relationship between the Euratom
   and European Community Treaties are the ECJ's Ruling in Case 1/78,
   ECR 1978, p. 2151; Case C-161/97 Kernkraftwerke Lippe-Ems GmbH v
   Commission of the European Communities, ECR 1999, pp. I-02057.

5. The Council decides unanimously with still very delimited consultative
   powers of the European Parliament.

6. These are the International Atomic Energy Agency (IAEA), Nuclear Energy
   Agency of the OECD, International Commission on Radiological Protection (ICRP), International Science & Technology Center, Association
   for Regional and International Underground Storage (Arius), and GMF—
   Group of Municipalities with nuclear facilities (for links to all these see
   http://ec.europa.eu/energy/nuclear/links/index_en.htm).

7. The establishment of WENRA was itself inspired by enlargement, it will
   hence be dealt with below; on the Convention on Nuclear Safety, see http://
   www.iaea.org/Publications/Documents/Infcircs/Others/inf449.shtml; on the
   Joint Convention on the Safety of Spent Fuel Management and on the Safety
   of Radioactive Waste Management, see http://www.iaea.org/Publications/
   Documents/Infcircs/1997/infcirc546.pdf (both accessed March 12, 2007).

8. The Commission decision is based on a Council Decision of December 15,
   2003, approving the accession of the European Atomic Energy Community
   to the Nuclear Safety Convention.

9. All member states with nuclear facilities have ratified the Convention.

10. "The Euratom treaty is very loosely drafted, you have a lot of flexibility within the Euratom Treaty to do things, you can do virtually anything. . . . That is why it does not change, you know, people talk about changing the Euratom Treaty, but in the end they never do, because you will never agree, you will never get a consensus, I think, certainly not for many years because of differences of views on nuclear dossiers you will never get a clear consensus on how you can modify the Euratom Treaty" (Interview 2007 DG TREN).

11. The *Report on the Evaluation of Nuclear Safety in the Context of Enlargement* states: "II.1 General observations: The methodology for the evaluation process is universal with respect to Candidate States. This means that: (a) it is not limited to Candidate States with nuclear power programmes in operation, (b) it is applicable to all types of reactor designs and other nuclear installations and to the varied regulatory environments encountered in the Candidate States. It was pointed out already in the original mandate1 given by Coreper to AQG that the demands made to the Candidate States to achieve the expected 'high level of nuclear safety' ought not to be stricter than the requirements in force in the EU. Furthermore, it is understood that this exercise does not lead to any transfer of competences from the Member States to the Community and that the competence and responsibilities relating to the safety of the design, construction, operation and decommissioning of a nuclear installation and for the safe management of radioactive waste, lie with the State which has jurisdiction for the installation concerned" (2001: 4–5).

12. The peer review process foreseen in the Council's report has since resulted in the publication of a progress report (ref. 9601/02) on the implementation of the Council's recommendations.

13. "The primary objective of the project was to develop a common format and general guidance for the evaluation of the current nuclear safety status in countries that operate commercial nuclear power plants. Therefore, one of the project team's first undertakings was to develop an approach that would allow for a consistent and comprehensive overview of the nuclear safety status in the CEEC, enabling an equal treatment of the countries to be evaluated. Such an approach, which did not exist, should also ensure identification of the most important safety issues of the individual nuclear power plants. The efforts resulted in the development of the 'Performance Evaluation Guide,' which focuses on important nuclear safety issues such as plant design and operation, the practice of performing safety assessments, and nuclear legislation and regulation, in particular the role of the national regulatory body" (EC-Project: Nuclear Safety in Central and Eastern Europe ENCONET/ES-konsult/NNC/NRG Final Report, December 2000: 2), http://ec.europa.eu/energy/nuclear/publications/doc/eur19895_main.pdf (accessed April 26, 2010).

14. Arguably it would also impose higher pressure to comply with the nonbinding reporting obligations under IAEA, which is not really being complied with very rigorously by all states.

15. The following reasoning by the Commission has therefore been considered not to be very fruitful in the end: "For those Member States that choose to go down the nuclear path, acceptability by the public will also be an important factor. The Community has a key role to play in ensuring that the nuclear industry develops in a safe and secure manner. In that respect, the Commission considers it a priority that the Community adopt a legal framework on nuclear safety, facilitating harmonisation and compliance with internationally acceptable standards and ensuring the availability of adequate funds for decommissioning NPPs at the end of their life and national policy plans on management of radioactive waste" (Commission of the European Communities 2006d).

16. The author continues pointing out the normative problems this kind of informal governance is linked to. "However, this form of informal governance constitutes also a major threat for the legitimacy of the Union, as there is no public and democratic accountability for the decisions taken by the Commission in this case. In search of expertise, the Commission has not consulted with anti-nuclear movements or environmentalist interest groups. The result is an imbalance between opinions presented which makes ex post control of decisions highly difficult" (Saurugger 2003: 224). I will return to this issue in the conclusions.

CHAPTER 8

1. Unité de coordination de la lutte anti-fraude (UCLAF) was founded in 1988 and since 1999 renamed and structured into the European Anti-Fraud Office (OLAF).
2. The Lisbon Treaty abolished the Convention tool for member state cooperation, but it is to date still unclear how the existing Conventions will be handled.
3. Eurojust cooperation was further enhanced in the Constitutional Treaty of 2004 and the Lisbon Treaty, respectively.
4. Although most public debate and also coercive means against corruption in the EU have been focusing almost exclusively on the Commission and have led, famously, even to the dismissal of the Santer College, every year "member states are the key target of the auditors' criticism due to 'the high level of error' in their dealings with the EU's budget. Member states manage and control 80 percent of the bloc's common budget, some €32.4bn in 2006. 'The supervisory and control systems in the member states were generally ineffective or moderately effective, and the [European] Commission maintains only a moderately effective supervision of their functioning,' noted Mr Weber [President of the European Court of Auditors]. The Court pointed out in its report that 'at least 12% of the total amount reimbursed to structural policies projects should not have been paid out,' particularly in the area of regional development and social cohesion" (http://euobserver.com/9/25128/?print=1, November 13, 2007).

5. Of the EU member states, Belgium, Cyprus, Czech Republic, Germany, Greece, Ireland, Italy, Luxembourg, Malta, Portugal, and the European Community have signed but not ratified.
6. Of the member states the following have not yet ratified: Czech Republic, Greece, Ireland, and Luxembourg. The European Community singed in 2000 and approved the Convention on May 21, 2004.
7. All 30 OECD countries and 6 nonmember countries have signed and ratified (not Malta and Cyprus).
8. Austria, France, Germany, Greece, Italy, Luxembourg, Spain, and Sweden have signed, but so far not ratified. The European Community is entitled to join but has not signed the Convention.
9. Besides an expected further elaboration in this direction in the next Commission Communication, cooperation with the World Bank is envisaged in the area of promoting anticorruption in external relations.
10. A further element in interservice cooperation in the Commission has been the reorganization and new creation of the DG Justice, Freedom and Security itself. Growing from a small task force for Justice, Freedom and Security when the Maastricht Treaty was signed in 1992, it was expanded into a full Directorate General in October 1999. From then on, the visibility and cooperation across the Commission has substantially increased, one example being the inclusion of anticorruption matters in the handling of sports policies in educational and cultural matters (Interview 2007 DG JFS).

CHAPTER 9

1. Quoted from Sullivan (1896).
2. Cases in point were standards on minority protection (Heidbreder and Carrasco 2003; Open Society Institute 2002a) and the standards on national anticorruption measures (Open Society Institute 2002b).
3. Beyond enlargement, Roma issues are dealt with by DG Employment and Social Affairs and Equal Opportunities, and the Commission representative on the Executive Board of the Fundamental Rights Agency is from DG Justice, Freedom and Security. While the *European Neighbourhood Policy* is directed by DG External Relations, the *Neighbourhood and Partnership Instrument* (ENPI) and within it cross-border cooperation has further moved on to *EurpeAid*; cross-border, transnational, and interregional cooperation among member states is dealt with by DG Regional Policy. Administrative capacity building, as most Roma initiatives, is financed by the European Social Funds directed by DG Employment and Social Affairs and Equal Opportunities.
4. Interestingly, the very term *acquis communautaire*—used to depict the sum of the Union's legal body—was promoted by the need to define what was the precise legal substance that candidate states were expected to transpose. Dealing with a request by an U.S. embassy, DG 1 requested clarification from

the legal service whether the (internally used) term *acquis communautaire* could be used in official communications for what in English had to be circumscribed as "the body of Community law, or the body of law and principles governing the EU" (internal note, October 1997, see Historical Archives of the European Union [EUI], GJLA 172—the Acquis of the Union).

REFERENCES

Ahrne, Göran, and Nils Brunsson. 2004. "Soft Regulation from an Organizational Perspective," in *Soft Law in Governance and Regulation,* edited by U. Mörth. Cheltenham, UK / Northampton, USA: Edward Elgar.

Aliboni, Roberto. 2005. "The Geopolitical Implications of the European Neighbourhood Policy," *European Foreign Affairs Review* 10 (1): 1–6.

Allan, David. 2005. "Cohesion and Structural Funds: Competing Pressures for Reform?" in *Policy-Making in the European Union,* edited by H. Wallace, W. Wallace and M. A. Pollack. Oxford: Oxford University Press.

Alston, Philip, and J. H. H. Weiler. 1999. "An 'Ever Closer Union' in Need of a Human Rights Policy: The European Union and Human Rights," in *The EU and Human Rights,* edited by P. Alston, et al. Oxford: Oxford University Press.

Amato, Giuliano, and Judy Batt. 1998a. *Final Report of the Reflection Group on the Long-Term Implications of EU Enlargement: The Nature of the New Border.* San Domenico di Fiesole: RSC European University Institute, Forward Studies Unit of the European Commission.

Amato, Giuliano, and Judy Batt. 1998b. *Minority Rights and EU Enlargement to the East. Report on the First Meeting of the Reflection Group on the Long Term Implications of EU Enlargement: The Nature of the New Border.* San Domenico di Fiesole: European University Institute.

Arbeitskreis Europäischer Grenzregionen (AGEG). 1997. *Die EU-Initiative INTERREG und zukünftige Entwicklungen* www.aebr.net/publikationen/pdfs/interreg_97.de.pdf (accessed July 31, 2010).

Arbeitskreis Europäischer Grenzregionen (AGEG). 1999. *Institutionelle Aspekte der grenzübergreifenden Zusammenarbeit* http://www.aebr.net/publikationen/pdfs/inst_asp_99.de.pdf (accessed July 31, 2010).

Bache, Ian. 1998. "Multi-level Governance and EU Regional Policy," in *Multi-level Governance,* edited by I. Bache. Oxford: Oxford University Press.

Bachtler, John, and Colin Wren. 2006. "Evaluation of European Union Cohesion Policy: Research Questions and Policy Challenges," *Regional Studies* 40 (2): 143–153.

Bailey, David, and Lisade Propris. 2004. "A Bridge Too Phare? EU Pre-Accession Aid and Capacity-Building in the Candidate Countries," *Journal of Common Market Studies* 42 (1): 77–98.

Balfour, Rosa, and Alessandro Rotta. 2005. "Beyond Enlargement: The European Neighbourhood Policy and its Tools," *The International Spectator* 40 (1): 7–20.

Balint, Tim, Michael W. Bauer, and Christoph Knill. 2008. "Bureaucratic Change in the European Administrative Space: The Case of the European Commission," *West European Politics* 31 (4): 677–700.

Banks, Jeffrey S., and Barry R. Weingast. 1992. "The Political Control of Bureaucracies under Asymmetric Information," *American Journal of Political Science* 36 (2): 509–524.

Barnes, Pamela M. 2003. "Nuclear Safety for Nuclear Electricity—the Search for a Solid Legal Basis for Nuclear Safety in an Enlarged Union," *Managerial Law* 45 (5/6): 115–143.

Batory, Agnes. 2010. "Post-accession Malaise? EU Conditionality, Domestic Politics and Anti-corruption Policy in Hungary," *Global Crime* 11 (2): 164–177.

Bauer, Michael W. 2008. "Introduction: Organizational Change, Management Reform and EU Policy-making," *Journal of European Public Policy* 15 (5): 627–647.

Benz, Arthur. 2007. "Accountable Multilevel Governance by the Open Method of Coordination?," *European Law Journal* 13 (4): 505–522.

Benz, Arthur, ed. 2004. *Governance—Regieren in komplexen Regelsystemen*. Wiesbaden: VS Verlag.

Benz, Arthur, Susanne Lütz, Uwe Schimank, and Georg Simonis. 2007. "Einleitung," in *Handbuch Governance,* edited by A. Benz, S. Lütz, U. Schimank and G. Simonis. Wiesbaden: VS Verlag.

Best, Edward, Thomas Christiansen, and Pierpaolo Settembri, eds. 2008. *The Institutions of the Enlarged European Union: Continuity and Change, Studies in EU Reform and Enlargement*. Cheltenham, UK / Northampton, USA: Edward Elgar.

Bignami, Francesca. 2004. "Foreword," *Law and Contemporary Problems* 68 (1): 1–17.

Blom-hansen, Jens. 2005. "Principals, Agents, and the Implementation of EU Cohesion Policy," *Journal of European Public Policy* 12 (4): 624–648.

Borrás, Susana, and Kerstin Jacobsson. 2004. "The Open Method of Coordination and New Governance Patterns in the EU," *Journal of European Public Policy* 11 (2): 185–208.

Börzel, Tanja A. 2008. "Der 'Schatten der Hierarchie'—Ein Governance-Paradox?" in *PVS Sonderheft 41—Governance in einer sich wandelnden Welt,* edited by G. F. Schuppert and M. Zürn. Wiesbaden: VS Verlag für Solzialwissenschaften.

Bossaert, Danielle, and Christoph Demmke. 2003. *Civil Services in the Accession States*. Maastricht: European Institute of Public Administration (EIPA).

Bossaert, Danielle, Christoph Demmke, Koen Nomden, Robert Polet, and Astrid Auer. 2001. *Civil Services in the European of Fifteen: Trends and New Developments*. Maastricht: EIPA.

Bradbury, Jonathan. 2003. "The Political dynamics of Sub-state Regionalisation: A Neo-functionalist Perspective and the Case of Devolution in the UK," *The British Journal of Politics and International Relations* 5 (4): 543–575.

Brandtner, Barbara, and Allan Rosas. 1998. The Human Rights and the External Relations of the European Community: An Analysis of Doctrine and Practice. *European Journal of International Law* (9): 468–490.

Brenner, P. 1993. "What Makes an Interregional Network Successful?" in *Regional Networks, Border Regions and European Integration,* edited by R. Chappelin and P. Batey. London: Pion.

Brunsson, Nils. 1989. *The Organization of Hypocrisy: Talk, Decisions and Actions in Organisations.* Chichester: John Wiley & Sons.

Capano, Giliberto. 1992. "Le Tipologie delle Scienze Politiche Pubbliche: Una Strada Senza Uscita?" *Rivista Italiana di Scienza Politica* 23 (3): 550–588.

Cardona, Francisco. 1999. European Principles for Public Administration. *SIGMA Papers: No. 27.*

Carrubba, Clifford J. 2003. "The European Court of Justice, Democracy, and Enlargement," *European Union Politics* 4 (1): 75–100.

Cassese, Sabino. 2004. "European Administrative Proceedings," *Law and Contemporary Problems* 68 (1): 21–36.

Checkel, Jeffrey T. 2000. "Compliance and Conditionality," in *ARENA Working Papers.*

Christiansen, Thomas, and Simona Piattoni, eds. 2003. *Informal Governance in the European Union.* Cheltenham, UK / Northampton, USA: Edward Elgar.

Church, Andrew, and Peter Reid. 1999. "Cross-border Co-operation, Institutionalization and Political Space across the English Channel," *Regional Studies* 33 (7): 643–655.

Cini, Michelle. 2000. "From Soft Law to Hard Law? Discretion and Rulemaking in the Commission's State Aid Regime," in Robert Schuman Centre for Advanced Studies: European Forum Series.

Cini, Michelle. 2001. "The Soft Law Approach: Commission Rule-making in the EU's State Aid Regime," *Journal of European Public Policy* 8 (2): 192–207.

Clapham, Andrew. 1999. "Where Is the EU's Human Rights Common Foreign Policy, and How is it Manifested in Multilateral Fora?" in *The EU and Human Rights,* edited by P. Alston et al. Oxford: Oxford University Press.

Commission of the European Communities. 1990. "Commission Decision concerning the conclusion on behalf of the European Atomic Energy Community of the Agreement between the European Economic Community and the European Atomic Energy Community and the Union of Soviet Socialist Republics on trade and commercial and economic cooperation (90/117/Euratom)," *OJ L 068* 15/03/1990 (February 27): 0020.

Commission of the European Communities. 1995. "White Paper," *On the Preparation of the Associated Countries of Central and Eastern Europe for Integration into the Internal Market of the Union* COM(95)163 final (May 3).

Commission of the European Communities. 1997a. "Agenda 2000—For a stronger and wider Union," *Bulletin of the European Union, Supplement 5/97* Document drawn up on the basis of COM (97) 2000 final (July 13, 1997).

Commission of the European Communities. 1997b. "Communication from the Commission to the Council and the European Parliament: On a Union Policy against Corruption," *COM 97/192 final.* Brussels: May 21.

Commission of the European Communities. 1999. "Europe's Agenda 2000: Strengthening and Widening the European Union." Draft of Commission information brochure for the general public on Agenda 2000, Priority Publications Programme 1999, X/D/5.

Commission of the European Communities. 2000a. "Contribution of the Commission Services to Question No 1 of the Questionaire Submitted on 13 September 2000 by the Presidency to the Atomic Questions Group in the Framework of the Mandate Given to It by the COREPER on 26 July 2000," in *Non-Paper* http://ec.europa.eu/energy/nuclear/safety/doc/non_binding_acquis.pdf (accessed 18 March 2007).

Commission of the European Communities. 2000b. "Nuclear Safety and the Environment: Nuclear Safety in Central and Eastern Europe," *ENCONET Consulting* EUR 19895 (April 2001).

Commission of the European Communities. 2001. European Governance. *A White Paper* Brussels, 25.7.2001 (COM(2001) 428 final).

Commission of the European Communities. 2002a. "Feasibility Study," in *Contribution to a Preliminary Draft Constitution of the European Union.*

Commission of the European Communities. 2002b. "Progress Report on the Communication from the Commission on the Impact of Enlargement on Regions Bordering Candidate Countries Community," *Action for Border Regions* COM(2002) 660 final (29 November).

Commission of the European Communities. 2003a. "Communication from the Commission to the Council and the European Parliament: Wider Europe—Neighbourhood: A New Framework for Relations with our Eastern and Southern Neighbours," *COM(2003) 104 final.*

Commission of the European Communities. 2003b. "Communication from the Commission to the Council, the European Parliament and the European Economic and Social Committee on a Comprehensive Policy against Corruption," *COM(2003) 317 final.*

Commission of the European Communities. 2003c. "Communication from the Commission: Paving the way for a New Neighbourhood Instrument," *COM(2003) 393 final.*

Commission of the European Communities. 2003d. *Enlargement of the European Union: An Historic Opportunity.* Belgium: European Communities.

Commission of the European Communities. 2003e. *Support for Roma Communities in Central and Eastern Europe.* Belgium: European Communities.

Commission of the European Communities. 2004a. "Amended proposal for a Council Directive (Euratom) laying down basic obligations and general principles on the safety of nuclear installations / Amended proposal for a Council Directive (Euratom) on the safe management of the spent nuclear fuel and radioactive waste," *(presented by the Commission pursuant to Article 119 (2) of the Euratom Treaty)* COM(2004) 526 final (September 8).

Commission of the European Communities. 2004b. "Amended proposal for a Regulation of the European Parliament and of the Council laying down general provisions establishing a European Neighbourhood and Partnership Instrument," *Adaptation following the agreement of 17 May 2006 on the Financial Framework 2007–2013 (presented by the Commission in accordance with Article 250(2) of the EC Treaty)* COM (2004) 0628 final/2—COD (2004) 0219 (September 29).

Commission of the European Communities. 2004c. "Commission Decision 2004/491/Euratom of 29 April 2004. Concerning the accession to the 1994 Convention on Nuclear Safety by the European Atomic Energy Community (Euratom) with regard to the Declaration attached thereto," *Official Journal* L 172 (May 6).

Commission of the European Communities. 2004d. "Communication from the Commission," *European Neighbourhood Policy: Strategy Paper* COM (2004)373 final (May 12).

Commission of the European Communities. 2004e. "Communication from the Commission to the Member States," *Laying down guidelines for a Community initiative concerning trans-European cooperation intended to encourage harmonious and balanced development of the European territory: INTERREG III* 2004/C 226/02 (September 2).

Commission of the European Communities. 2004f. *The Situation of Roma in an Enlarged European Union.* Brussels: European Communities, Directorate General for Employment and Social Affairs.

Commission of the European Communities. 2004g. "White Paper on services of general interest Review of services of general interest" *Communication from the Commission to the European Parliament, the Council, the European Economic and Social Committee and the Committee of the Regions* (COM(2004) 374 final).

Commission of the European Communities. 2005. "Communication from the Commission," *Cohesion Policy in Support of Growth and Jobs: Community Strategic Guidelines, 2007–2013* COM(2005) 0299.

Commission of the European Communities. 2006a. *Commission Decision of 13/XII/2006 Establishing a Mechanism for Cooperation and Verification of Progress in Bulgaria to Address Specific Benchmarks in the Areas of Judicial Reform and the Fight against Corruption and Organised Crime.* Brussels, 13/XII/2006, C (2006) 6570 final.

Commission of the European Communities. 2006b. *Commission Decision of 13/XII/2006 Establishing a Mechanism for Cooperation and Verification of Progress in Romania to Address Specific Benchmarks in the Areas of Judicial Reform and the Fight against Corruption.* Brussels, 13/XII2006, C (2006) 6569 final.

Commission of the European Communities. 2006c. "Commission Decision of 20 January 2006 establishing a high-level advisory group on social integration of ethnic minorities and their full participation in the labour market," *Official Journal of the European Union* L 21/20 (25 January) (2006/33/EC): 20–21.

Commission of the European Communities. 2006d. *Communication from the Commission to the Council and the European Parliament: Nuclear Illustrative Programme Presented under Article 40 of the Euratom Treaty for the opinion of the European Economic and Social Committee.* COM(2006) 844 final Brussels: January 1.

Commission of the European Communities. 2006e. *Communication from the Commission: Implementing the Community Lisbon Programme: Social Services of General Interest in the European Union.* COM(2006) 177 final Brussels: 26. April (SEC(2006)516).

Commission of the European Communities. 2006f. *Institutional Capacity: Public Administrations and Services in the European Social Fund 2007–2013.* Brussels: Information service DG Employment, Social Affairs & Equal Opportunities.

Commission of the European Communities. 2006g. Regional Policy—Inforegio. In *PART III—The EU Budget and the Contribution of Structural Policies and Social Cohesion.*

Commission of the European Communities. 2006h. *Strengthening Institutional Capacity and Efficiency of Public Administrations and Public Services in the Next Programming Period (2007–2013).* Brussels: DG Employment Social Affairs and Equal Opportunities.

Commission of the European Communities. 2007a. *Commission Acts to Close Gaps in Race Equality Rules* (Commission press release: 27 June) http://europa.eu/rapid/pressReleasesAction.do?reference=IP/07/928&format=HTML&aged=0&language=EN&guiLanguage=en (accessed July 31, 2010).

Commission of the European Communities. 2007b. *Nuclear Safety and Enlargement* http://ec.europa.eu/energy/nuclear/legislation/safety_en.htm (accessed July 31, 2010).

Commission of the European Communities. 2007c. *Progress Report on the Cooperation and Verification Mechanism—Procedural Aspects.* MEMO/07/260.

Commission of the European Communities. 2007d. *Report from the Commission to the European Parliament and the Council on Bulgaria's progress on Accompanying Measures Following Accession.* Brussels: June 27.

Commission of the European Communities. 2007e. *Report from the Commission to the European Parliament and the Council on Romania's Progress on Accompanying Measures Following Accession.* Brussels: June 27.

Commission of the European Communities 2008a. *Communication from the Commission on the Creation of a Forum for discussing EU Justice Policies in Practice Communication of the Commission,* COM(2008) 38 final, Brussels, Feburary 2.

Commission of the European Communities. 2008b. *Interim Report from the Commission to the European Parliament and the Council on Progress in Bulgaria under the Co-operation and Verification Mechanism.* Brussels: February 14, COM(2008) 63 final/2.

Commission of the European Communities. 2008c. *Interim Report from the Commission to the European Parliament and the Council on Progress in Romania under the Co-operation and Verification Mechanism.* Brussels: February 14, COM(2008) 62 final/2.

Commission of the European Communities. 2008d. *Press release* http://europa. eu/rapid/pressReleasesAction.do?reference=IP/08/210&format=HTML& aged=1&language=EN&guiLanguage=en (accessed July 31, 2010).

Commission of the European Communities. 2010a "Communication from the Commission to the Council, the European Parliament, the European Economic and Social Committee and the Committee of the Regions: The social and economic integration of the Roma in Europe," *COM/2010/0133 final.* Brussels: April 7.

Commission of the European Communities. 2010b. "Communication on Roma in Europe and Progress Report on Roma inclusion 2008–2010," *Rress Release RAPID.* MEMO/10/121: April 7, <http://europa.eu/rapid/press ReleasesAction.do?reference=MEMO/10/121&format=HTML&aged=0& language=EN&guiLanguage=en> (accessed November 18, 2010).

Commission of the European Communities. 2010c. "Statement by Viviane Reding, Vice-President of the European Commission and EU Commissioner for Justice, Fundamental Rights and Citizenship, on the Roma situation in Europe," *MEMO/10/384*, <http://europa.eu/rapid/pressReleasesAction.do? reference=MEMO/10/384&type=HTML> (Accessed on: November 18, 2010).

Council of Europe. 1995. *Framework Convention for the Protection of National Minorities.* Strasbourg: H(1995)010.

Council of the European Communities. 1975. "Council Resolution. On the technological problems of nuclear safety," *OJ C 185, 14/08/1975* (July 22): 0001–0002.

Council of the European Communities. 1988. "Council Decision on the conclusion of the Joint Declaration on the establishment of official relations between the European Economic Community and the Council for Mutual Economic Assistance," *OJ L 157, 24/06/1988* 88/345/EEC (June 22): 34.

Council of the European Communities. 1989. "Council Regulation on economic aid to the Republic of Hungary and the Polish People's Republic," *OJ L 375, 23/12/1989* (EEC) No. 3906/89 (December 18): 0011–0012.

Council of the European Communities. 1992. "Council Resolution on the technological problems of nuclear safety," *OJ C 172, 8.7.1992* (June 18): 2–3.

Council of the European Communities. 1999. "Council Regulation on coordinating aid to the applicant countries in the framework of the pre-accession strategy and amending Regulation," *(EEC) No 3906/89 (OJ L 161, 26/06/1999, pp. 0068–0072)—Regulation (EEC) No 3906/89 amended by adding a new paragraph 3 to Article 3.* (EC) No 1266/1999 (June 21).

Council of the European Communities. 2000. "Council Decision of 27 November 2000 establishing a Community action program to combat discrimination (2001 to 2006)," *OJ L 303* (February 2): 0023–0028.

Council of the European Union. 1988a. Council Regulation. *Laying down provisions for implementing Regulation (EEC) No 2052/88 as regards the European Regional Development Fund* (EEC) No 4254/88 (December 19).

Council of the European Union. 1998b. "Joined Action of 22 December 1998 adopted by the Council on the Basis of Article K.3 of the Treaty on European

Union, on Corruption in the Private Sector (98/43/JHA)." *Official Journal* 358/2 (December 31).

Council of the European Union. 2000a. "Council Directive Establishing a General Framework for Equal Treatment in Employment and Occupation," *2000/78/EC* (November 27).

Council of the European Union. 2000b. "Council Directive Implementing the Principle of Equal Treatment between Persons Irrespective of Racial or Ethnic Origin," *2000/43/EC* (June 29).

Council of the European Union. 2001. "Report on Nuclear Safety in the Context of Enlargement," *9181/01* (May 27).

Council of the European Union. 2002a. "Council Decision. Setting up Eurojust with a view to reinforcing the fight against serious crime," *2002/187/*JHA (February 28).

Council of the European Union. 2002b. "Peer Review Status Report" *(9601/02)*.

Council of the European Union. 2003. "Council Framework Decision 2003/568/JHA of 22 July 2003 on Combating Corruption in the Private Sector," *OJ L 192* (July 31): 54–56.

Council of the European Union. 2005a. "A Strategy for the External Dimension of JHA : Global Freedom, Security and Justice," *RELEX 628* 14366/05 (November 11).

Council of the European Union. 2005b. "Council and Commission Action Plan implementing the Hague Programme on strengthening freedom, security and justice in the European Union," *Official Journal of the European Union 2005/C 53/01* (March 3).

Council of the European Union. 2005c. "Outcome of Proceedings, Article 36 Committee: Subject, Communication from the Commission to the Council, the European Parliament and the European Economic and Social Committee on a Comprehensive EU Policy against Corruption," *OJ 6902/05* (March 2).

Council of the European Union. 2005d. "The Hague Programme: Strengthening Freedom, Security, and Justice in the European Union," *OJ 2005/C 53/01* (March 3).

Council of the European Union. 2006a. "Council Regulation (EC) No 1083/2006 of 11 July 2006 laying down general provisions on the European Regional Development Fund, the European Social Fund and the Cohesion Fund and repealing Regulation (EC) No 1260/1999," *OJ L 210/25* (July 31): 25–77.

Council of the European Union. 2006b. "Council Regulation No 1084/2006 of 11 July 2006 establishing a Cohesion Fund and repealing Regulation (EC) No 1164/94," *OJ L 210/79* (July 31): 79–81.

Council of the European Union. 2006c. "Council Regulation No 1085/2006 of 17 July 2006 establishing an Instrument for Pre-Accession Assistance (IPA)," *OJ L 210/82* (July 31): 82–93.

Council of the European Union. 2009. "Council Directive 2009/71/ Euratom of 25 June 2009 establishing a Community framework for the nuclear safety of nuclear installations." *OJ L 172* (July 2): 18–22.

Court of Auditors. 1999. "Special Report No 25/98 concerning operations undertaken by the European Union in the field of nuclear safety in central and eastern Europe (CEEC) and in the new independent States (NIS) (1990 to 1997 period) together with the Commission's replies," *OJ C (35/01)*: 1–48.

Court of Auditors. 2003a. Special Report No 5/2003 Concerning PHARE and ISPA funding of environmental projects in the candidate countries together with the Commission 's replies. *OJ C (167/01)*: 1–20.

Court of Auditors. 2003b. "Special Report No 6/2003 concerning twinning as the main instrument to support institution-building in candidate countries together with the Commission's replies (pursuant to Article 248(4), second subparagraph, of the EC Treaty)." *OJ C (167/02)*: 21–45.

Court of Justice of the European Communities (CJEC). 1991. Judgment of 19 November 1991, Andrea Francovich and Others v Italian Republic, Joined Cases C-6/90 and C-9/90, in *Reports of Cases Before the Court of Justice and the Court of First Instance*. 1991: 5357.

Cremona, Marise. 2004. "The European Neighbourhood Policy: Legal and Institutional Issues," *CDDRL Working Paper: Freeman Spogli Institute for International Studies (Stanford)*.

Cremona, Marise. 2006. "A Constitutional Basis for Effective External Action?" *EUI-LAW Working Paper: 30*.

Cremona, Marise, and Christophe Hillion. 2006. "L'Union fait la force? Potential and Limitations of the European Neighbourhood Policy as an Integrated EU Foreign and Security Policy." in *EUI-LAW Working Paper: 39*.

D'Orta, Carlo. 2003. "What Future for the European Administration Space?" *EIPA Working Paper: 15*. Maastricht: European Institute for Public Administration.

Daams, Claire A. 1999. "Regional Initiatives: European Union against Corruption," in *9th International Anti-Corruption Conference (IACC)*. Durban, South Africa: October 10–15.

Dashwood, Alan. 1996. "The Limits of European Community Powers," ELR *European Law Review* 23 (2): 113–128.

de Boer, Rob, Hester Benedictus, and Marc van der Meer. 2005. "Broadening without Intensification: The Added Value of the European Social and Sectoral Dialogue," *European Journal of Industrial Relations* 11 (1): 51–70.

De Esteban, Fernando 2002. "The Future of Nuclear Energy in the European Union" *Background paper for a speech made to a group of representatives from nuclear utilities in the context of a "European Strategic Exchange."* Brussels: May 23.

de Filippis, Fabrizio. 2003. "The Eastward Enlargement of the European Union and the Common Agricultural Policy: The Direct Payments Issue," in *The Economics of Enlargement,* edited by S. Manzocchi. Basingstoke, UK/New York/Rome: Palgrave Macmillan in association with Rivista di Politica Economica, SIPI.

de la Porte, Caroline. 2002. "Is the Open Method of Coordination Appropriate for Organising Activities at European Level in Sensitive Policy Areas?" *European Law Journal* 8 (1): 38–58.

De Witte, Bruno. 2000. "Politics Versus Law in the EU's Approach to Ethnic Minorities," *EUI Working Papers* (RCS No 2000/4).

De Witte, Bruno. 2004. "The Constitutional Resources for an EU Minority Protection Policy," in *Minority Protection and the Enlarged European Union: The Way Forward*, edited by G. N. Toggenburg. Budapest: Open Society Institute.

De Witte, Bruno. 2007. "Saving the Constitution?" n *Genèse et destinée de la Costitution européenne; Genesis and Destiny of the European Constitution*, edited by G. Amato, H. Bribosia and B. De Witte. Brussels: Bruylant.

Del Sarto, Raffaella A., and Tobias Schumacher. 2005. "From EMP to ENP: What's at Stake with the European Neighbourhood Policy towards the Southern Mediterranean?" *European Foreign Affairs Review* 10 (1): 17–38.

Delcour, Laure. 2007. "Does the European Neighbourhood Policy Make A Difference? Policy Patterns and Reception in Ukraine and Russia," *European Political Economy Review* 5 (7): 118–155.

Dimitrova, Antoneta L. 2002. "Enlargement, Institution-Building and the EU's Administrative Capacity Requirement," *West European Politics* 25 (4): 171–190.

Dimitrova, Antoneta L. 2005. "Europeanization and Civil Service Reform in Central and Eastern Europe," in *The Europeanization of Central and Eastern Europe*, edited by F. Schimmelfennig and U. Sedelmeier. Ithaca/London: Cornell University Press.

Donahue, John D., and Mark A. Pollack. 2001. "Centralization and Its Discontents: The Rhythms of Federalism in the United States and the European Union," in *The Federal Vision: Legitimacy and Levels of Governance in the United States and the European Union*, edited by K. Nicolaïdis and R. Howse. Oxford: Oxford University Press.

Duke, Simon. 1999. "Consistency as an Issue in EU External Activities," *EIPA Working Paper: 99/W/06*. Maastricht: European Institute for Public Administration.

Eiselt, Isabella, Johannes Pollak, and Peter Slominski. 2007. "Codifying Temporary Stability? The Role of Interinstitutional Agreements in Budgetary Politics," *European Law Journal* 13 (1): 75–91.

Eiselt, Isabella, and Peter Slominski. 2006. "Sub-Constitutional Engineering: Negotiation, Content, and Legal Value of Interinstitutional Agreements in the EU," *European Law Journal* 12 (2): 209–225.

Eisl, Gerhard. 1999. "EU Enlargement and Co-operation in Justice and Home Affairs," in *Back to Europe: Central and Eastern Europe and the European Union*, edited by K. Henderson. London: UCL Press.

Ellinas, Antonis, and Ezra Suleiman. 2008. "Reforming the Commission: Between Modernization and Bureaucratization," *Journal of European Public Policy* 15 (5): 708–725.

Epstein, David, and Sharyn O'Halloran. 1994. "Administrative Procedures, Information, Agency Discretion," *American Journal of Political Science* 38 (3): 697–722.

Epstein, David, and Sharyn O'Halloran. 1999a. "Asymmetric Information, Delegation, and the Structure of Policy-making," *Journal of Theoretical Politics* 11 (1): 37–56.

Epstein, David, and Sharyn O'Halloran. 1999b. *Delegating Powers: A Transaction Cost Politics Approach to Policy Making under Separate Powers*. Cambridge: Cambridge University Press.

Europe.bg. 2008. *News Report*. http://www.europe.bg/en/htmls/page.php?id=7337&category=5. (accessed: April 20, 2008).

European Commission. 2006. "Opinions on Organised, Cross-border Crime and Corruption," *Special Eurobarometer* 245 (Wave 64.3).

European Commission. 2008. "The Attitudes of Europeans towards Corruption," *Special Eurobarometer* 291 (Wave 68.2).

European Commission. 2009. "Attitudes of Europeans towards Corruption," *Special Eurobarometer* 325 (Eurobarometer 72.2).

European Council. 1993. *Presidency Conclusions*. European Council Meeting in Copenhagen: June 21–22.

European Council. 1999. *Presidency Conclusions*. European Council Meeting in Helsinki: December 10–11.

European Council. 2000a. "Charter of Fundamental Rights," *Presidency Conclusions*. Nice European Council Meeting: December 7–10.

European Council. 2000b. *Presidency Conclusions*. Lisbon European Council: March 23–24.

European Council. 2007. "Treaty of Lisbon: Amending the Treaty on the European Union and the Treaty establishing the European Community." *OJ* 50 (C 306).

European Court of Justice. 1996. "Opinion of the European Court of Justice," *Opinion 2/94* March 28 (Rec. 1996-I): 1759.

European Court of Justice. 2002. "Judgment of the Court of 10 December 2002," *Commission of the European Communities v Council of the European Union: International agreements—Convention on Nuclear Safety—Accession decision—Compatibility with the Euratom Treaty—External competence of the Community—Articles 30 to 39 of the Euratom Treaty.* Case C-29/99 (European Court reports 2002): I- 11221.

European Economic and Social Committee. 2003. Opinion of the European Economic and Social Committee. *On the Draft proposal for a Council Directive (Euratom) setting out basic obligations and general principles on the safety of nuclear installations and the Draft proposal for a Council Directive (Euratom) on the management of spent nuclear fuel and radioactive waste COM(2003) 32 final* 2003/0021 (CNS) – 2003/0022 (CNS) (Brussels, 26 March).

European Parliament. 2003. *European Parliament resolution on the communication from the Commission to the Council, the European Parliament and the European Economic and Social Committee—On a Comprehensive EU Policy Against Corruption.* COM(2003) 317–2003/2154(INI).

European Parliament. 2005. "European Parliament resolution on the situation of the Roma in the European Union," in *Roma in the European Union*. Brussels: April 28.

European Parliament. 2006. "Report on the proposal for a Council decision on the conclusion, on behalf of the European Community, of the United Nations Convention against Corruption," in *Consultation Procedure: Final A6-0380/2006* of October 26.

European Parliament, and Council. 2006a. "Regulation (EC) No 1080/2006 of the European Parliament and of the Council on the European Regional Development Fund and repealing Regulation (EC) No 1783/1999," *OJ L 210/1* (July 5): 1–11.

European Parliament, and Council. 2006b. "Regulation (EC) No 1081/2006 of the European Parliament and of the Council of 5 July 2006 on the European Social Fund and repealing Regulation (EC) No 1784/1999." *OJ L 210/12* (July 5): 12–18.

European Parliament, and Council. 2006c. "Regulation (EC) No 1082/2006 of the European Parliament and of the Council of 5 July 2006 on a European grouping of territorial cooperation (EGTC)." *OJ L 210/19* (July 31): 19–24.

European Parliament, and Council of the European Union. 2004. "Decision No 804/2004/EC of the European Parliament and of the Council. Establishing a Community action programme to promote activities in the field of the protection of the Community's financial in-terests (Hercule programme)," *OJ L 143/10–14* (April 21).

Fagan, Colette, Jill Rubery, Damian Grimshaw, Mark Smith, Gail Hebson, and Hugo Figueiredo. 2005. "Gender mainstreaming in the Enlarged European Union: Recent Developments in the European Employment Strategy and Social Inclusion Process," *Industrial Relations Journal* 36 (6): 568–591.

Falkner, Gerda, Oliver Treib, Miriam Hartlapp, and Simone Leiber. 2005. *Complying with Europe: EU Harmonisation and Soft Law in the Member States.* Cambridge: Cambridge University Press.

Farrell, Henry, and Adrienne Héritier. 2003. "Formal and Informal Institutions Under Codecision: Continuous Constitution-Building in Europe," *Governance: An International Journal of Policy, Administration, and Institutions* 16 (4): 577–600.

Farrell, Henry, and Adrienne Héritier. 2007. "Introduction: Contested Competences in the European Union," *West European Politics* 30 (2): 227–243.

Florio, Massimo. 2006. "Cost—benefit Analysis and the European Union Cohesion Fund: On the Social Cost of Capital and Labour," *Regional Studies* 40 (2): 211–224.

Franchino, Fabio. 2000. "The Commission's Executive Discretion, Information and Comitology," *Journal of Theoretical Politics* 12 (2): 155–181.

Franchino, Fabio. 2001. "Delegation and Constraints in the National Execution of the EC Politics: A Longitudinal and Qualitative Analysis," *West European Politics* 24 (4): 169–192.

Franchino, Fabio. 2005. "A Formal Model of Delegation in the European Union," *Journal of Theoretical Politics* 17 (2): 217–247.

Franchino, Fabio, and Anne J. Rahming. 2003. "Biased Ministers, Inefficiency, and Control in Distributive Policies," *European Union Politics* 4 (1): 11–36.

Froman, Lewis A. Jr. 1967. "An Analysis of Public Policies in Cities," *Journal of Politics* 29 (1): 94–108.

Froman, Lewis A. Jr. 1968. "The Categorization of Policy Contents," in *Political Science and Public Policy,* edited by A. Ranney. Chicago: Markham Publishing.

Gadowska, Kaja. 2010. "National and International Anti-corruption Efforts: The Case of Poland," *Global Crime* 11 (2): 178–209.

Gaja, Giorgio. 1996. "Opinion 2/94, Accession by the Community to the European Convention for the Protection of Human Rights and Fundamental Freedoms, given on March 28 1996, not yet reported," *Common Market Law Review* 33: 973–989.

Ganghof, Steffen. 2005. "Kausale Perspektiven in der vergleichenden Politikwissenschaft: X-zentrierte und Y-zentrierte Forschungsdesigns," in *Vergleichen in der Politikwissenschaft*, edited by S. Kropp and M. Minkenberg. Wiesbaden: Westdeutscher Verlag.

Geddes, Andrew, and Guiraudon, Virginie. 2004. "Britain, France, and EU Anti-Discrimination Policy: The Emergence of an EU Policy Paradigm," *West European Politics* Vol. 27 (2): 334–353.

General Secretariat of the Council. 2007. "European Policy Needs for Data on Crime and Criminal Justice: State of Play (Draft)," in *Directorate General H/3A (Justice and Home Affairs)*.

Goetschy, Janine. 1999. "The European Employment Strategy: Genesis and Development," *European Journal of Industrial Relations* 5 (2): 117–137.

Goetz, Klaus H., and Hellmut Wollmann. 2001. "Governmentalizing Central Executives in Post-communist Europe: A Four-country Comparison," *Journal of European Public Policy* 8 (6): 864–887.

Gold, Michael, Peter Cressey, and Evelyne Léonard. 2007. "Whatever Happened to Social Dialogue? From Partnership to Managerialism in the EU Employment Agenda," *European Journal of Industrial Relations* 13 (1): 7–25.

Grabbe, Heather. 2001. "How does Europeanization affect CEE Governance? Conditionality, Diffusion and Diversity," *Journal of European Public Policy* 8 (6): 1013–1031.

Greenberg, George D., Jeffrey A. Miller, Lawrence B. Mohr, and Bruce C. Vladeck. 1977. "Developing Public Policy Theory: Perspectives from Empirical Research" *American Political Science Review* 71 (4): 1532–1543.

Grunwald, Jürgen. 1998. "Neuere Entwicklungen des Euratom-Rechts," *Zeitschrift für Europarechtliche Studien (ZEuS)* 1 (3): 275–311.

Grunwald, Jürgen. 2007. "Assessing Euratom—50 Years of European Nuclear Policy: Panel 3." *European Parliament: Committee on Industry, Research, and Energy Public Hearing*, http://www.europarl.europa.eu/hearings/20070201/itre/grunwald_de.pdf (Accessed March 9, 2007).

Gugliemlo, Rachel, and Timothy William Waters. 2005. "Migrating Towards Minority Status: Shifting European Policy Towards Roma," *Journal of Common Market Studies* 43 (4) 763–86.

Guy, Will. 2001. "Romani Identity and post-Communist policy," in *Between Past and Future: The Roma and Eastern Europe*, edited by W. Guy. Hertfordshire: University of Hertfordshire Press.

Haas, Ernst B. 1968. *The Uniting of Europe*. first edited 1958 ed. Stanford, California: Stanford University Press.

Haas, Ernst B. 1975. *The Obsolence of Regional Integration Theory.* Edited by U. o. B. Institute of International Studies. Berkley: Institute of International Studies.

Haas, Ernst B. 2001. "Does Constructivism Subsume Neo-functionalism," in *The Social Construction of Europe,* edited by T. Christiansen, K. E. Jørgensen and A. Wiener. London / Thousand Oaks / New Delhi: Sage Publications.

Haas, Ernst B. 2004a. "Introduction: Institutionalism or Constructivism?" in *The Uniting of Europe: Political, Social, and Economic Forces 1950–1957,* edited by E. B. Haas. Notre Dame, Indiana: University of Notre Dame Press.

Haas, Ernst B. 2004b. *The Uniting Europe: Political, Social, and Economic Forces 1950–1957.* First edited 1958 ed. Notre Dame, Indiana: University of Notre Dame Press. Original edition, 1958.

Hall, Peter A., and Paul C. R. Taylor. 1996. "Political Science and the Three New Institutionalisms," *Political Studies* 44 (5): 936–957.

Hayes, Michael T. 1978. "The Semi-Sovereign Pressure Groups: A Critique of Current Theory and an Alternative Typology," *The Journal of Politics* 40 (1): 134–161.

Heckathorn, Douglas D., and Steven M. Master. 1990. "The Contractual Architecture of Public Policy: A Critical Reconstruction of Lowi's Typology," *The Journal of Politics* 52 (4): 1101–1123.

Heclo, Hugh H. 1972. "Policy Analysis" *British Journal of Political Science* 2 (1): 83–108.

Heidbreder, Eva G. 2011. "Structuring the European Administrative Space: Policy Instruments of Multi-level Administration" *Journal of European Public Policy* 18 (5).

Heidbreder, Eva G., and Laura Carrasco. 2003. "Assessing the Assessment: A Review on the Application Criterion Minority Protection by the European Commission," *EIPA Working Paper 03/W/04.* Maastricht: European Institute for Public Administration.

Héritier, Adrienne. 1999. *Policy-Making and Diversity in Europe: Escape from Deadlock.* Edited by R. E. Goodin, *Theories of Institutional Design.* Cambridge: Cambridge University Press.

Héritier, Adrienne. 2002. "New Modes of Governance in Europe: Policy-Making without Legislating?" in *Common Goods: Reinventing European and International Governance,* edited by A. Héritier. Lanham: Rowman and Littlefield.

Héritier, Adrienne. 2003. "New Modes of Governance in Europe: Increasing Political Efficiency and Policy Effectiveness?" in *The State of the European Union,* edited by T. A. Börzel. Oxford: Oxford University Press.

Héritier, Adrienne, and Dirk Lehmkuhl. 2008. "The Shadow of Hierarchy and New Modes of Governance (Introduction)," *Journal of Public Policy* 28 (1): 1–17.

Hillion, Christophe. 2002. "Enlargement of the European Union: A Legal Analysis," in *Accountability and Legitimacy in the European Union,* edited by A. Arnull and D. Wincott. Oxford: Oxford University Press.

Hillion, Christophe. 2005. " 'Thou Shalt Love thy Neighbour': The Draft European Neighbourhood Policy Action Plan between the EU and Ukraine," in *Wider Europe Research Papers*. http://www.wider-europe.org/research/papers/UkraineandENPHillion.pdf (accessed July 31, 2010).

Hix, Simon. 2002. "Constitutional Agenda-Setting through Discretion in Rule Interpretation: Why the European Parliament Won at Amsterdam," *British Journal of Political Science* 32 (2): 259–280.

Hoffmann, Stanley. 1982. "Reflections on the Nation-State in Western Europe Today," *Journal of Common Market Studies* 21 (1): 21–37.

Hoffmeister, Frank. 2004. "Monitoring Minority Rights in the Enlarged European Union," in *Minority Protection and the Enlarged European Union: The Way Forward*, edited by G. N. Toggenburg. Budapest: Open Society Institute.

Hofmann, Andreas, and Alexander Türk. 2006. *EU Administrative Governance*. Cheltenham, UK / Northampton, USA: Edward Elgar.

Hofmann, Herwig C. H., and Alexander Türk, eds. 2009. *Legal Challenges in EU Administrative Law: Towards an Integrated Administration*. Cheltenham, UK / Northampton, USA: Edward Elgar.

Homeyer Von, Ingmar. 2004. "Differential Effects of Enlargement on EU Environmental Governance," *Environmental Politics* 13 (S1): 52–76.

Hooghe, Liesbet, and Gary Marks. 2001. *Multi-Level Governance and European Integration*. "Governance in Europe Series." Lanham/Oxford: Rowman & Littlefield Publishers.

House of Lords. 2006a. "European Scrutiny—Twenty-Third Report, Chapter 9: Draft Decision on the setting up of a European Anti-Corruption Network," in *Home Office*. Basis of Consideration: EM of 27 March.

House of Lords. 2006b. "Managing Nuclear Safety and Waste: The Role of the EU," in *European Union Committee*. Volume I: Report, Ordered to be printed 27 June 2006 and published 6 July.

Hug, Simon. 2003. "Endogenous Preferences and Delegation in The European Union," *Comparative Political Studies* 26 (1/2): 41–74.

Hughes, James, and Gwendolyn Sasse. 2003. "Monitoring the Monitors: EU Enlargement Conditionality and Minority Protection in the CEECs," *Journal on Ethnopolitics and Minority Issues*: European Centre for Minority Issues (ECMI).

Hughes, Jim, Gwendolyn Sasse, and Claire Gordon. 2001. "The Regional Deficit in Eastward Enlargement of the European Union: Top Down Policies and Bottom Up Reactions," in *ESRC "One Europe or Several?" (Sussex European Institute) Working Paper 27*.

Idema, Timo, and Daniel R. Kelemen. 2006. "New Modes of Governance, the Open Method of Co-ordination and Other Fashionable Red Herrings," *Perspectives on European Politics and Society* 7 (1): 108–123.

Ingham, Mike, Hilary Ingham, Hasan Bicak, and Mehmet Altinay. 2005. "The impact of (more) enlargement on the European Employment Strategy," *Industrial Relations Journal* 36 (6): 546–477.

INTERACT Managing Transition. 2005. *Study on Selected Monitoring Systems in use by INTERREG III Programmes across EU-25* http://www.interact-eu.net/913123/911627/0/0 (accessed: June 12, 2006).

INTERACT Programme Secretariat. 2002. *Community Initiative Programme 2002–2006* Available from http://www.interact-eu.net/download/application/pdf/452610. (accessed June 12, 2006).

INTERREG II. 1994–1999. *Programm Outline.* http://ec.europa.eu/regional_policy/interreg3/inte2/inte2.htm (accessed June 6, 2006).

INTERREG IIIA. 2000–2006. *Strand (Cross-border Cooperation)* http://www.interact-eu.net/604900/604902/656368/0 (accessed April 9, 2008).

Ivanov, Kalin. 2010. "The 2007 Accession of Bulgaria and Romania: Ritual and Reality," *Global Crime* 11 (2): 210–219.

Ivanova, Maria N. 2007. "Why There Was No 'Marshall Plan' for Eastern Europe and Why This Still Matters," *Journal of Contemporary European Studies* 15 (3): 345–376.

Jachtenfuchs, Markus. 2001. "The Governance Approach to European Integration," *Journal of Common Market Studies* 39 (2): 245–264.

Jacobsson, Kerstin. 2004. "Soft Regulation and the Subtle Transformation of States: The Case of EU Employment Policy," *Journal of European Social Policy* 14 (4): 355–370.

Jones, Robert A. 2000. "The European Union," in *Comparative Public Administration,* edited by J. A. Chandler. London / New York: Routledge.

Kassim, Hussein. 2008. "'Mission Impossible', but Mission Accomplished: The Kinnock Reforms and the European Commission," *Journal of European Public Policy* 15 (5): 648–668.

Kassim, Hussein, and Anand Menon. 2002. "The Principal-Agent Approach and The Study Of The European Union: A Provisional Assessment," *The European Research Institute Working Paper Series 14.* University of Birmingham: The European Research Institute: The University of Birmingham (July).

Kassim, Hussein, and Anand Menon. 2003. "The Principal–Agent Approach and the Study of the European Union: Promise Unfulfilled?" *Journal of European Public Policy* 10 (1): 121–139.

Kassim, Hussein, and Anand Menon. 2004. "European Integration Since the 1990s: Member States and the European Commission," *ARENA Working Papers: WP 04/06.*

Kelemen, Daniel R. 2002. "The Politics of 'Eurocratic' Structure and the New European Agencies," *West European Politics* 25 (4): 93–118.

Keller, Berndt, and Bernd Sörries. 1998. "The Sectoral Social Dialogue and European Social Policy: More Fantasy, Fewer Facts," *European Journal of Industrial Relations* 4 (3): 331–348.

Keller, Berndt, and Bernd Sörries. 1999. "The New European Social Dialogue: Old Wine in New Bottles?" *Journal of European Social Policy* 9 (2): 111–125.

Kelley, Judith. 2006. "New Wine in Old Wineskins: Promoting Political Reforms through the New European Neighbourhood Policy," *Journal of Common Market Studies* 44 (1): 29–55.

Kennard, Ann. 2002. "The Changing Role of Border Regions in Central and Eastern Europe," in *EU Expansion to the East,* edited by H. Ingham and M. Ingham. Cheltenham, UK / Northampton, USA: Edward Elgar.

REFERENCES   209

Keohane, Robert O. 1984. *After Hegemony: Cooperation and Discord in the World Political Economy.* Princeton, N.J.: Princeton University Press.
Keohane, Robert O. 1989. *International Institutions and State Power: Essays in International Relations Theory.* Boulder, Colorado: Westview Press.
Keohane, Robert O., and Helen V. Milner, eds. 1996. *Internationalization and Domestic Politics.* Cambridge: Cambridge University Press.
Keohane, Robert O., and Joseph S. Nye. 1974. "Transgovernmental Relations and International Organizations," *World Politics* 27 (1): 39–62.
Kietz, Daniela, and Andreas Maurer. 2007. "The European Parliament in Treaty Reform: Predefining IGCs through Interinstitutional Agreements," *European Law Journal* 13 (1): 20–46.
Kinnock, Neil. 2004. "Reforming the European Commission: Organisational Challenges and Advances," *Public Policy and Administration* 19 (3): 7–12.
Kjær, Anne Mette. 2004. *Governance.* Cambridge UK / Malden: Polity Press.
Kohler-Koch, Beate, and Rainer Eising, eds. 1999. *The Transformation of Governance in the European Union, ECPR Studies in European Political Science.* London and New York: Routledge.
König, Thomas, and Dirk Junge. 2006. "Die räumliche Modellierung von EU-Entscheidungssituationen: Akteure, Dimensionen, Interessen, Stimmengewichte und die Natur des Politikraums," *FÖV Discussion Papers 25,* June 10.
Kooiman, Jan. 1993. *Modern Governance.* London: Sage.
Kramer. 2004. "EU Enlargement and the Environment: Six Challenges," *Environmental Politics* 13 (Supplement 1): 290–311.
Kymlicka, Will. 2000. "Nation-building and Minority Rights: Comparing West and East," *Journal of Ethnic and Migration Studies* 26 (2): 183–212.
Kymlicka, Will, and Magda Opalski. 2002. *Can Liberal Pluralism be Exported?—Western Political Theory and Ethnic Relations in Eastern Europe.* Oxford: Oxford University Press.
Laffan, Bridgid, and Johannes Lindner. 2005. "The Budget: Who Gets What, When and How?" in *Policy-making in the European Union,* edited by H. Wallace, W. Wallace and M. A. Pollack. Oxford: Oxford University Press [fifth edition].
Leisink, Peter. 2002. "The European Sectoral Social Dialogue and the Graphical Industry," *European Journal of Industrial Relations* 8 (1): 101–117.
Lindberg, Leon N. 1963. *The Political Dynamics of European Economic Integration.* Stanford: Stanford University Press.
Lindberg, Leon N. 1965. "Decision Making and Integration in the European Community," *International Organization* 19 (1): 56–80.
Lindberg, Leon N. 1966. "Integration as a Source of Stress on the European Community System," *International Organization* 20 (2): 233–265.
Lindberg, Leon N. 1967. "The European Community as a Political System: Notes toward the Construction of a Model," *Journal of Common Market Studies* 5 (4): 344–387.
Lindberg, Leon N., and Stuart A. Scheingold, eds. 1971. *Regional Integration: Theory and Research.* Cambridge, Mass.: Harvard University Press.

López-Santana, Mariely. 2006. "The Domestic Implications of European Soft Law: Framing and Transmitting Change in Employment Policy," *Journal of European Public Policy* 13 (4): 481–499.

Lowi, Theodore J. 1964. "American Business, Public Policy, Case-Studies, and Political Theory," *World Politics* 16 (4): 677–715.

Lowi, Theodore J. 1972. "Four Systems of Policy, Politics and Choice," *Public Administration Review* 74 (2): 298–310.

Lowi, Theodore J. 1985. "The State in Politics: The Relation Between Policy and Administration," in *Regulatory Policy and the Social Sciences*, edited by R. G. Noll. Berkley/ Los Angeles/ London: University of California Press.

Lowi, Theodore J. 1988. "Foreword: New Dimensions in Policy and Politics," in *Social Regulatory Policy,* edited by R. Tatalovich and B. W. Daynes. Boulder / London: Westview Press.

Lowi, Theodore J. 2008. *Arenas of Power, Edited and Introduced by Norman K. Nicholson.* Boulder, London: Paradigm Publishers.

Mabbett, Deborah, and Waltraud Schelkle. 2009. "The Politics of Conflict Management in EU Regulation," *West European Politics* 32 (4): 699–718.

Magen, Amichai. 2006. "The Shadow of Enlargement: Can the European Neighbourhood Policy Achieve Compliance?" *CDDRL Working Paper.* Freeman Spogli Institute for International Studies (Stanford).

Mair, Peter. 2007. "Political Opposition and the European Union," *Government and Opposition* 42 (1): 1–17.

Majone, Giandomenico. 1996. *Regulating Europe.* London: Routledge.

Majone, Giandomenico. 2001a. "Nonmajoritarinan Institutions and the Limits of Democratic Governance: A Political Transaction-Cost Approach," *Journal of Institutional and Theoretical Economics* 157 (3): 57–78.

Majone, Giandomenico. 2001b. "Two Logics of Delegation: Agency and Fiduciary Relations in EU Governance," *European Union Politics* 2 (1): 103–122.

Majone, Giandomenico. 2002. "Delegation of Regulatory Powers in a Mixed Polity," *European Law Journal* 8 (3): 319–339.

Mangenot, Michel, ed. 2005. *Public Administrations and Services of General Interest: What Kind of Europeanisation?* EIPA, *EIPA 2005/05.* Maastricht: European Institute of Public Administration.

Maniokas, Klaudijus. 2004. "The Method of the European Union's Enlargement to the East: A Critical Appraisal," in *Driven to Change: The European Union's Enlargement Viewed from the East,* edited by A. Dimitrova. Manchester / New York: Manchester University Press.

Marchetti, Andreas. 2007. "Consolidation in Times of Crisis: The European Neighbourhood Policy as Chance for Neighbours?" *European Political Economy Review* 5 (7): 9–23.

Marks, Gary, Liesbet Hooghe, and Stephen J. Blank. 1996. "European Integration from the 1980s: State v. Multi-level Governance," *Journal of Common Market Studies* 34 (3): 341–378.

Marks, Gary, Fritz Wilhelm Scharpf, Philippe C. Schmitter, and Wolfgang Streeck. 1996. *Governance in the European Union.* London / Thousand Oaks, Calif.: Sage.

Mayhew, Allan. 1998. *Recreating Europe: The European Union's Policy towards Central and Eastern Europe.* Cambridge: Cambridge University Press.

Mayntz, Renate. 2004. "Governence im modernen Staat," in *Governance: Regieren in komplexen Regelsystemen,* edited by A. Benz. Wiesbaden: VS Verlag.

Mayntz, Renate. 2008. "Von der Steuerungstheorie zu Global Governance," in *PVS Sonderheft 41—Governance in einer sich wandelnden Welt,* edited by G. F. Schuppert and M. Zürn. Wiesbaden: VS Verlag für Solzialwissenschaften.

Mayntz, Renate, and Fritz W. Scharpf. 1995a. "Steuerung und Selbstorganisation in staatsnahen Sektoren," in *Gesellschaftliche Selbstregulierung und politische Steuerung,* edited by R. Mayntz and F. W. Scharpf. Frankfurt a. M. / New York: Campus.

Mayntz, Renate, and Fritz W. Scharpf, eds. 1995b. *Gesellschaftliche Selbstregulierung und politische Steuerung.* Frankfurt a. M. / New York: Campus.

McCubbins, Mathew D., Noll G. Roger, and Barry R. Weingast. 1987. "Administrative Procedures as Instruments of Political Control," *Journal of Law, Economics and Organizations* 3 (2): 243–277.

McInerney, Siobhan. 2002. "Bases for Action against Race Discrimination in the E.U. Law," *European Law Review* 21 (1): 72–79.

Meyer-Sahling, Jan-Hinrik. 2001. "Getting on Track: Civil Service Reform in Post-communist Hungary," *Journal of European Public Policy* 8 (9): 960–979.

Meyer-Sahling, Jan-Hinrik. 2009. "Sustainability of Civil Service Reforms in Central and Eastern Europe Five Years after EU Accession," *SIGMA Paper: No. 44* GOV/SIGMA 2009/1.

Moe, Terry. 1990. "Political Institutions: The Neglected Side of the Story," *Journal of Law, Economics and Organisations* (6): 213–253.

Moe, Terry M. 1984. "The Economics of Organization," *American Journal of Political Science* 28 (4): 739–777.

Monar, Jörg. 2003. "Justice and Home Affairs after the 2004 Enlargement," *The International Spectator: Istituto Affari Internazionali* (1/2003): 1–19.

Moravcsik, Andrew. 1998. *The Choice for Europe: Social Purpose and State Power from Messina to Maastricht.* London: UCL Press.

Moravcsik, Andrew. 2002. "In Defence of the 'Democratic Deficit': Reassessing Legitimacy in the European Union," *Journal of Common Market Studies* 40 (4): 603–624.

Morgenthau, Hans J. 1960. *Politics Among Nations: The Struggle for Power and Peace.* 3rd ed. New York: Alfred Knopf.

Mörth, Ulrika. 2004a. "Conclusions," in *Soft Law in Governance and Regulation,* edited by U. Mörth. Cheltenham, UK / Northampton, USA: Edward Elgar.

Mörth, Ulrika. 2004b. "Introduction," in *Soft Law in Governance and Regulation,* edited by U. Mörth. Cheltenham, UK / Northampton, USA: Edward Elgar.

Nicholson, Norman. 2002. "Policy choices and the uses of state power: The work of Theodore J. Lowi," *Policy Science* 35 (2): 163–177.

Nizzo, Carlo. 2001. "National Public Administrations and European Integration," *SIGMA.* http://unpan1.un.org/intradoc/groups/public/documents/nispacee/unpan007286.pdf (accessed March 14).

Nowak, Manfred. 1999. "Human Rights 'Conditionality' in Relation to Entry and Full Participation in the EU," in *The EU and Human Rights,* edited by P. Alston et al. Oxford: Oxford University Press.

Nugent, Neill, and Sabine Saurugger. 2002. "Organizational Structuring: The Case of the European Commission and its External Policy Responsibilities," *Journal of European Public Policy* 9 (3): 345–364.

Nye, Joseph S. 1988. "Neorealism and Neoliberalism," *World Politics* 40 (2): 235–251.

Open Society Institute. 2001. *EU Accession Monitoring Program: Minority Protection in the EU Accession Progress.* Budapest/New York: Central European University Press.

Open Society Institute. 2002a. *EU Accession Monitoring Program. Monitoring the EU Accession Process: Minority Protection.* Budapest/New York: Central European University Press.

Open Society Institute. 2002b. *Monitoring the EU Accession Process: Corruption and Anti-corruption Policy.* Budapest/New York: Central European University Press.

Panke, Diana, and Tanja A. Börzel. 2007. "Policy-Forschung und Europäisierung," in *Die Zukunft der Policy-Forschung: Theorien, Methoden und Anwendung,* edited by F. Janning and K. Toens. Wiesbaden: VS Verlag.

Papadimitriou, Dimitris, and David Phinnemore. 2004. "Europeanization, Conditionality and Domestic Change: The Twinning Exercise and Administrative Reform in Romania," *Journal of Common Market Studies* 42 (3): 619–639.

Pechstein, Matthias. 2001. "Elektrizitätsbinnenmarkt und Beihilfekontrolle im Anwendungsbereich des Eurato-Vertrags," *Europäische Zeitung für Wirtschaftsrecht* 12 (10): 307–311.

Perkmann, Markus. 1999. "Building Governance Institutions across European Borders," *Regional Studies* 33 (7): 657–667.

Peters, Guy B. 2000. "Governance and Comparative Politics," in *Debating Governance,* edited by J. Pierre. Oxford: Oxford University Press.

Peterson, John. 2008. "Enlargement, Reform and the European Commission. Weathering a Perfect Storm?" *Journal of European Public Policy* 15 (5): 761–780.

Peterson, John, and Andrea Birdsall. 2008. "The European Commission: Enlargement as Reinvention?" in *The Institutions of the Enlarged European Union: Continuity and Change,* edited by E. Best, T. Christiansen and P. Settembri. Cheltenham, UK / Northampton, USA: Edward Elgar.

Pierre, Jon, and Guy B. Peters. 2000. *Governance, Politics and the State.* London: Palgrave.

Pierson, Paul. 1996. "The Path to European Integration: A Historical Institutionalist Analysis," *Comparative Political Studies* 29 (2): 123–163.

Pierson, Paul. 2000. "Increasing Returns, Path Dependence, and the Study of Politics," *American Political Science Review* 94 (2): 251–267.

Pollack, Mark A. 1994. "Creeping Competence: The Expanding Agenda of the European Community," *Journal of Public Policy* 14 (2): 95–145.

Pollack, Mark A. 1997. "Delegation, Agency, and Agenda Setting in the European Community," *International Organization* 51 (1): 99–134.

Pollack, Mark A. 1998. "The Engines of European Integration? Supranational Autonomy and Influence in the European Union," in *European Integration and Supranational Governance*, edited by W. Sandholtz and A. Stone Sweet. Oxford: Oxford University Press.

Pollack, Mark A. 2000. "The End of Creeping Competence? EU Policy-Making since Maastricht," *Journal of Common Market Studies* 38 (3): 519–538.

Pollack, Mark A. 2002. "Learning from the Americanists (Again): Theory and Method in the Study of Delegation," *West European Politics* 25 (1): 200–219.

Pollack, Mark A. 2003. *The Engines of Integration: Delegation, Agency, and Agency Setting in the European Union*. Oxford: Oxford University Press.

Preston, Christopher. 1995. "Obstacles to EU Enlargement: The Classical Community Method and the Prospects for a Wider Europe," *Journal of Common Market Studies* 33 (3): 451–463.

Prieto Serrano, Nuria. 2006. "Wakening the Serpent: Reflections on the Possible Modification of the Euratom Treaty," *International Journal of Nuclear Law* 1 (1): 11–18.

Rasmussen, Anne. 2007. "Challenging the Commission's right of initiative? Conditions for institutional change and stability," *West European Politics* 30 (2): 244–64.

Redmond, John, and Glenda G. Rosenthal, eds. 1998. *The Expanding European Union. Past, Present, Future*. London: Lynne Rienner Publishers.

Rhodes, R.A.W. 1997. *Understanding Governance: Policy Networks, Governance, Reflexivity, and Accountability*. Buckingham / Philadelphia: Open University Press.

Rieger, Elmar. 2005. "Agricultural Policy: Constrained Reforms," in *Policymaking in the European Union*, edited by H. Wallace, W. Wallace and M. A. Pollack. Oxford: Oxford University Press [fifth edition].

Rollo, Jim. 2003. "Agriculture, the Structural Funds and the Budget after Enlargement," *SEI Working Paper* No 68.

Salisbury, Robert H. 1968. "The Analysis of Public Policy: A Search for Theories and Roles," in *Political Science and Public Policy*, edited by A. Ranney. Chicago: Markham Publishing.

Saurugger, Sabine. 2003. "Governing by Informal Networks? Nuclear Interest Groups and the Eastern Enlargement of the EU," in *Informal Governance in the European Union*, edited by T. Christiansen and S. Piattoni. Cheltenham, UK / Northampton, USA: Edward Elgar.

Schäfer, Armin. 2004. "Beyond the Community Method: Why the Open Method of Coordination was Introduced to EU Policy-making," *European Integration Online Papers 8, No. 13*, http://eiop.or.at/eiop/texte/2004-013a.htm (accessed November 11, 2011).

Schäfer, Armin. 2006. "Resolving Deadlock: Why International Organisations Introduce Soft Law," *European Law Journal* 12 (2): 194–208.

Scharpf, Fritz. 2006. "The Joint-Decision Trap Revisited," *Journal of Common Market Studies* 44 (4): 845–864.

Scharpf, Fritz W. 1985. "Die Politikverflechtungs-Falle: Europäische Integration und deutscher Föderalismus im Vergleich," *Politische Vierteljahresschrift* 26 (4): 323–356.

Scharpf, Fritz W. 1993. "Positive und negative Koordination in Verhandlungssystemen," in *Policy-Analyse. Kritik und Neuorientierung*, edited by A. Héritier. Opladen: PVS Sonderheft 24.

Scharpf, Fritz W. 1997. *Games Real Actors Play*. Boulder, Colo.: Westview Press.

Scharpf, Fritz W. 1999. *Governing in Europe. Effective and Democratic?* Oxford: Oxford University Press.

Scharpf, Fritz W. 2002. "The European Social Model: Coping with the Challenges of Diversity," *Journal of Common Market Studies* 40 (4): 645–670.

Schattschneider, Elmer Eric. 1975. *The Semisovereign People: A Realist's View of Democracy in America (with an Introduction by David Adamany)*, first edition 1960. Hinsdale, Illinois: The Dryden Press.

Schimmelfennig, Frank, and Ulrich Sedelmeier. 2002. "Theorizing EU Enlargement: Research Focus, Hypotheses, and the State of Research," *Journal of European Public Policy* 9 (4): 500–528.

Schmidt, Vivien Ann. 2006. *Democracy in Europe: The EU and National Polities*. Oxford: Oxford University Press.

Schmitter, Philippe C. 1970. "A Revised Theory of Regional Integration," *International Organization* 24 (4): 836–868.

Schmitter, Philippe C. 1971a. "A Revised Theory of Regional Integration," in *Regional Integration: Theory and Research*, edited by L. N. Lindberg and S. A. Scheingold. Cambridge, Massachusetts: Harvard University Press.

Schmitter, Philippe C. 1971b. The "Organizational Development of International Organizations," *International Organization* 24 (4): 917–937.

Schmitter, Philippe C. 2003. "Neo-Neofunctionalism," in *European Integration Theory*, edited by A. Wiener and T. Diez. Oxford: Oxford University Press.

Schön-Quinlivan, Emmanuelle. 2008. "Implementing Organizational Change—The Case of the Kinnock Reforms," *Journal of European Public Policy* 15 (5): 726–742.

Schuppert, Gunnar Folke, and Michael Zürn, eds. 2008. *PVS Sonderheft 41—Governace in einer sich wandelnden Welt*. Wiesbaden: VS Verlag für Sozialwissenschaften.

Scott, Joanne. 1996. "Nuclear Health and Safety: Legal Aspects of the Euratom Treaty," *Review of European Community & International Environmental Law* 5 (4): 225–230.

Scott, Joanne, and David M. Trubek. 2002. "Mind the Gap: Law and New Approaches to Governance in the European Union," *European Law Journal* 8 (1): 1–18.

Senden, Linda. 2004. *Soft Law in European Community Law*. Oxford / Portland Oregon: Hart Publishing.

SIGMA—European Union and Council of Europe. 2005. *Reform Areas: External Audit and Financial Control*. www.sigmaweb.org (accessed March 19).

Simhandl, Katrin. 2006. " 'Western Gypsies and Travellers'—'Eastern Roma': The Creation of Political Objects by the institutions of the European Union," *Nations and Nationalism* 12 (1): 97–115.

Sisson, Keith, and Paul Marginson. 2001. " 'Soft Regulation'—Travesty of the Real Thing or New Dimension?" in *ESRC "One Europe or Several?" (Sussex European Institute) Working Paper 32/01.*

Sjursen, Helen. 1998. "Enlargement and the Common Foreign and Security Policy: Transforming the EU's External Policy?" *ARENA Working Papers* WP 98/18.

Smismans, Stijn. 2006. "New Modes of Governance and the Participatory Myth," in *European Governance Papers* (EUROGOV), http://www.connex-network.org/eurogov/pdf/egp-newgov-N-06-01.pdf (accessed November 11, 2010).

Smismans, Stijn. 2008. "New Modes of Governance and the Participatory Myth," *West European Politics* 31 (5): 874–895.

Stone Sweet, Alec, and James Caporaso. 1998. "From Free Trade to Supranational Polity: The European Court and Integration," in *European Integration and Supranational Governance,* edited by W. Sandholtz and A. Stone Sweet. Oxford: Oxford University Press.

Stone Sweet, Alec, Neil Fligstein, and Wayne Sandholtz. 2001. "The Institutionalization of European Space," in *The Institutionalization of Europe,* edited by A. Stone Sweet, W. Sandholtz and N. Fligstein. Oxford: Oxford University Press.

Streeck, Wolfgang. 1994. "European Social Policy after Maastricht: The 'Social Dialogue' and 'Subsidiarity,' " *Democracy Economic and Industrial Democracy* 15 (2): 151–177.

Sullivan, Louis. 1896. "The Tall Office Building Artistically Considered," *Lippincott's Magazine* (March).

Sushko, Oleksandr. 2006. "EU Initiatives for Border Management in its Eastern Neighbourhood," *The International Spectator* 41 (4): 43–53.

Süßmuth, Rita. 2007. "An Urgent Call for Better Social Inclusion," in *Report of the High Level Advisory Group of Experts on the Social Integration of Ethnic Minorities and Their Full Participation in the Labour Market,* December. Brussels: European Commission.

Tallberg, Jonas. 2002. "Delegation to Supranational Institutions: Why, How, and with What Consequences?" *West European Politics* 25 (1): 23–46.

Thatcher, Mark. 2002. "Delegation to Independent Regulatory Agencies: Pressures, Functions and Contextual Mediation," *West European Politics* 25 (1): 125–147.

Thatcher, Mark, and Alec Stone Sweet. 2002. "Theory and Practice of Delegation to Non-Majoritarian Institutions," *West European Politics* 25 (1): 1–22.

Tivig, Andrea, and Andreas Maurer. 2006. "Antikorruptionspolitik," *SWP Diskussionspapier der FG 1,* Vol. 3. SWP Berlin: March.

Toggenburg, Gabriel. 2000. "A Rough Orientation Through a Delicate Relationship: The European Union's Endeavours for (its) Minorities," *EIOP* 4: 16.

Toggenburg, Garbriel N. 2006. "A Remaining Share or a New Part? The Union's Role vis-à-vis Minorities after the Enlargement Decade," in *EUI Law Working Paper 2006: No. 15.*

Tömmel, Ingeborg. 2007. "Governance und Policy-Making im Mehrebenensystem der EU," in *PVS Sonderheft 40—Die Europäische Union: Governance und Policy-Making,* edited by I. Tömmel. Wiesbaden: VS Verlag für Solzialwissenschaften.

Trondal, Jarle. 2010. *An Emergent European Executive Order.* Oxford: Oxford University Press.

Trubek, David M., and Louise G. Trubek. 2005. "Hard and Soft Law in the Construction of Social Europe: the Role of the Open Method of Co-ordination," *European Law Journal* 11 (3): 343–364.

True, Christiane. 2003. "Legislative Competences of Euratom and the European Community in the Energy Sector: The Nuclear Package of the Commission," *European Law Review* 28 (5): 664–685.

Trüe, Christiane. 2006. "The Euratom Community Treaty's Prospects at the Start of the New Millenium," *International Journal of Nuclear Law* 1 (3): 247–260.

Tsebelis, George, and Geoffrey Garrett. 2001. "The Institutional Foundations of Intergovernmentalism and Supranationalism in the European Union," Review of pdf filed. *International Organization* 55 (2): 357–390.

Tsilevich, Boris. 2001. "EU Enlargement and the Protection of National Minorities: Opportunities, Myths, and Prospects," in *EUMAP Articles: October 1,* http://www.eumap.org/journal/features/2001/oct/euenlarge/ (accessed June 10, 2001).

Turner, Lowell. 1996. "The Europeanization of Labour: Structure before Action," Review of pdf filed EJIndR. *European Journal of Industrial Relations* 2 (3): 325–344.

Utstein Anti-Corruption Resource Centre. 2005. *FAQs: Cures—at International Level: International Law, Crime Prevention and Assistance.* http://www.u4.no/document/faqs3e.cfm (accessed March 19, 2005).

van den Broek, Hans. 1999. "Time for Enlargement," in *The Second Decade: Prospects for European Integration after Ten Years of Transition,* edited by Ministry of Economic Affairs of the Netherlands/Directorate General for Foreign Economic Relations. The Hague: Ministry of Economic Affairs.

van der Beek, Gregor, and Larry Neal. 2004. "The Dilemma of Enlargement for the European Union's Regional Policy," *The World Economy* 27 (4): 587–607.

Verheijen, Antony J.G. 2000. "Administrative Capacity Development: A Race against Time?" in *Scientific Council for Government Policy* (The Hague), Working Document, W 107, http://www.ut.ee/SOAH/kursused/w107.pdf.

Verheijen, Antony J.G. 2007. "Administrative Capacity in the New EU Member States: Limits of Innovation?" *World Bank Working Paper* Washington D.C., No. 115.

Vermeersch, Peter. 2004. "Minority Policy in Central and Eastern Europe: Exploring the Impact of the EU's Enlargement Strategy," *The Global Review of Ethnopolitics* 3 (2): 3–19.

Verwilghen, Stephane. 2007. "De Quelques Autres Politiques," in *Genèse et destinée de la Constitution européenne—Genesis and Destiny of the European Constitution,* edited by G. Amato, H. Bribosia and B. De Witte. Bruxelles: Bruylant.

Wallace, Helen. 2005. "An Institutional Anatomy and Five Policy Modes," in *Policy-making in the European Union,* edited by H. Wallace, W. Wallace and M. A. Pollack. Oxford: Oxford University Press [fifth edition].

Wallace, Helen. 2007. "Adapting to Enlargement of the European Union: Institutional Practice since May 2004," in *Trans European Policy Studies Association (TESPA)* November.

Wallace, Helen, William Wallace, and Mark A. Pollack, eds. 2005. *Policy-making in the European Union.* Oxford: Oxford University Press [fifth edition].

Wallace, William. 1983. "Less than a Federation, More than a Regime: The Community as a Political System," in *Policy-Making in the European Community,* edited by H. Wallace and C. Webb. Chichester: John Willey.

Wallace, William. 2005. "Post-Sovereign Governance: The EU as a Partial Polity," in *Policy-Making in the European Union,* edited by H. Wallace, W. Wallace and M. A. Pollack. Oxford: Oxford University Press.

Walt, Stephen. 1987. *The Origins of Alliances.* Ithaca, N.Y.: Cornell University Press.

Waltz, Kenneth N. 1979. *Theory of International Politics.* Reading, Mass.: Addison-Wesley.

Warner, Carolyn M. 2003. "Common Market Institutions, Fraud and Informal Networks," in *Informal Governance in the European Union,* edited by T. Christiansen and S. Piattoni. Cheltenham, UK / Northampton, USA: Edward Elgar.

WENRA. 1999. *Mission Statement* http://www.wenra.org/extra/pod/?id=14& module_instance=1&action=pod_show (accessed July 30, 2010).

Western European Nuclear Regulators' Association (WENRA). 2000. "Nuclear Safety in EU Candidate Countries," http://www.wenra.org/dynamaster/file_ archive/050630/c80a3ff3f07543faca024150e648efed/wenratotal2000.pdf (accessed July 30, 2010).

Wiener, Antje. 2002. "Finality vs. Enlargement: Constitutive Practices and Opposing Rationales in the Reconstruction of Europ," *Jean Monnet Working Paper (NYU School of Law)* 8/02.

Wiener, Antje, and Thomas Diez. 2009. *European Integration Theory.* 2nd edition ed. Oxford: Oxford University Press.

Wiener, Antje, and Guido Schwellnus. 2004. "Contested Norms in the Process of EU Enlargement: Non-Discrimination and Minority Rights," *Constitutionalism Web-Papers* ConWEB No. 2/2004.

Wight, Martin. 1991. *International Theory: Three Traditions.* Leicester: Leicester University Press.

Wilks, Stephen, and Ian Bartle. 2002. "The Unanticipated Consequences of Creating Independent Competition Agencies," *West European Politics* 25 (1): 148–172.

Williams, Andrew. 2000. "Enlargement of the Union and Human Rights Conditionality: A Policy of Distinction?" *European Law Review* 25 (6): 601–617.

Williams, R. H. 1996. *European Union Spacial Policy Planning*. London: Paul Chapman.

Wilson, James Q. 1973. *Political Organizations*. New York: Basic Books, Inc.

Wolf, Sebastian. 2010. "Assessing Eastern Europe's Anti-corruption Performance: Views from the Council of Europe, OECD, and Transparency International," *Global Crime* 11 (2): 99–121.

World Bank. 2006. "EU-8: Administrative Capacity in the New Member States: The Limits of Innovation?" in *Poverty Reduction and Economic Management Unit Europe and Central Asia.* Report Number: 36930-GLB.

Ziller, Jacques. 2006. "L'autorité administrative dans l'Union Européenne," in *L'Autorité de l'Union Européenne,* edited by L. Azoulai and L. Burgorgue-Larsen. Buxelles: Bruylant.

INDEX

"NOTE: **Bold** page numbers indicate principal discussion".